GETTING AND SPENDING:
The Consumer's Dilemma

This is a volume in the Arno Press collection

GETTING AND SPENDING:
The Consumer's Dilemma

Advisory Editor
Leon Stein

*See last pages of this volume
for a complete list of titles*

THE CONSUMPTION OF WEALTH

BY
ELIZABETH ELLIS HOYT

ARNO PRESS
A New York Times Company
1976

.320562

Editorial Supervision: EVE NELSON

———◆———

Reprint Edition 1976 by Arno Press Inc.

Reprinted from a copy in
  The Newark Public Library

GETTING AND SPENDING: The Consumer's Dilemma
ISBN for complete set: 0-405-08005-0
See last pages of this volume for titles.

Manufactured in the United States of America

———◆———

Library of Congress Cataloging in Publication Data

Hoyt, Elizabeth Ellis, 1893-
    The consumption of wealth.

    (Getting and spending)
    Reprint of the ed. published by Macmillan, New York.
    1. Consumption (Economics) 2. Consumers. I. Title.
II. Series.
HB801.H6 1976   339.4'7   75-39249
ISBN 0-405-08023-9

THE CONSUMPTION OF WEALTH

THE MACMILLAN COMPANY
NEW YORK . BOSTON . CHICAGO . DALLAS
ATLANTA . SAN FRANCISCO

MACMILLAN & CO., Limited
LONDON . BOMBAY . CALCUTTA
MELBOURNE

THE MACMILLAN CO. OF CANADA, Ltd.
TORONTO

THE CONSUMPTION
OF WEALTH

BY

ELIZABETH ELLIS HOYT, A.M., Ph.D.

PROFESSOR OF ECONOMICS, IOWA STATE COLLEGE

New York

THE MACMILLAN COMPANY

1928

PRINTED IN THE UNITED STATES OF AMERICA

BY T. MOREY & SON

PREFACE

For the ordinary man or woman consumption is the most significant part of economics. We are all consumers and we are consumers every day of our lives. All of us want to get more out of life, and it is through our choices of goods and services that we improve our living standards.

The following chapters seek an answer to four questions. What is the psychology by which our wants arise? What influences are acting on our choices all the time, unrecognized by us? How and to what extent can we control our wants for our welfare? And, finally, just what goods and services do we consume in the United States and how do our choices compare with the choices made by other peoples? Perhaps the newest aspect of the following pages is the discussion of our limitations in acquiring new interests, and the discussion of the culture-idea as determining for a people what they consider worth consuming.

Home economics and euthenics are asking science what it has to give to the everyday life of ordinary normal people. These "homelier" applications of science, however, have always come late. Consumption, in particular, has been too commonplace to excite curiosity. The man speculates about the comet and the whirlwind, but not about the course of life in his own village. The child wonders about the frog and the spider, but not about its bread and milk. We are all of us more or less like the old ploughman who remarked on his deathbed: "Look at the sky! I never noticed that it was so blue."

Even in economics, such discussions as there are under the name of consumption turn out frequently to be discussions of some other part of economics in which consumers are inter-

ested. Consumption is, in fact, a unique field, a field distinct
from value but bearing the same relation to it on the one side
that production bears on the other. It is the explanation and
the interpretation of the demand side of value: the nature of
demand, the causes of demand, and the consequences of demand in so far as we can ascertain them. Arbitrary and analytical study of marginal utility, which may be excellent as
far as it goes, is but the point of departure for the study of
consumption.[1] In consumption we must be realistic and
concrete.

It is impossible for the author to enumerate her obligations.
It was in Professor Carver's classes that she began to appreciate the importance of consumption. Its wide field of study
was first suggested to her in a book review by Professor Dickin-
son.[2] Professor Young has given her many suggestions. Col-
leagues at Iowa State College have read and criticized several
of the chapters. Her students have helped to build them all.

E. E. H.

Seattle, Washington,
September, 1928.

[1] Miss Hazel Kyrk broke ground with *A Theory of Consumption*, Boston,
1923.

[2] *Quarterly Journal of Economics*, XXXVIII, pp. 343–346.

CONTENTS

PART I. INTRODUCTION

PART II. THE PSYCHOLOGY OF CONSUMPTION

PART III. FACTORS UNCONSCIOUSLY
AFFECTING CONSUMPTION

CHAPTER PAGE
VI. ECOLOGY: MAN'S INTERESTS AND THE GEOGRAPHIC
ENVIRONMENT 53
Consumption and Culture Zones 53
Culture Traits Supplied by the Immediate Environment 55
Culture and Climate 59
The Economic Value of Natural Resources . . 59

VII. THE HERITAGE OF BIRTH AND RACE 62
What Is Race? 62
Race and Culture 63
The Biological Inheritance of Individuals . . 68
Eugenics and Culture 70

VIII. THE DIFFUSION OF CULTURE 72
The Merging of Whole Cultures 73
The Diffusion of Separate Traits 75
Diffusion Today 77
Diffusion and Democracy 80

IX. TRADE AND CULTURE 83
History of the Market 84
Contributions from Abroad to American Consumption 88
Expansion of Markets Over the World . . 90
Efforts of the United States Department of Commerce 92
Social and Political Effects of Foreign Trade . 94

X. AGGRESSIVE METHODS OF SALES-MAKING . . . 97
The "Science" of Selling 99
Recognition and Creation of Demand . . . 99
Aggressive Sales Methods as Social Gain . . 103
Aggressive Sales Methods as Social Waste . . 105
A Specific Illustration of Advertising as It Is . 108
The Way Out 109

XI. PRODUCTION AND CONSUMPTION 111
Some Pictures of Consumption at Various Stages
of Production 112

PART IV. CONSUMPTION DELIBERATELY CONTROLLED BY THE CONSUMER

TABLES

PART I

INTRODUCTION

THE CONSUMPTION OF WEALTH

CHAPTER I

CONSUMPTION AND CULTURE

"'Their pockets are full of money,' said the Keeper of the Inn, 'but there is not a mother's son of them that knows what to do with it.' "—*Old Tale.*

Let us suppose that some scientific society on the planet Mars sends a man to the planet Earth to make a study of its civilization. Can we not say that the first thing that would astonish him would be the great number of different ways of living all going very much their own way on the surface of one small globe?

If he happened to arrive in Asia he would see in China an ancient and dignified civilization which five thousand years before had built a Great Wall to keep other influences out,— a civilization emphasizing the graces and courtesies of life. He would see it still clinging to its own old ways in spite of the efforts and influences of foreigners of one type or another who had penetrated within it.

As he moved westward he would find a manner of living of another type in India. He would certainly take note of the measure of psychic development attained in a country so backward along material lines and by men who apparently despised material "progress."

Further west still he would enter Europe and observe the efforts of the people to bring all nature under their control by harnessing her powers and transforming her materials for human purposes. Yet further west, across the Atlantic, he would find that this line of endeavor was reaching its most complete expression in a certain geographic region which he would describe as bounded on east and west by the Atlantic and Pacific oceans and on north and south by parallels 48 and 25 north latitude and known as the United States. "This country," he might jot in his notebook, "is the most active and enthusiastic of any I have hitherto visited. The inhabitants, who are known as Americans, have lately become masters of the means for producing considerable wealth, but as yet they have made little progress in the art of using it."

If during his visit in the United States he asked some of the Citizens' Committees, which welcomed him in the various cities, in which lands he had best continue his observations, he would doubtless be informed that he had already seen everything essential. Canada, to the north, was representative of the best European and American culture; Latin America to the south was rapidly falling into line. Australia was already redeemed and Africa very nearly so. The cultures of the islands of the Indian and Pacific oceans were hardly worth mentioning.

Our scientist from Mars, however, being an acute man, would doubtless ask himself: What do they mean by "hardly worth mentioning"? "Falling into line" from what? And off he would go again; visiting Baffin Land, the headwaters of the Amazon, Patagonia, the Congo, Borneo—every place where men had applied themselves in their own way to the problems of living. And he would enter in his notebook:

"The single most striking thing about the inhabitants of the Planet Earth is the extraordinary narrowness of their lives. Although, in the judgment of their scientists, men have been present on the planet some hundreds of thousands of years, they are still living in groups in large measure unfamiliar with one another's culture; indeed, often contemptuous of it. The groups which have suffered the greatest geographic isolation and whose culture is scantiest, are treated by the rest as intrinsically inferior beings. Although the men of Earth should be credited with having achieved very considerable development within their separate cultures, these separate cultures are all narrow and imperfectly understood by those who profess them; and the men of each behave like spoiled children in their attitude toward the men and the cultures of other groups."

But the men of the Planet Earth are at least anxious to learn, and before the visiting scientist left us there is no doubt that scientific men and others here would ask him for his frankest criticisms. "How would you suggest that we become more intelligent about living? How can we reach a better understanding?" they would ask. "We do try, but it is slow."

"Have you studied *why* you want the things you do?" he would answer. "What wants are common to you all? When do your interests begin to diverge? What makes them diverge? You've got a science called psychology—put it to work. You've got something named economics—wealth in its relation to man, you call it. Why not give some effort to studying how men use wealth and how they can best use it, instead of so much to how they get it?"

CONSUMPTION AND ITS DEVELOPMENT

Consumption, the study of the use of wealth, has been the last of the three great divisions of economics to be developed. Production, the study of the general principles governing the creation of wealth, began to claim chief emphasis from the appearance, in 1776, of Adam Smith's *Wealth of Nations*. This was during one of the most important periods of the Industrial Revolution, when the attention of men of affairs was beginning to be intensively directed toward greater production, particularly by the use of the new machines.

Problems of production continued to dominate economic writing for seventy-five years, although the beginnings of industrial legislation and the struggles of the laborers for organization indicate that practical, if not theoretical, interest was being directed toward problems of the distribution of wealth as early as the last years of the eighteenth century. In the year 1848, with the development of Socialism, this interest reached a crisis in several countries of Europe; and it was in this very year, with the publication of J. S. Mill's *Principles*, that an economist of note first turned his serious attention to the problems of distribution, or the study of the division of

wealth among the "factors" which produce it—land, capital,
labor, and management. With the words "It is doubtful if
all the machines that have ever been invented have lightened
the day's labor of a single human being," Mill called striking
attention to a fact that had been obscured in the rush for
wealth: increased production is certainly not the ultimate
goal of economic effort if it does not result in improving the
condition of ordinary men.

From the day of Mill to the present, interest in the distribution of wealth has taken precedence over interest in
production in most theoretical economic study.

The problems of production and distribution are by no
means solved, but better business, on the one hand, and, on
the other hand, the efforts of social reformers and that long-
time equalization to which the early economists trusted so
much have gradually brought about a state of society in the
United States, at least, in which labor has begun to share
richly in the material returns from production.

In the nine years immediately following the beginning of the
War there took place an increase of 25% in the purchasing
power of the American people.[1] Such an increase was unprece-
dented, and substantial changes in consumption and standards
of living were bound to follow. Some of these changes, from
1919 to 1926, are given in Table I (pp. 6–7).[2] This table presents the brightest side of the picture. There were increases
in the consumption of other things not so beneficial as these.

Still, to be sure, all groups and classes are crying for more
money. "A' complain o' want o' siller; nane o' want o' sense"
runs a Scotch proverb. Nevertheless, for an increasingly
large number of persons the more important problem has
become, not how to get a larger return from production or a
larger share from distribution, but how to spend wisely the
money that they have. Indeed, to paraphrase the words of

[1] National Bureau of Economic Research. Preliminary estimate in News
Bulletin 23, p. 1.
[2] United States Department of Commerce. Annual Report of the Secretary
of Commerce for the Year Ended June 30, 1927, p. xxxvii.

Mill and say, it is doubtful if all the wealth that has ever been produced and distributed has led any human being to a richer experience of life, would not be so gross an exaggeration as at first it may seem to be.

The fact is, we have scarcely as yet begun to realize that we have been consuming the form rather than the substance of wealth. We have been so occupied in securing the wherewithal to get more things that we have not paid much attention to what things we should get.

Professor Meiklejohn in *The Liberal College* states the case thus: [1]

"More difficult yet than the distributing of values is the human task of using them. And the most serious aspect of the difficulty is that we do not feel it . . . In the realm of use, in apprehension of the necessity of taste and insight and appreciation of value, we are hardly conscious of difficulty at all. We have a certain blind faith that if only the opportunities of life are given they will be taken and human lives will be in general what they ought to be. Nothing could be more obvious than the falseness of such a faith as this. Wealth has not very generally brought to those who have it the fineness of taste and the niceness of discrimination which the use of it demands. Quite as often it has brought coarseness of feeling and dullness of appreciation. Our civilization does not very clearly become more fine as it becomes more rich. We are in danger of having the world in our hands and losing it because our fingers slip."

The chief reason for the relatively late development of the study of consumption undoubtedly lies in the fact that so long as wealth was small and variety of goods was meagre, and so long as men knew little about other peoples' ways of living, there was slight reason for considering alternative ways of spending money, and certainly not much practical incentive to do so. As wealth and knowledge increased, the inertia of customary consumption, like all inertias, lifted but slowly. As Professor Meiklejohn says, we have been slow in apprehending the necessity of taste and insight. Wealth comes, appreciation lingers.

[1] Boston, 1920, pp. 54-55.

TABLE I

INDICATIONS OF MATERIAL PROGRESS OF THE UNITED STATES, 1919–1926

(United States Department of Commerce)

Item		1919	1926	
Life insurance in force, total excluding fraternal....	dollars	369	712	Per capita
Savings deposits in banks and trust companies....	"	(a) 144	211	"
Assets of building and loan associations....	"	20	(b) 48	"
Members of building and loan associations....	number	41	85	Per 1,000 pop.
Residential buildings constructed during year, floor space (c)....	sq. feet	3.4	5.4	Per capita
Meat consumed during year....	pounds	138	156	"
Sugar consumed during year....	"	84	117	"
Butter consumed during year....	"	15.4	16.7	"
Fruit, fresh, carried by railroads during year....	"	(a) 125	134	"
Vegetables, fresh, carried by railroads during year..	"	(a) 41	48	"
Silk, imports, during year....	"	530	660	"
Farms receiving electric service from central stations (c)....	number	(e) 30	56	Per 1,000 farms
Residence electric customers, total....	"	76	135	Per 1,000 pop.
Electricity generated during year, public utility plants....	kilowatt hours	371	630	Per capita

Item	Unit		
Electrical household appliance manufactures during year, value	cents	37	55
Washing machines, domestic use, manufactures during year, value	"	39	60
Electric refrigerators sold during year	number	(d)	2.1 Per 1,000 pop.
Bathtubs sold during year	"	3.9	10.2
Furniture, new, carried by railroads during year	tons	7.0	8.4
Telephones, total	number	(a) 122	151
Radio receiving sets, sold during year	"	(d)	15
Motor vehicle registrations	number	72	189
Roads, rural, surfaced, total	miles	2.9	4.8
Pupils in high schools, public and private, total	number	20	35
Students in universities, colleges, and professional schools, total	"	4.3	7.0
Death rate	"	12.9	12.2
Deaths of infants under 1 year of age	"	87	73 Per 1,000 births

(a) 1920　(b) 1925　(c) 27 states　(d) Insignificant　(e) 1923

It used to be said that one reason for the slow development of the study of consumption was that the production and distribution of wealth could be considered either impersonally or on broad social principles, whereas the consumption of wealth was an individual matter and subject to the whims and idiosyncrasies of a thousand different consumers. Consumption is, to be sure, more subject to individual idiosyncrasy than production or distribution, but it is not nearly so subject thereto as at first appears. It, too, is largely dependent on broad principles and laws, which we have not recognized because the separate sciences of which they are a part have been, at these particular points, undeveloped. Hence a second important reason for the delayed appearance of consumption as a science lies in the fact that the various sciences and branches of knowledge on which an understanding of consumption rests have themselves been delayed in development. That portion of psychology on which consumption leans most heavily—the study of interest—has even yet received relatively little attention from psychologists. The study of cultural anthropology, which is so important for giving the student a detached view of human institutions, is, as an organized body of knowledge, a product of the last few years. It is only within the last few years that we have had the beginnings of a science of human geography; we have only just commenced to understand what is implied, or not implied, in the biological basis of race. Scholars are still disagreeing over the most fundamental problems of population. The possibilities of those physiological sciences to which the well-being of the body should be entrusted are only just becoming known. The conception of consumption as an art is only hinted at in the works of a few of the more daring philosophers. And, finally, our knowledge of comparative standards of living is as yet very slight. We know little enough about any peoples other than our own, and very little indeed about other peoples' standards of living. It is clear that if we want to improve our consumption we should pool the experiences of all human beings who have something to contribute.

THE RELATION OF CULTURE TO CONSUMPTION

This brings us, in fact, to another aspect of our problem, another difficulty in connection with it. We need considerable insight into the culture of other peoples, their general way of living, their point of view and their attitude before we can understand the significance of their experiences in using goods, or what their consumption means to them. What a people gets from its consumption depends partly on its point of view, its general attitude toward life and living. The common definition of culture in the sense we use it is the mode of living that distinguishes one large group of mankind from another. Yet a "culture" is not a mere sum of beliefs, practices, and goods and services consumed. It is beliefs, practices, goods and services linked and bound together first by a mutual dependence on some common point of view, and second by a mutual interdependence on one another. A culture, in other words, is organic.

Our culture is not the sum of the visible aspects of life here in the United States nor is the culture of India the sum of the visible aspects of life there. The meaning of the begging bowl in actual life in India depends on something that goes deeper than appearance; it is a symbol of something believed to be significant. In the same way, a tunnel under the Hudson River is to us not a mere tunnel, though we may think so. It is one symbol of our domination over the powers of nature. An American would condemn the begging bowl, and an East Indian of the old school would condemn the tunnel. Neither would be right, for the condemnation in each case would be based on what the bowl or the tunnel would signify in his own culture; each should be judged in the light of what it means to the people who have it.

All goods and services consumed except the very simplest—air, light, and the food and protection necessary to keep a man alive—enter human experience not as things in themselves but as things refracted by a point of view, as light is refracted by passing through a prism.   As yet each main type of culture is its own dome of many colored glass.

A simple figure will illustrate this influence of culture.   In this diagram, the lines between Nature and Man represent

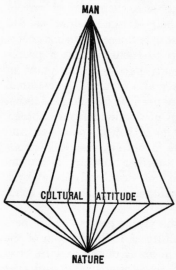

the course that is taken by the various factors which enter our experience.   Only the very simplest things proceed directly, as by the heavy black vertical line.   Almost everything is deflected by cultural attitude, some things more and some things less, and therefore reach man by an indirect route.

This fact we should make note of at the outset, since it is essential for the understanding of culture and hence for the complete understanding of consumption. We shall not, however, consider it particularly again until, at the end of the book, we take up cultures again and compare them.   For the time being we are chiefly concerned with the lines of connection between wealth and man's use of it, not with the refraction of these lines by culture.

THE FIELD OF CONSUMPTION

It seems scarcely necessary to stress the importance of the study of consumption, but it is perhaps well to note that, after we know what actually is consumed, the study falls logically into two main divisions, first what causes it to be what it is, and, second, what is the consumption of different groups and different peoples in the world today.   So far as possible, also, we should consider a third question, the evaluation of consumption in terms of maximum satisfactions.

Human psychology, individual and social, provides the mechanism by means of which choices arise and consumption takes place. Choices are influenced by biological and environmental factors which human beings take very much as a matter of course and do not stop to analyze. They are influenced also to some extent by deliberately exercised reason. In our discussion we use the term *interests* to refer to economic choices concretely expressed. A less colorful term than wants or desires, it avoids their implications of need or of longing.

When we have surveyed the field of causes we are in a better position to understand our own consumption and the consumption of other peoples throughout the world. We should be able also to make a few generalizations as to the effects of consumption according to the nature of the satisfactions it produces and their enduring character.

This last aspect of our study is of course the most difficult. It has sometimes been maintained that it takes us out of the field of economics and into the field of ethics. This misconception is due to some mistakes of economists themselves, whose moral fervor has led them out of their own province. Ruskin, for instance, took his own personal and subjective conceptions of what was good and tried to introduce them under the name of economic truth. But economics has no business with the personal prejudices that so endanger the moral preacher. If he is to study satisfactions, the economist must approach them in the spirit not of the pulpit but of the laboratory, and render his verdict as impartially as if he were passing on the relative merits of coal and oil for running a ship.

At present, economics can do very little indeed to tell a man what is best; what are the greatest satisfactions, and how we may obtain them. The important thing, however, is that we have at last reached the place where economics can do something. With a further development of the sciences from which the science of consumption is derived and with a further study and appreciation of cultures other than our own, our problems in making choices will be led to more and more intelligent solutions.

CHAPTER II

THE BEGINNINGS OF CULTURE

"What is man that thou art mindful of him?"—The Book of Psalms.

The demands and exercises and interests of life call into use but a fraction of man's mental powers. Post-mortem examinations of our brains show that at best we use only part of their capacities. Perhaps we do as well as we can under the circumstances in which we find ourselves, but our potential achievement, from a physiological standpoint, is but started.

Yet we have achieved something. Our earliest human ancestors had apparently about the same mental capacity as we; but they knew and could do very much less. Let us imagine the earliest of these, some hairy creature with clouded eyes, a man without clothing, without tools, without weapons, without fire, a man living in a cave or in the trees, a man terrified by wind and thunder, a man at the mercy of wild animals, a man who could make noises but not speak, and yet a man with a brain like our brains and with all our capacities latent in him; the same man, in fact, of whom the Psalmist sings: "Thou hast put all things in subjection under his feet."

The consumption of the stooping, groping creature we have described was limited, like the consumption of animals, to a narrow variety of foods and to shelter. How did the consumption of something else begin? With what did it begin? At what points and how did men first control nature or "cultivate" it in the broad meaning of the word? When "cultivation" in this sense began, human culture became engrafted on animal consumption.

OUR SOURCES OF INFORMATION

Man in this earliest stage we have described has never been met. We have never seen him. We can only imagine him.

12

Our imagination is aided, however, by two sources of information: first, by those actual records of prehistoric man which archaeologists and anthropologists have unearthed; second, by the customs and interests of the more primitive peoples living on earth today or who have lived here and been studied recently.

It will help us to examine these sources of information for two reasons. First, primitive cultures are so remote from ours that we can approach them without prejudice; one of the most difficult things we can do is to look without prejudice into the origin of our own interests. From the very fact that they are ours we assume they arose from some justifiable and good cause. Even, however, when we clearly accept the fact that some of them originated blindly or foolishly, and when we resolve that we will examine the source of all others with an entirely open mind, we find it almost impossible to keep to our resolve consistently, for our interests are too closely bound up with all that we hold dear to our own nature.

For this reason it is easiest and simplest to lead up to the study of the origin of our own interests by beginning with a study of the interests of other persons so remote from ourselves that we can approach them with unbiased minds. When the origins of the interests of other peoples are obvious to us, and we see the general principles on which these origins rest, we can gradually be induced to contemplate our own interests in the light of these same principles. It is true also that we can look with less prejudice into primitive than into contemporary civilized cultures; for primitive cultures are in no sense competitors of our own. We can study a culture complex in Borneo far more dispassionately than a culture complex in Germany or England.

In the second place, primitive cultures, though by no means simple, are far simpler than our own or contemporary "civilized" cultures. The people whose interests are most amenable for study purposes are those whose interests are relatively few. Among them we meet with the smallest number of complicating conditions and circumstances, and origins are traced more clearly. Ideally we should like to go back to the very dawn of the human race and follow men's interests as they awoke one by one. We cannot do this, it is obvious, since we have few records of these prehistoric centuries. We can, however, use what knowledge of prehistoric interests we do possess, and supplement this very largely with our knowledge of the interests of the more primitive peoples living today or within recorded history. When we have discovered the principles lying behind the rise of these interests we shall be in a position to pick out from our contemporary life material which illustrates these same principles; and, if we know something of other cultures, we shall be prepared to answer the question: which of these principles in our own culture are most predominant, and why?

Of prehistoric man's affairs we know too little. What we do know comes to us very largely from the actual remains of his tools or other possessions. We have found these, perhaps with his bones, hidden away in caves or buried deep in the earth or under lakes or rivers. Within fifty years much interesting material has come to light by uncovering the kitchen middens, or, as we should say, the kitchen dumps of these prehistoric peoples. Obviously these remains must all be of articles fashioned of the most durable materials. Everything of perishable material has vanished. We have gained some knowledge of these men also from the paintings, relatively few in number, which they left on the walls of caves. Here we have their own pictures of what was engaging their attention.

We have a great mass of information regarding the interests of primitive peoples living within historic times, and, in fact, many of these so-called primitive peoples are living today. The Australians, some of the American Indians, and some of the South Sea islanders, for instance, are frequently called "primitive." The truth is, however, that all groups living within historic times have a considerable development of culture and are not primitive in any but a relative sense.

Now, in the first place, we should like to know what interests or types of interests are common to all known human cultures of whatever time and of whatever place. When we have determined this we shall have the universal substratum of cultures, and shall have set ourselves the problem of what is the relationship between human nature and these interests, that they should be found everywhere. In the second place, having isolated the first elements in culture, we shall be able more intelligently to study those that remain. Why are not these universal also? And why does one group develop its culture in one direction, and another in another?

It is clear we lack the materials to draw a picture of the development of men's interests one after another. The chances are, in fact, that these first interests did not appear in the same order in different places. Of course we cannot prove this, but the more primitive cultures we do find are so distinct from one another as to suggest that quite different influences bore upon each. Here one thing came first, and there, no doubt, another.

The most striking thing about the more primitive cultures is not that they have certain things in common, but that they are so extremely different. Nevertheless, a few traits and interests have been found to be common to all historic cultures, and evidences of the same traits and interests go far back in prehistoric times.

The First Useful Interests

Of the directly useful traits and interests, we find that all known men had learned to eat a wider variety of foods than were probably familiar to their pre-human ancestors and lived in a wider variety of types of home. Those in colder climates wore some kind of clothing. They all, moreover, had some sort of a cutting instrument. All men of historic cultures have known the use of string and the use of fire, and most have tamed the dog. Ashes and the bones of the dog have been found with the prehistoric, though not with the most ancient, remains of men.

How did men learn the use of these things? First of all,

it must be noted that these culture traits are all quite simple
and obvious.   If man is to begin anywhere, here is a good place.
Suggestions of these culture traits and interests are all around
us in nature.   A man has only to put forth his hand and take
what is offered.   Different sorts of food are all about him and
he sees every sort eaten by some kind of animal or bird or fish.
Why not extend his own dietary in this way?   So why not copy
the shelters of animals, their dens and houses?   The shelters,
caves, and huts of primitive men are not necessarily better
than those animals use or make, but animals merely follow
their instinct, as we say, and use or make exactly the same
kind of shelter generation upon generation, while our early
men, without showing more skill, exhibit slightly more in-
genuity.   Our primitive friends have several kinds of shelters,
according to circumstances, although the original models of
dens and wattled huts were all undoubtedly furnished by
animals or birds.

It would be hard to name any three interests more useful
to man than a cutting instrument, string, and fire.   It is worthy
to note, however, that not only are these few inventions very
useful; they are also, as primitive inventions go, fairly easy
ones to make or utilize.   So far as fire is concerned, nature
offers it to man in several ways: in volcanoes, and in forest
or grass fires set by lightning or caused by the friction of dead
tree branches.   Man has only to take the fire that is offered,
and suggestions for making it are given by sparks and friction.
It is a distinct step in advance of animals, which do not cook
food, although some of them deliberately seek the enjoyment
of a fire's warmth.

How this interest—the use of fire to cook—arose we can only
conjecture, but its most probable source is accident.   It may
even be that fire was worshipped before it was used to cook
food.   Fruits or vegetables accidentally baked in the ashes,
flesh roasted by the same means, must many times have been
eaten and found good.   Such food, too, it would be discovered,
in many cases kept better than raw food, and it might also be

realized that the body required less of it for nourishment. It would then seem to be a short step to the deliberate roasting of food, but we cannot know how many hundreds of times the accident was repeated before some one took the hint and cooked his meat by set purpose.

We do not know how far back man began to use string, but here again nature gives the suggestion. Creepers and vines bind together grasses and sticks in the forest. It does not seem to us a long step for a man passing through the forest to bind his burden in the same way, but again the purpose, ceremonial or directly practical, for which string was first used, can only be conjectured.

As for the cutting instrument, it is not at all uncommon for apes to use stones as missiles, so the differentiation between man and beast must come not in the use of stones but in the chipping or fashioning of stone to suit a purpose. Very many rude stone implements are found among the remains of prehistoric peoples, for stones are of all possible remains least subject to decay. The form of these implements gets rougher and rougher as we go further back into the dim past, until finally we reach the stage, hundreds of thousands of years ago, which causes archaeologists to debate as to whether certain more or less pointed stones, the so-called eoliths, are really fashioned by man at all.

That stones could cut man must have discovered by sad experience. No doubt he often cut his feet on the sharp edges of rocks over which he climbed, or scraped the skin from his fingers as he handled stones. Nature gave him the hint so far as the use of stones was concerned; and she gave him the hint also for fashioning stones by showing him how they were chipped if they fell or were knocked together. Whether these first implements were used for a practical purpose, like cutting meat, or scraping skins, or whether they were used in some ceremonial observance, who can say?

The primitive hunter must often have killed the mother wolf or jackal and then have come upon the orphaned little ones. The little ones may indeed, led by the familiar odor of their mother, have followed him home. Francis Galton suggests that the domestication of the dog began with the pleasure of watching puppies at their play. The useful friend, in other words, may well have developed from a playmate.

When an interest is once started, it tends to become a center from which spring other closely related interests, or extensions of itself. If it once succeeds in getting in, it may be worked to death as the saying goes. To this we shall refer in Chapter III.

The Not-Directly-Useful Interests

It is easier to talk about these useful interests common to primitive men than it is to explain the fact that not all of men's first interests were useful. Every primitive group ever studied has had interests of another type: interests that served no directly useful purpose at all. Cultures swerved from the directly utilitarian path almost as soon as they started; or they swerved first and started second, for all we know.

There are no concrete universal interests in this not-directly-useful class, but as a class it is probably larger than the useful class, and an enormous part of men's energies went to sustain it. It cannot but seem very strange indeed that man should spend his dawning intelligence so widely on other than utilitarian interests. He made fetishes and charms; he painted pictures, perhaps for aesthetic reasons but more probably because of his belief in sympathetic magic. He adorned himself in curious ways: various explanations have been suggested for the origin of this, but emulation was certainly present in it very early. In fact, among the most primitive peoples lately studied, clothing for self-adornment appears to take precedence over clothing for warmth or for so-called decency.

We must not dismiss the great mass of immaterial or unpractical culture among primitives as serving no useful purpose, for much of it did and does serve a useful purpose in a round-about and indirect way. Over and over again, as in this case of clothing, it provided the means by which practical ends were, as by accident, found to be efficiently accomplished; and means which so proved themselves efficient were adopted into the rational culture of the group. Of this we shall hear more later when we come to emulation.

The self-conscious and imaginative faculties of man, differentiating him from animals and at the same time showing him foolish as they are not—leading him often to useless, wasteful, or even harmful self-expression—are human qualities we take for granted, but which deserve more serious study than has ever been given them. The possession of these faculties, and not his utilitarian perceptions, may indeed prove to be the dividing line between man and his pre-human ancestors. There are some grounds for suspecting that utilitarian perceptions themselves grew out of these. The first man was perhaps not *homo sapiens* but *homo somnians;* not a man of discernment but a man of idle imaginings. It is a subject on which we should like to linger.

THE COMMON MATERIAL BASIS OF CULTURES

Enough has been said to show how meagre is the common material basis of cultures. From this common basis of the merest physical necessities of life and three simple inventions, or even before this common basis is reached, all the various cultures of the world shoot off in a hundred different ways. Indeed, when we come to study cultures we are overwhelmed and confused by the differences and the variety of culture traits disclosed. A generation ago, scholars thought they could classify cultures into savage, semi-savage, barbarous, and so on, using such tests as a knowledge of pottery or of metals, or the institution of agriculture, to mark the transition points from one stage to another. We know better than that now. To trace the reasons why one group is rich in this respect, and a second group in that, is one of the most fascinating tasks of the anthropologist.

As cultures develop do they tend to grow more or less like

one another? This all depends on circumstances, but for a time there are very definite tendencies making isolated cultures, at any rate, more and more peculiar along the lines of interest which originally secured a foothold.

In the next chapters we shall be concerned with the psychological mechanism behind our interests and the basic factors which contribute to the building up of cultures.

PART II

THE PSYCHOLOGY OF CONSUMPTION

CHAPTER III

HOW AN INTEREST ESTABLISHES ITSELF

*"The only freedom we can attain for our souls is through know-
ing and governing the activities of our bodies."—Preface to an old
Physiology.*

There is a story told of a young foreign correspondent of
unusually engaging manners. He was remarkably successful
in obtaining interviews with distinguished men and often did
not bother with the usual formality of a letter of introduction.
When he was asked how he managed it, he replied, "A smile
and an air of determination are the most useful passports."

Unfortunately the keepers who guard the doors by which
interests come through into our lives are beguiled neither by
the charms nor the virtues of potential new interests. Some
of these doorkeepers are more willing to take a chance than
others, but even those who are most open to conviction require
the new interest to show its pedigree. And a potential new
interest fares the better, the more relationships it can prove
it has with interests that have already succeeded in passing
the threshold. We like to think of ourselves as free to choose
what we will, but these doorkeepers of ours interfere, with
their own prejudices. In short, we are inhabiting bodies in
which free spirits become somewhat restive at times. "The
Lord let the house of a brute to the soul of a man," said Tennyson, and we have to make the best of it.

THE PHYSICAL MECHANISM INVOLVED IN INTEREST

We learn from psychology that there is a physical mechanism,
the nervous system, for transmitting the impressions of the
outer world to the brain. The impression travels over a well-
defined path from the outer sense organ to the brain, where
the impression more or less consciously enters the life of the

21

man, and becomes a part of his acquired equipment, or a part of his interest in the broad sense of that word. We know of no way in which anything can get into the mind without using the physical mechanism of the nervous system. Apparently, then, our culture and all the various interests composing it have entered our lives by passing along the nerve currents by which there is communication between the outer world and the human mind.

It would seem that a knowledge of the nature of the nerve currents and how they respond to outer stimuli must throw light on the study of human interests. The world is full of potential interests, but in Chapter II we have seen how slowly they get into consciousness, and how one-sided, how narrow, how peculiar, are the ways in which they are grouped when once they are found within. It is possible that the study of psychology can explain to us the reason for such peculiarities. Indeed, psychology can do a great deal to explain them to us; and its explanation is given fundamentally in terms of the law of the conservation of energy.

We saw from Chapter II how rare was the introduction of a new interest, and we know that men must have lived many thousands of years on this earth with practically no interests beyond the inborn interests of animals. We saw, too, that the use of the first material interests of men—fire, a cutting instrument, string—had undoubtedly been suggested by the environment over and over again before anything happened in man himself to get the suggestion into consciousness. Indeed, the accomplishment of acquiring the first conscious and intelligent interest may well have been relatively much greater for primitive man than for us would be the accomplishment of communicating with the planets. In his case, it was a problem of establishing a simple interest for which there were no precedents; in our case it is the problem of a complex invention for which there are altogether inadequate precedents, but nevertheless many of them. It is only by very gradual stages that we can proceed to an interest in the unfamiliar.

It takes a great genius to go forward without the encouragement of many precedents.

But what, from a psychological point of view, is the advantage of precedent? It is this. When a channel of communication is once established between the outer world and the brain, or the brain and the outer world, it is like the making of a path from one point to another. If one wants to travel the same way again it is easier to do so; if one wants to travel a similar way, the first path will help in part. Even if one wants to travel in a quite different way by a new path, it is something to know that paths have been made before; for at least one has the encouragement of the example of other pioneers. A new connection established between the outer world and the brain is like the first trail that an explorer makes through an uncharted wilderness: the more it is trodden, the easier it is to follow. Or it is like the first course of the spring rains down a hillside, a course which becomes a deeper bed with each succeeding flood.

HABIT AND INTEREST

This account, as an explanation of habit, is familiar to students of elementary psychology. By repetition in this way, interests become "vested" and relatively secure. Thus there is always a presumption in favor of an habitual interest and a presumption against a new idea that has its own new way to make.

How an habitual interest ofttimes refuses to budge when conditions change is very well illustrated when people move from one locality to another. They cling, for instance, to old diets which may be difficult to obtain, and hesitate to try new foods. Boas tells us that although the Eskimos have adapted themselves very well to their habitat, they yet have a law forbidding the promiscuous use of caribou-meat and of seal-meat.

"Another example is presented by the reindeer-breeding Chukchee, who carry about in their nomadic life a tent of most complicated structure, which corresponds in its type to the older permanent house of the coast dwellers, and which contrasts in the most marked way with the simplicity and light weight of the Eskimo tent." [1]

Some of our own first settlers in America tried for a time to make their houses of stone, like the cottages they had left in England, regardless of the fact that wood was a far more economical material in the new country.

Such illustrations are examples of habits which have been carried or which might have been carried into social life to become customs or conventions. The general subject of customs and conventions with particular reference to its social significance is left to Chapter V; at this point we are concerned only with the physical basis of habit in the nervous system of the individual.

Instances of habits which affect primarily the interests of single individuals are found in the personal experiences of all of us. A man "gets used" to riding without a saddle, a woman "gets used" to sewing without a thimble. "I don't care if the thing is more efficient," they say. "It isn't for me." Or, "I learned to eat with one kind of knife and fork and one kind is enough." "My mother taught me to do it this way." "I don't like the feeling of overshoes. I never wore them." "No, I never read books. I guess they never taught me to read right." The personal idiosyncrasies which affect interest tend to disappear under the pressure of society, but they are frequently important in the lives of the middle-aged and the old. Habit as affecting interest is more important when it has established itself as custom and convention, for then it binds all society, as we shall later see.

New Interests and the Extension of Old Ones

Our explanation of the physical basis of interest casts light on more than simple habit. It illuminates in two other important ways the question of interest in general and culture

[1] Boas, Franz, *The Mind of Primitive Man*, New York, 1911, p. 162. The latter example is quoted by him from Waldemar Bogoras.

traits in particular. In the first place it explains how one
trait leads to another new and unrelated new one which
happens to have something in common with it, as is shown
in Figure A. If a possible new trait has some point of sim-

OLD TRAIT A ━━━━━━━━━➤ NEW TRAIT B ━━━━━━━━━➤ SECOND NEW TRAIT C

FIGURE A

ilarity to an old trait, it can travel part of the way by a
road already made.

In the second place, it explains how, when once a new trait
has really got in, has become a "vested" interest, it is likely
to expand and enlarge; to send out branches of itself. New
possibilities appear in it, and it may grow into what is known
as a trait complex. A trait complex, which is seen as a group
of interests related to a single trait as in Figure B, has its
basis in a system of nerve connections within the human body.

While new traits or interests are coming in and old ones
are expanding in these two fashions, other traits and interests,
perhaps better, perhaps more useful, are not recognized at all;
they do not succeed in getting
in because they are too strange
and unfamiliar; they are not
sufficiently akin to anything
gone before so that there is
enough road for them to travel
on.

It is easy to see that all this is
an expression of the same law
of conservation of energy that
one meets in all departments
of science and of life. In psy-

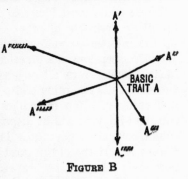

FIGURE B

chology its application is attested to in the phenomena of
habit and in the phenomena of so-called associationism and
of conditioned reflexes.

New Interests

Now let us go back to man's actual interests and see how this helps us to understand some of their peculiarities. In the first place, as to new interests: how is it that some interests get in and some do not? Chance has a good deal to do with presenting possibilities for culture traits, and men often show an immediate reaction of superficial interest to anything new that is brought to their attention. Animals do this as well. A proverb tells us that curiosity has killed cats. Wise parents know that one way to divert crying children is to show them something new. Yet, novelty alone and by itself would never install interests for cats, for children, or for men. When novelty is the only attraction, interest diminishes as novelty wears off, and each succeeding minute makes the new thing less desirable. An exploring expedition made presents of fish hooks, hatchets, and bright utensils to a party of aborigines who had never seen the like before. The savages seemed delighted, but the next day the explorers found all their gifts lying discarded on the sand. The same fate befalls one hundred of the hundred and one fads human beings chase after every year.[1]

Those traits most likely to get in have characteristics found useful or desirable in other connections. Men actually take up the interests recommended to them by other associations. We have seen how the practical uses of fire, the cutting instrument, string, were all suggested by the environment many times. Fruits like other fruits known to be edible will be tested and enjoyed. If a man likes plums, which are blue, round, soft, and juicy he will be disposed to try grapes which are blue, round, soft, and juicy, too. This is illustrated in our preceding Figure A. If the old interest in this figure is plums, the first new trait, B, may be grapes, and the second new trait, C, may be blueberries. But an already established interest for plums or grapes or blueberries will not help a man to discover the edibility of chestnuts.

[1] Cf. p. 41.

It is only within a few decades that the tomato has been regarded as good to eat. For many years it was popularly believed to be poison, since the plant resembled its cousin, the deadly night-shade. People who consider spring lamb a great delicacy scorn the woodchuck, that has fed on the most delicate garden vegetables. What is wrong with the woodchuck? He is related to our sinister neighbor, the rat. The creatures branded as unclean in the Mosaic law, the pig, the vulture, the oyster, and others, were considered such primarily because of the unappetizing food they ate or were believed to eat, and with which they themselves were therefore associated. When the United States Bureau of Fisheries instituted a change in the name of the small shark, dogfish, and gave it the commercial appellation of grayfish it was found, as was expected, that people became willing to buy it. An eel tastes all right to the man who has never seen one.

What applies to foods applies equally clearly in other cases. The first textile fabrics in most parts of the world were made of wool. The white fuzz of the cotton plant, tree wool, as the Germans say, suggested that it also might be used as wool was used. We know how hard the Western World tried to discover the source of silk. The Chinese were able to keep it secret a long time because there was nothing in the cocoon of a caterpillar to suggest the basic textile materials with which the Western World was already familiar.

Well-intentioned missionaries who have tried to introduce new tools into primitive economies have often had great difficulty unless the new tool was fashioned to resemble the old one. A sharp new steel axe, for example, would not be used unless its head was moulded in the shape of the clumsy old stone axe with which the natives were familiar. In placing on the market more efficient electric cooking devices today, producers have met an unexpected objection from housewives who want something in the kitchen that reminds them of the old-fashioned cooking stove.

We remember that the first automobiles looked very much

like buggies. Stream-line effects would not have been popular in 1902. All our modern new interests and inventions are, in fact, the offspring of the associations lying about us, and what we are able to do depends very obviously on what we have already done. The mind of a genius can move more speedily and take longer leaps than the mind of an ordinary person, but even the action of the mind of a genius is dependent on the nature of the materials it can lay hold of. Our cultural advance is held back because of a lack of sufficient desirable associations on which to build; in some cases it is checked also because of illogical associations—such as that of the tomato and the night-shade, the eel and the snake—already formed; and thus many good interests still wait outside the threshold of recognition.

THE EXTENSION OF OLD INTERESTS

One of the most peculiar things that we noticed when we glanced at primitive cultures in Chapter II was that they appeared so one-sided. Anthropologists have given up trying to arrange primitive cultures in an orderly sequence from lower to higher because to a very large extent they are not comparable. Group or tribe A attains great perfection in one thing, let us say bead-work, but gets nowhere with something else, let us say basketry, which tribe B does better than civilized man; but tribe B, so proficient in basket-making, may have neither pottery nor blankets. The New Britishers, who apparently had the most highly developed money economy of any primitive people, went about wearing no clothes at all. We can find many examples of extreme development in one direction combined with complete lack of development in another.

The fact is, each more or less isolated group of mankind gets started with a few ideas or interests over and above those necessary for sustaining life, and goes on developing those few further and further and more and more; while the group may be absolutely blind to the existence or desirability of others which would be far more useful to them.

"The mind, it would seem, when once started on a track develops that, and the utmost refinements along one line may appear before we have developments along other lines at all. The obsessional use of certain materials, such as wood, by some peoples and their refusal to see the possibilities in other materials; the exclusive use, in one area, of birch bark for baskets, for tepees, for canoes, and the exclusive use of skins in an adjoining area for the same purposes; the insistence on a variation of one type of utensil for all uses; the recurrence of certain basic forms on which all weapons are modelled: all these are instances as to how great an extent a culture is due to a relatively few themes, which, however they get started in the first place, are repeated over and over. The thing that once succeeds in arriving has a very good chance of arriving again." [1]

We have all heard of the Stone Ages. Why were they so called? Simply because a significant part of their culture was the extension of various uses of stone. In the Stone Age we have points, scrapers, scratchers, cleavers, flakes, disks, gravers, drills, spokeshaves, saws, hammerstones, knives, and bolas, all of stone. [2] In time this basic substance was supplanted or supplemented by organic materials such as bone, ivory, and reindeer horn, from which in turn a vast number of implements were made. [3] In the beginning most of the whole meagre culture may be the immediate offspring of some one thing, of which stone is the best example. As culture advances, however, complexes center around a number of different traits.

American anthropologists have made clear to us the importance of certain trait complexes among American Indians. [4] Let us look, for instance, at the Indian corn complex, which our first settlers took over almost without change. Maize was the great food of the North American Indians in the Plains region; it was continually before their eyes, and their culture came very largely to center about it. They made various inventions to utilize it more fully—the corn crib, the husking pin, the mortar, the mush ladle; they applied it and

[1] Hoyt, E. E., *Primitive Trade*, London, 1926, p. 48.
[2] MacCurdy, G. G., *Human Origins*, New York, 1924, Vol. I, p. 133.
[3] Ibid., Vol. II, Chapter XII, " The Stone Age Culture Complex."
[4] See Wissler, G., *Man and Culture*, New York, 1923, pp. 121–125.

its products to solve problems that arose in other connections—cornhusk mats, corncob pipes; and they experimented with it to make new dishes. It is obvious how the law of the conservation of energy through association is working here. It was easier for Indians in the cornbelt to think about corn than to think about walnuts or potatoes; they got started on corn and they became corn-minded.

There is no particular point in drawing our illustrations from primitive culture except that it is somewhat more easy to perceive trait complexes among primitive peoples. We in the United States have our own trait complexes. The automobile, the radio, ice cream, are each the center of a trait complex. A trait may send off its rays and from the ends of the rays, in turn, new rays may be sent off. Let us take electricity as a culture trait. It branches into electricity for

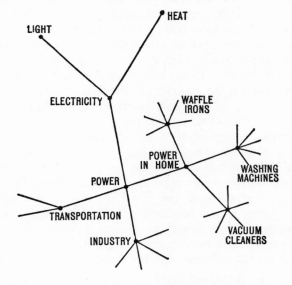

light, heat, power. One branch of electricity for power leads to domestic equipment. One branch of domestic equipment

leads to waffle irons. Different types of waffle irons follow;
and different recipes for making waffles and similar delicacies.
A figure based on Figure B on page 25 makes this plain. The
mind runs in tracks and its expansion is closely circumscribed
by them. Since electricity is the center of an important trait
complex with us, it is easier for us to think of new kinds of
electric waffle irons than of new kinds of harps or lyres. If
we had started on music instead of electricity, the idea of
waffle irons would make us laugh. A waffle iron for every
home would seem as absurd as a lyre for every home today,
and probably more so.

Most of the trait complexes of the American people are
bound together in one great industrial or material culture
complex. We are industrially minded and proud of it. What
we do not see, of course, is how one-sided our culture appears
in the eyes of other peoples, as their cultures likewise appear
one-sided to us. The keepers who stand guard over the thresh-
olds of our interests are, of course, letting interests of a certain
type in, and holding others out. One type gains admittance
in Borneo, another type gains admittance in India, and another type in the United States.

The Culture-Centric Predicament

It would seem, would it not, that we are pretty well caught
in a web of our own spinning? We can see that we are caught
but we cannot see how to get out nor what to do if we could
get out. As our experiences are bound by our own egos, so
our interests are bound by our own cultures. And no amount
of cultural psycho-analysis will help us either.

Looking back in cultural history we can see prejudices we
have escaped. The twentieth century descendants of the
Puritans, for example, are doubtless less prejudiced than the
Puritans were, and, indeed all mankind has presumably thrown
off some shackles since then. But it is very hard indeed to
give many important examples of prejudices we are suffering
today, and even harder to point out desirable interests that

have not yet been able to gain an entrance into our lives. The very fact of the recognition of a prejudice, or the perception of a new and desirable interest, even by one person alone, is the first and longest step towards the elimination of the prejudice or the establishment of the new interest.

A man who has come in contact with cultures other than his own should be able to make suggestions for the improvement of his own, but no one can see far into the untrodden future of culture as a whole. The worst prejudices and the best new interests of all are recognized by nobody. No one knows what marvellous things are waiting for passports outside the threshold of recognition!

The first intelligent step to emancipation is the consciousness of bondage. We cannot do away with our nervous systems, but we may be clever enough to command and cajole them, and so find a speedier way

"Tomorrow to fresh woods and pastures new."

CHAPTER IV

HOW GROUP LIFE STIMULATES THE INTERESTS OF ITS MEMBERS

"The Joneses, they got a Cadillac; and I says to my wife, 'Well, maybe we can go them one better.'"—Heard on a street corner.

Robinson Crusoe is said to be the economists' favorite character in fiction. It would be hard to find a person more suited to be the hero in a discussion of marginal utility. As we stand on the threshold of this chapter we recall his careful, intelligent and unbiased choices with admiration—and with a sigh. If all men were like him, and if all were hermits on desert islands, this chapter would not have been written. But the ordinary man lives in society, and even Robinson Crusoe eventually went back to his kind.

The "Group Spirit"

Men in groups act differently from men on desert islands. They are stimulated to resemble one another; they are handicapped by social restraint. They want what their neighbors have and they are afraid to be independent in their wants; in fact, it hardly occurs to them to be independent. Men in groups are subject to one another's enthusiasms and prejudices. The ideas and interests of the group are contagious within the group, while new ideas and interests have a hard time getting started.

When, in Chapters I and II, we took a brief survey of the various cultures throughout the world, we saw that the surface of the globe was divided into more or less distinct culture areas. In our last chapter we cast some light on the peculiarities of those areas by showing that new interests depended very largely on old ones. So far, however, we have made our explanations in terms of the psychology of an individual man, alone and by himself, and all that was said in Chapter III

would apply just as much to the psychology of our friend
Robinson as to the psychology of a Chicagoan or a citizen
of Los Angeles.

It is the purpose of this and the next chapter to go a step
further and to set forth additional psychological factors that
work in society.

The curious way in which a man is influenced by those
around him, to such an extent, at times, that members of one
particular group come to resemble one another in all interests
and beliefs, so that they act as one man against outsiders,
and against the interests and beliefs of outsiders, has led
some students to speak of a group mind or a group spirit
and some have gone so far as to say there must be a group mind
or spirit separate and distinct from, but nevertheless including,
the various minds and spirits of the individuals composing
the group.   Such words or phrases as alma mater, Britannia,
the spirit of California, indicate how this idea grips the popular
imagination.

Count Hermann Keyserling states the case for a culture
"soul" in this way: [1]

> "All aggregations of individuals necessarily create a true super-in-
> dividual unity which transforms the individual into something other
> than it was before . . . So collective souls emerge at every moment,
> and a collectivity increases its mastery over its component parts in
> proportion as a relationship is more enduring and many-sided and as
> it faces as a whole other collectivities. And thus when we keep the
> state of things in view, we are by no means concerned in our acceptance
> of the culture-soul, with postulates, but with a more or less felicitous
> designation for indubitable truths. It depends on this alone as far
> as we are concerned. . . . Collective states and thus cultures, too, are
> true, independent life-unities, no matter if they present primary or
> secondary formations."

People who are members of the same group are, as we have
said, both stimulated and restrained by their connection with
the group. How are they stimulated?

[1] *The World in the Making*, (Samuel, Maurice, trans.) New York, 1927, pp.
121–122.

EMULATION DEFINED

The spirit of the group, in the first place, directs the form and type taken by new interests along the lines of interests already established and approved by society. In the second place, the spirit of the group facilitates the diffusion of old interests among all the members of the group. These two aspects of the reaction of group life on interests may both be considered under the head of emulation. Emulation is distinctly a phenomenon of group life. It is a man's desire, on the one hand to excel, on the other hand to equal or keep pace with his fellows.

Robinson Crusoe seems to have kept at work, but constructive activity is not a usual characteristic of hermits. Most hermits lack incentive. Group life tends to foster progress because it provides a standard by which progress may be estimated. A man ordinarily looks at his neighbors to find the milestones by which he judges the extent and the rapidity of his advance. There is more incentive to try to get ahead in a group because within a group one can see whether one has made progress or not. Family A has a definite measuring stick for its own achievements in the house and lot, the car, the radio, and the fur coats of the B family.

At the same time that group life in general fosters the progressive spirit, it tends to direct the form that the progressive spirit shall take. By deflecting creative activity into socially approved channels it may economize it; it may save it from being thrown to the winds of the individual's own obstinate, perverse, or restless fancy. The group seeks to make the outstanding individual conform to its own standards and carry its own interests further. In many cases this is doubtless a bad thing; in many other cases it is doubtless a good one. Have we not all seen creative energy wasted by some individual who was too proud, too wise in his own conceits to recognize the spirit of his age or his community? On the other hand, we have all seen many who did not dare to be original.

In its aspect of desire to equal, emulation effects the spread of interests throughout a group with the greatest possible speed. While the leaders are trying to excel, the great mass of the members of a group are trying to bring their interests up to the number and kind of interests that are fostered by their leaders. Because of the strong sympathy existing between members of a group, such conformity in interest is comparatively easy. It is hard for one member to adopt an interest not socially approved, but almost no effort is required for him to buy a car or install a radio set or an electric refrigerator. Indeed, the difficult thing may be to refrain from adopting these new interests. Society almost forces them upon one.

As the desire to equal, emulation stimulates men to an ever-changing conformity with their fellows; as the desire to excel, emulation stimulates men to get ahead of their fellows in socially approved lines.

How Emulation Affects Interests

Emulation may affect almost any interests and in an active society full of material interests it does affect almost all. Nevertheless, it is obvious that it is of greatest importance in introducing and diffusing such interests as may be conspicuously exhibited—its chief service is to encourage "conspicuous consumption," in Veblen's excellent phrase. It affects people's clothing more than it affects their cooking utensils, it affects their cars more than it affects their furnaces, and it affects their window draperies more than it affects the mattresses on their beds. I congratulate myself if my grandmother's -pie plates, her mattresses, and her furnace are still in good condition but I should hate to attend an afternoon tea in her best bombazine gown.

Apparently men begin to emulate as soon as they begin to be men. We have already noted the resort to artificial means for distinction as one of the characteristics that sharply distinguish man from animals. An ape is usually content as nature made him, but a man-ape must stick a red feather in his hair. Personal ornaments, such as necklaces of animals' teeth, are found among very ancient prehistoric remains, and practically all living tribes indulge in some form of adornment of the body. These decorations often form, indeed, a considerable part of the material culture of the people, and we have a very extensive literature dealing with various types of primitive decoration. The wearing of clothing itself may have originated as a form of decoration. We know what extensive use primitives make of ornaments in all possible ways in which they can be attached to their persons, and of the various malformations and mutilations of the body practiced by primitives to secure distinction of one sort or another.

As civilization advances there is relatively less tendency to call attention to oneself by the obvious and somewhat naïve method of personal adornment. It is usually the less developed races, or at least the less developed individuals, who mutilate their bodies or bedeck themselves with gold and jewels. At the same time, with the advance of civilization, there is more tendency to resort to somewhat more subtle means of distinction. The economic world provides a very rich field from which material for this purpose may be drawn.

The display of expensive goods of any sort testifies to the economic distinction of the owner. They proclaim him a person of wealth, and in a pecuniary society like ours in the United States today, this is a distinction worth achieving. At the same time the display of particular economic goods testifies to the style or to the presumptive good taste of the owner. A man may achieve distinction either by having many and expensive things or by having things of an approved or well-chosen type.

As soon as it is learned by experience that economic goods may be of great service in setting one man off from another, a strong stimulus is given to displaying goods and to searching for more and other economic goods which shall extend the possibility of emulation in yet more refined ways.

PECUNIARY EMULATION

For a brilliant exposition of the way in which emulation
in number and expense of goods and services has affected
economic life, we are indebted to Veblen's *Theory of the Leisure
Class.*

In primitive groups, where all the members of the group
are well acquainted, there are many ways of obtaining distinction other than by the use of economic goods. A man's
skill in hunting, bravery in fighting, are well known to all his
associates, and win him glory. But as population increases,
as society grows more complex, and as the number of people
with whom a man is thrown in contact becomes larger, the
non-material means of attaining distinction, while they doubtless become no less important absolutely, do become relatively
less important. The extent of a man's native gifts, his wisdom,
his courage, and the other endowments or capacities by which
he might win the esteem of his fellows are ordinarily known
only within his immediate circle, and if he wishes to impress
others outside he can do this most easily by resorting to a
display of material possessions which are vicarious testimony
of his distinction. In a pecuniary society, where wealth-getting
is an indication of superiority, the mere display of material
possessions is in itself a token of wealth-getting ability. In
fact, as pecuniary valuations become more widespread and
significant, the display and use of goods becomes increasingly
important not only outside one's intimate circle, but to a large
extent within it.

It is amazing to what a great extent pecuniary valuations
enter into our lives and control or affect our interests, and to
what an extent our potential sources of satisfaction are limited,
because pecuniary emulation uses up our resources. We expect
some of the newly-rich to behave foolishly, but what about
college students? Pecuniary emulation affects their dress,
of course, but it goes much further. A group of college girls
confessed that pecuniary emulation entered even into their

purchases of pencils and notebook paper. "I'd be ashamed
to take my notes with a cheap pencil," one girl said. But,
worse than this, pecuniary emulation led many of them to
buy what they did not want in other ways at all. It affected
their spending at soda-fountains and in tea-rooms. "If the
bunch order sundaes, I think I must. And if they order banana
splits at thirty cents, I feel I have to pay thirty cents too,
even though I don't want to eat and am trying to reduce.
I don't want the others to think I am stingy." Another said:
"My crowd have all been getting expensive perfumes, and I
couldn't go home over the holiday because I spent so much
for an ounce bottle. And the worst of it is, I don't care for
perfumes myself."

Certain advantages to society do, however, arise from
pecuniary emulation, so far as the introduction of new interests
is concerned. The newly rich do no more than display quantities of goods, expensive goods, and variety of goods, and yet
as a potential market for such goods they stimulate the production of some things which are bound to prove later of
substantial value in other ways. To possess a variety of goods
means that a person must become familiar with a number of
different things, and some of these may turn out to be highly
desirable in themselves.

The automobile is an excellent example of an expensive
good the use of which was greatly stimulated by pecuniary
emulation. To be sure, the automobile is of practical service
also, but emulation has had much to do with establishing it
as a practical necessity for half the American people. The
group that first bought their automobiles for pecuniary emulation have come to accept automobiles as an essential part of
their standard of living and the emulative principle now works
chiefly in influencing what make of car they will buy. For
them, perhaps, pecuniary emulation in airplanes will come
next.

Emulation in expense has indirectly had something to do
with developing tastes for music and for art. It has stimulated

the introduction of pianos, phonographs, and radios. It has led people to seek art that is costly, and at the same time of some aesthetic value. It has been partly responsible for costly and sometimes beautiful houses, and it has been one means of introducing fine furniture and even bathrooms into our homes. Certain refinements of service, originally desired because they were expensive, have brought with them improvements in manners.

EMULATION IN NOVELTY: FASHION

Emulation in expense is not the only type of emulation for which economic goods are useful. Through economic goods one may show his superiority as a person who recognizes the latest thing, who knows what is up to the minute. This sort of emulation prevails to some degree in primitive societies as well. One man throws a mat across his pony's back, and presently a whole tribe rides on mats. Another makes a fireplace in his hut; all his visitors desire fireplaces in their huts, and so the whole tribe come to make fireplaces. A trader complains that the styles are always changing among the primitive groups he visits, and what is desired eagerly on one voyage will not be looked at on the next. It is discouraging, indeed, to carry a cargo of red beads to people who are clamoring for yellow feathers.

Emulation in novelty, or fashion, often requires that a good deal of money should be spent, but the emphasis is put not on the money cost, but on the style. In the United States today emulation in novelty is perhaps quite as important as pecuniary emulation. Few of us are aware of the extent to which fashion dictates to us. It dictates in literature, for instance. Most popular new books make their sales in their first year or two and then drop to nothing. "Have you read So and So? Everybody's doing it. Oh, *that!* Why nobody's reading *that* now." Fashion very greatly influences house building. We know the bay windows, turrets and towers of the late Victorian period. A few years ago the prevailing architecture was

Dutch colonial, but an adapted French cottage is now taking its place. With fashion in furniture and furnishings we are all familiar, and some of us remember when sturdy mission chairs and tables were discarded as clumsy and ugly, and Grand Rapids colonial moved in. Straight draperies—"the only possible artistic method of draping"—suddenly disappeared from our windows and loops and scallops appeared again. "But I thought they were inartistic," pleaded an amateur. "Our taste was not sufficiently developed to appreciate them," replied the interior decorator. "To be sure our mothers used loops long ago, but they put them in the wrong place." Fashion in dress is now more important than pecuniary emulation in dress, except for a few aristocratic old ladies and gentlemen who still examine goods to determine their quality. The modern woman does not care half so much about the quality of her silk as she cares about the width of the hem and the shape of the neckline. "It's being worn," is the salesman's best recommendation to the modern man.

What a merry-go-round it is! And it is the merriest merry-go-round of all in the case of fads, which today are and tomorrow are forgotten. Professor Bogardus and his collaborators made up annually for ten years a list of fads, which totalled 735 different ones for the whole period. He found that not more than 2% of all appeared on three successive annual lists. For most there was a curve showing "a somewhat rapid incline or quick adoption, an extreme popularity or plateau of perhaps two or three months, and a sloping decline." [1] A mere handful of the 735 were permanently retained.

The people who keep up with fads and fashions are often very able people who want to be doing something and don't know just what. They welcome the effort to keep dashing along with the crowd because they find it uses up all their superfluous energy. But it is a display of power that has failed to find a creative outlet, a sound and fury signifying nothing.

[1] Bogardus, E. S., "Social Psychology of Fads," *Journal of Applied Sociology.* VIII, pp. 239–243.

Occasionally, however, fashion and fad quite by accident hit upon something so useful that people insist on keeping it, and then the novelty joins the slowly increasing ranks of our permanent interests. It was a turn of the wheel of fashion, for instance, that brought in low shoes, short skirts, and short hair, and now all the style-mongerers in Christendom are having a hard time to turn these things out again.

Occasionally, too, fashion may be a means by which the introduction of some good new interest is hastened. Home economists tried to set a style for serving a salad at dinner, and they succeeded. Ten years or so ago it would be asked in small town circles: "Did you go to Mrs. Brown's luncheon? Did she have salad? They say it has vitamins or something. It certainly gives a lot of style to a meal."

EMULATION IN TASTE

Emulation in the display of taste is not so common as pecuniary emulation or fashion, but it has probably the greatest permanent good results, for ordinarily it is the least wasteful expression of emulation. It is the means people choose to get credit for good taste or good judgment; and sometimes they really acquire good taste or judgment in the process. The desire to be thought superior is influential in introducing a style of living rather above the real tastes and judgment of the people affecting it. A style of living persisted in, however, in the course of time really transforms those who attempt to follow it. It has been said that, no matter how crude are the tastes of self-made millionaires, their children and grandchildren cannot escape achieving some distinction from their schools, social contacts, and even their material surroundings, which a wise self-made man leaves to the choice of someone better taught than himself. Indeed, when people are striving for emulation in true good taste they should look well to be sure they follow the best models. What the multitude calls good taste is too often merely the prevailing aspect of fashion.

Many witty sallies are pointed at good folk who go religiously to Symphony concerts without knowing Bach from Offenbach, and visit art galleries to exclaim about the wrong things. Yet such procedure is certainly not entirely absurd, for, if we have time enough, we will show in ourselves the character of the surroundings we have sought for ourselves. Even a college education is desired by some people as a means of social distinction, but no one ever went to college without getting at least a little something more from it than that. Our dress, our furniture, and our architecture have all been influenced for the good by our desire to show ourselves appreciative of the best. Emulation in character of interests is, in fact, very closely related to the deliberate discipline and control of tastes, which will be taken up in a later chapter.

How Powerful Is Emulation in Culture?

Emulation affecting interests is most powerful where group feeling is, consciously or unconsciously, a strong force. It flourishes everywhere, but it is seen at its height in relatively well-knit groups, the members of which regard themselves essentially as equals. A true hermit does not emulate at all. In a country where there are several social classes the citizen in the lowest rank will probably be influenced a little to emulate those remote from him, but his strongest stimulus will come from the group most like himself. Democracy is one of the strongest influences favoring emulation. There is far more emulation in the United States than in Europe, and far more in Europe than in India.

One of the best places to observe emulation is on a college campus. On a campus students are known to one another and group spirit is consciously and deliberately fostered, sometimes even beyond its normal development. At the same time college students are at an age where social approval seems unusually desirable, for social approval is greatly esteemed in adolescence and the years immediately following. We have spoken of the influence of emulation on college girls, and college boys are not very different.

So powerful is the influence of emulation at the college age under the wing of alma mater that young people on the whole incline to overestimate its importance as a driving force in progress. Important it is, but it kicks up a tremendous amount of dust for every millimeter it leads men forward. It is not progress to keep jumping from straight draperies to looped draperies and back again, nor is it progress to change the lines of a car every six months. If one swings around in a circle he can cover a good many miles and still end at his starting point.

Some cultural advance results from emulation, as we have seen, but emulation is by no means the only motive that leads men to good work and new interests.

CHAPTER V

HOW GROUP LIFE RESTRAINS THE INTERESTS OF ITS MEMBERS

"The despotism of custom is everywhere the standing hindrance to human advancement."—John Stuart Mill, *Essay on Liberty.*

Though life in a group encourages emulation, the net effects of the psychology of group life are probably more conservating than they are stimulating. It is true that group life gets interests established with a minimum of effort and guards the new interests faithfully. Sometimes it guards them too faithfully. The group spirit is like a dog that growls at the approach of either foe or friend.

The Mores

Because we have no equivalent English word, the Latin word mores is used to cover the sum total of traditions, customs, and conventions, the culture traits and the culture complexes, approved by any society. The mores are social habits, based on individual habits as explained in Chapter III. But in Chapter III we saw that any unconventional habit acquired by an individual tended to disappear under pressure from society, or was retained only by the middle-aged or the old. When, however, individuals' habits are confirmed and authorized by society, their tenure is doubly secure.

The most important forms of the mores are tradition, custom, and convention, although even emulation to a certain degree comes under this head as well. Emulation, though always characterized by great social activity, is truly progressive by accident only. At all times emulation is held down by the mores to certain socially approved channels. College students, for example, emulate one another in the socially approved ways of "collegiate" cars and marcel waves; there is very little, if any, emulation in the ownership of dictionaries or encyclopaedias. There is a point, too, where emulation and convention are not distinguishable. When most people are trying to get a thing, it is a case of emulation; but after most people already have it, it is a convention. The possession of some sort of a car has passed from the emulational to the conventional stage within a few years.

It is not easy to draw a strict line of division between custom and tradition on the one hand, and convention, on the other. Sometimes the word custom is used in a wide sense, as Mill uses it in his *Essay on Liberty*, to include traditions and conventions as well. More explicitly, however, customary and traditional interests are the institutionalized interests we derive from our ancestors and those who have gone before us, while conventional interests are the institutionalized interests we derive from contemporary society. Custom and tradition look back and convention looks around. The former two are more important in old societies, as China for example. The latter is more important in new societies, such as the United States. Tradition may be defined as affecting ways of thinking; custom, ways of doing; convention, both.

Custom and tradition, having a longer history behind them than convention, are more deep-seated, though they may not be less tyrannical at any given time. They change less frequently than convention. They are most deep-seated with regard to those interests in which the emotions, the sentiments, and affections are involved—the interests least subject to reason. In our own society, for instance, tradition affects our thoughts on political, social, and religious subjects, and science has to wage a hard fight even here to open the eyes of all of us to simple and easily demonstrated truths. Custom is most strongly engrained in church and religious and other formal ceremonies, and above all on the occasions of marriages and funerals. Our brides, for instance, in the language of the old established marriage services promise to obey because there is so much sentiment connected with marriage. On account of this sentiment one hesitates to change the form of the ceremony, fearing perhaps that the spirit of the ceremony must suffer as a result; not considering, of course, at least not under the emotional influence of the occasion, that the elusive spirit waits for no such ceremonial permission.

In this case, however, though the custom survives, it has no particular influence. It is merely an outworn survival, along with folklore, proverbs, and superstitions. Some surviving customs continue to exercise real influence, however; funeral customs, for instance. It has been said that our funerals are the most barbaric part of our culture. As conducted in many sections of the United States they emphasize and increase grief and mourning; our usual burial practices, too, would seem dreadful to us if we looked at them straight. But we cannot look straight at customs so intimately tied up with the emotional experience of the group. In the same way it is very hard indeed to look straight at the religious practices for which we may have formed an affection.

The people of the United States, however, are perhaps freer from the influence of tradition and custom than any other large national group. Our case with regard to convention is somewhat different.

The root of mores is the same as the root of morals, and the mores are accepted not only as the usual, but the right and proper thing.

> "It is most important to notice that, for the people of a time and place, their own mores are always good, or rather that for them there can be no question of the goodness or badness of their mores. The reason is . . . the standards of good and right are in the mores." [1]

For the most part, people acquire the mores of their group so unconsciously that it is only when they compare themselves with others that they realize they have any mores at all. Writers on the mores usually pay a good deal of attention

[1] Sumner, W. G., *Folkways*, Boston, 1913, p. 58.

to their beneficent aspects.   They keep men from being fanatics
and revolutionaries and they economize energy.   Speaking of
these conserving aspects of the group spirit, Professor William MacDougall writes as follows: [1]

> "In a thousand situations it is a source of settled opinions and of defi-
> nite guidance of conduct, which obviates the most uncomfortable and
> difficult necessity of exerting independent judgment and of making
> up one's mind."

So far as thoughts and conduct are concerned it is doubtless
a good thing that society should have some restraining influences upon it.   It would be unfortunate, for instance, for
every man to have his own individual theory of government,
which he insisted on putting into operation.   The mores of
democracy, however "old-fashioned," are better than a pot
pourri of the principles of tyrants, oligarchs, bolsheviks, and
communists, and those who, on the other hand, would throw
tyrants, oligarchs, bolsheviks, or communists into the Bastille.
We should find it hard to get along at all.

But we, of course, are concerned with the mores chiefly as
they affect the consumption of goods and services, and it is
not so obvious that they are serviceable here.   In fact, it is
hard to see that they are usually directly serviceable in any
way, except as a protection against high-pressure salesmanship.   A man is not at all likely to become a fanatic or a revolu-
tionary in the use of things that cost money.   His interests
here are tested immediately in their use.   An impossible theory
of government may last a hundred years, but a flying-machine
that will not fly will not last a week.   A man requires of his
material interests that they demonstrate they can serve some
purpose.   It is not the mores that keep a man from buying
perpetual-motion tops and soap-bubble projectors.   He won't
buy them anyway.

At the same time, when people have once learned how to
keep warm, how to be well fed, and how to enjoy themselves,
they do not need the mores to encourage them to continue

[1] *The Group Mind*, New York, 1920, p. 96.

with their useful interests. Once having learned, they have
sense enough to keep on, unless, indeed, another set of mores
interferes. It's a dull horse that must be dragged twice to a
green pasture.

A man, then, does not ordinarily need the mores to keep
his head on his shoulders in the market-place. He wants
guidance there, it is true, but custom and convention do not
usually supply it. On the contrary, by continually barking at
his heels they distract him from exercising his economic judgment. They restrain him where restraint is a disadvantage.

Our Tribute to the Mores in Every-day Life

Naturally enough, it is easier for us to see the consumption
mores of others than it is to see our own. Take primitive men,
for example. Visitors to them are always quoting them as
saying: "Our fathers made their soup—or their pots, or their
hammocks—in such a way. Why should we change?" Or,
take the Chinese. Why will they insist on the extra effort
involved in building a curved roof instead of a straight one?
Curved roofs were formerly supposed to be efficacious in preserving the house from devils, but after the devils have gone
the curved roof remains. Why are they so slow about adopting the use of milk? Or, take the English cottage housewife,
who still does her cooking over an open fire. "A stove would
be so much more convenient," the author once observed. "I
suppose so," was the reply. "But you see nobody likes stoves
around here." Almost all peoples are over-influenced by
the mores in the forms of their architecture. Mores in Scan-
dinavia cluster about the drinking of coffee, in England about
the drinking of tea, in France, though to a less degree, about
the drinking of chocolate.

We have said that the mores influence us in the United
States more obviously by convention than by custom. It is
custom to use holly and mistletoe at Christmas and put candles
on birthday cakes, but these things are unimportant. In conventions, however, the mores are tyrannous. The power of

their sway among us can best be shown by an account of an unconventional family who sought to make their lives as intelligent as possible. They lived in a college town where people were supposed to have some measure of breadth of mind. But what exclamations there were, first, over the house the family built. The living room was much too large, the kitchen was much too contracted to suit the neighbors, and there was a small conservatory, which looked as if the family thought themselves rather superior to the common crowd. They had roller curtains but no draperies at their windows, believing that draperies collected dust and could not be well-adjusted to the light. "But everybody else has draperies!" exclaimed the neighbors. The women of the family did not spend nearly enough on clothes. They wore flat-soled shoes and their things were "funny." "They may be artistic all right," said the other women, "but they'd show more sense to look like Americans and not like ancient Greeks." The men of the family were much interested in art, which their neighbors regarded as hardly a "masculine" taste. Guests at the house were entertained with philosophy, poetry, and humor, but they were given paper cups and paper napkins, and got nothing better to eat than milk, lettuce, and canned beans. "Oh, yes, we had a good time, but what a peculiar dinner!" In short, the family provided a never-failing topic of amused and critical conversation for the whole town.

It is easy to see that only a very extraordinary family would be able to endure the comments that our friends received, though in almost every respect their economic interests were more intelligent than those of their conventional critics. And these critics, moreover, felt themselves quite justified. They had the majority with them, and honestly believed it better to be fools with the majority than sages apart from it.

We usually think of the mores as interfering only with the establishment of new interests. This is bad enough, but they are yet more unintelligent than this. There is no excuse for them at all when they try to drive out useful old interests, yet they do it. In progressive societies, emulative convention is always at war with old practices, even good ones. Some college girls were asked to illustrate how the mores interfered with their own economic interests. In almost every case their examples were of old useful interests on which new conventions were frowning. Several wished they could ride bicycles. Several would have liked to wear warm underwear on cold days. Several wanted to put on rubber overshoes when they had to tramp through the wet. One thought longingly of mittens. But no! The mores of the campus would not permit the gratification of such homely desires.

It should be observed that groups within groups and groups partially interpenetrating other groups have their own peculiar mores. For college students and up-to-date young people we have a set of mores rather different in some respects from that which prevails for their elders. We have mores prevailing for one group within a country: baked beans and brown bread in New England. We have mores for a whole nation or group of nations: bull fights in Spain, chopsticks in the Far East. We have mores for the ceremonially religious groups of any country: the use of vestments in worship. Finally we have a few mores nearly universal for all mankind: the wearing of clothing for the sake of a presumptive decency.

THE MORES AS RESTRAINTS ON CREATION

The new interests that enrich society must originate in somebody's brain. We should have few enough of them at best, for most men are not original. Yet if it were not for the mores we might have more. The mores discourage original self-expression.

Men are afraid to be different. They do not ordinarily dare to stand alone and offer society something new. They seek to deflect their creative energy into old channels. It is often said that one finds far more originality and difference in personality among children than among adults, since children have not yet learned the force of social approval or disapproval.

College freshmen are usually more interesting than college seniors.

Some great men, of course, positively insist on expressing themselves. We must note, however, that the great new contributions of any age are all more or less along the same lines. The great men, whatever they might have been or done, are moulded by the age early. In Periclean Athens the potential inventors became philosophers, dramatists, and artists, if they became anything at all. Up to now in America the potential philosophers have become inventors and captains of finance, or else perhaps have languished by the wayside. Not more light from philosophy but more light from electricity is the cry of our generation.

From the point of view of the great men themselves, recognition of the demand of the group is sensible. It is better to live as an artist than sink to oblivion as an inventor; or vice versa. From the point of view of society, it is better to get a second-rate picture out of a man than it is to get a first-rate invention that will never be used at all. But it is a pity that society cannot yet use first-rate gifts in their most spontaneous form of expression.

PART III
FACTORS UNCONSCIOUSLY AFFECTING CONSUMPTION

CHAPTER VI

ECOLOGY: MAN'S INTERESTS AND THE GEOGRAPHIC ENVIRONMENT

"Now the earth is our Mother, and to her we must offer praise and prayer and sacrifice, for all that we have comes from her."—Greek Myth.

Nobody knows precisely where man first appeared on this planet. Seven cities contended for the honor of being the birthplace of Homer, but there are champions for more than seven birthplaces of the Genus Homo. Was it in North Africa, France, Arabia, Ceylon, Java, some island or continent now submerged by the sea? Or did man make an independent appearance in several places? Students agree on one thing, however: it was in a region where the climate was warm. The chances of getting a culture started were greater in a warm climate, for here there is ordinarily less struggle with the elements and here the food supply is usually the richest, most abundant, and most easily secured. Thus men living in a warm climate would probably have some energy and some leisure for culture building.

CONSUMPTION AND CULTURE ZONES

As soon as man acquired a few tools and some means of protection from the weather he was able to seek more adventureful habitats. The geographical conditions which he found most favorable for the development of culture were in fairly dry regions, not too warm, where the natural surroundings were full of variety and suggestion to his expanding mind. Anthropologists tell us that the original great cultures of the world arose not in jungle but in mesa regions, that is to say

53

they were found in the highlands, stretching roughly from the Pyrenees through the Alps and Himalayas, and, in America, through the Rockies and the Andes. This extensive belt is known as the chief culture zone and is contrasted with the jungle zone, generally to the south of it, and the tundra zone, the forests and treeless steppes and plains in the north of America, Europe, and Asia.[1]

It is noteworthy that the original great cultures of the world, those of the eastern Mediterranean and China in the old world, of the Aztecs, Mayas, and Incas in the new, all arose in the mesa. These early mesa cultures were in fairly warm regions, but still not so warm as the region of man's origin seems to have been. The early mesa cultures were able to profit also from a fairly abundant food supply; but what they seem to have excelled in above all was their wealth of suggestions. The northern regions were too barren or covered with snow too large a portion of the year to be fertile in suggestion. The jungle, though luxuriant, was monotonous. It was the mesa which presented man with the largest variety of ideas. It seems possible that man could have adapted himself to a hot or cold climate if other conditions had been most favorable for him in torrid or frigid regions. Man was probably more able to adjust himself to climate than to triumph over a meagre and monotonous environment; the first is a matter of physical adaptation; the second involves the more vital question of having a rich source of suggestions on which culture can be built. So we see the tendency of the chief culture regions has been to move a little north or south away from the equator, from regions where nature is easy to regions where she is more suggestive.

Today our cultures no longer derive their impetus from direct suggestions in the geographic environment, so they now include regions of monotonous plains. However it was at the beginning, man now finds his greatest stimulus to activity in a temperate climate.

[1] Wissler, *Man and Culture*, op. cit., pp. 228–232.

Culture Traits Supplied by the Immediate Environment

In our second chapter we saw that the material for the three universal useful interests: a cutting instrument, string, fire—was found all over the world. Everywhere there are fire materials, something from which string can be made, stone. Then, too, the ancestors of the dog have been found almost everywhere.

The material for other simple interests is not so generally nor so obviously distributed all over the world. In one place nature seems to be emphasizing one thing, and in another place she emphasizes another. The character of the food here or there clearly depends on what nature offers to eat; the character of the home or shelter depends on the presence or absence of certain materials for its construction. The character of clothing is determined by the presence or absence of animals with suitable skins or wool, or of fibrous or other plants; the character of weapons is a matter of the kinds of stone available or the accessibility of mineral deposits. All this seems too obvious to mention, and it goes a long way to explain the differences in men's interests. Let us illustrate it more in detail in the case of four types of receptacles found in primitive societies, those of pottery, basketry, bark, and skins.

Clays vary much in adaptability to pot-making. The deposits vary also in their accessibility and their obviousness to view. We should not expect pot-making to develop early among a people dwelling in a land covered with snow most of the year. We should expect it to appear where there were considerable clay deposits in plain sight along the banks of streams and where the weather was dry and the sun hot for days at a time. What were the original pottery models no one knows, but it is likely they were the clay nests of birds—and such birds frequently build near the water—or the structures of certain semi-aquatic animals. In such cases as these nature puts the material and the model before man's eyes as if she were tempting him to use it.

In the case of baskets the determining factor would be the presence of reeds or cane or rushes adaptable to weaving. Again it may have been birds that furnished the model. Following the birds, again, the interstices in the baskets might be spread with clay and thus rendered waterproof; another way, in fact, in which a knowledge of pottery may have arisen. There are some Indians who mark their pottery with a design simulating a basket weave, suggesting that their pottery developed from baskets.

When we come to bark receptacles, we can easily see how important was the presence of trees from which the pliable bark easily detached itself. One often sees in the woods a piece of bark which has become partially separated from a birch and which has curled tightly about at the bottom, making a receptacle which holds moss or plants or sometimes even water. A man has only to hold out his hand and take what nature offers.

In the same way we should expect that people in cold lands, who lived largely on animal food and who needed many animal skins to keep them warm, would see the possibility of using skins to make various receptacles. The presence of skins before their eyes would suggest various possibilities for which skins could be used.

These expectations as to the geographic environment where certain traits are found are borne out by the cultural facts. On the whole, early useful culture traits are traits clearly suggested by the environment. The converse is not so true. The apparently clear suggestions of the environment do not necessarily produce culture traits.

Not only do separate suggestions of the environment become culture traits, but traits group themselves definitely into areas in primitive society. To confine our discussion to North America, which has possibly been studied most fully from this point of view, students tell us that in what is now the United States and Canada we had, on the arrival of the white man, an Eskimo culture area; a MacKenzie culture area (now central and northern Canada); the area of the Northwest Coast; the California area; the Southwestern area; the Plateau area; the Plains area; and the Southeastern and Eastern Woodland areas. These were inhabited in all by hundreds of tribes to be sure, but they represented nevertheless nine very distinct culture types.[1] In all of these cases the type of culture bears a direct relation to the physical environment. Clark Wissler, an authority on this matter, tells us that he has superimposed an ecological map of North America on a map of culture areas, and notes "several remarkable coincidences."[2]

"For example, a large irregular area in Arizona and New Mexico is delineated as a specific type of semi-desert . . .; and when the distribution of the Indian tribes is regarded, it will be found that all of the living Pueblo culture is, therefore, an affair of this semi-desert area and confined to it. . . . Ethnographers have been puzzled by the fact that throughout a long narrow belt from Nova Scotia to Wisconsin, the original Indian inhabitants showed a close similarity in habits and customs, in contrast to differences between themselves and those immediately to the north and south; but when the ecological map is consulted, we note that such a belt is indicated, or to put the matter in another way, the environmental conditions were much the same throughout this entire belt. Again, a tongue of true prairie land reaches across Illinois and expands over northern Indiana, a geographical fact often overlooked; but ethnic phenomena did not overlook it, because we find in this pocket a tribe of Indians having striking prairie characteristics, though, for the most part, surrounded by forest tribes. Our test is, therefore, conclusive, for it proves that there is a close correlation between the geographical area and the type of culture."

Do we have such culture areas dependent upon the immediate suggestions of the environment in modern civilized culture? With the development of intercourse, especially trade, such general area differences tend to disappear, though differences in traits linger yet. The relation is not nearly so obvious as it used to be, but it is still there.

The connection between environment and the consumers' goods it directly offers is perhaps most clearly seen in the

[1] Wissler, *Man and Culture*, op. cit., pp. 15, 56.
[2] *The Relation of Nature to Man in Aboriginal America*, New York, 1926, pp. 213-214.

case of things difficult to transport, as building materials.
Houses are customarily of wood in districts of the country
near forests. Nearly all houses in rural Maine, for instance,
are of wood. In the Middle West, brick and stucco are con-
tending with wood for supremacy. In southern California,
brick and stucco have won.

The geographic environment is responsible also for certain
differences of diet by sections of the country. What does one
eat in rural Maine? Griddle cakes and maple syrup, and
certainly a great deal of codfish, stewed cranberries, and blue-
berry pie. The per capita consumption of corn-fed pork is
greatest where we should expect it to be—in the Middle West;
and the Middle West is both geographically and gastronomically the home of the black walnut. In southern California,
naturally enough, one feasts on oranges, grapefruit, and avocado
pears.

Between nations we see very considerable differences in the
relative per capita consumption of textile fabrics. One thinks
at once of the consumption of linen in England and Europe,
relatively to other fabrics much greater per capita than in the
United States. Linen sheets, which, in spite of our greater
income, are a luxury among us, are fairly common abroad. One
thinks of the many uses to which silk is put in China. Men's
clothing, for instance, is made of it. One thinks of the jute,
sisal, and hemp, and other fibers of the tropics from which rough
household fabrics are woven.

The fact that different building materials, different foods,
and different textiles are consumed in different parts of the
country and of the world may be explained immediately by
differences in cost of transportation and manufacture, or it
may be immediately explained by the influence of custom.
In either case, however, it is clear that geographic environment is at the root of it.

The most significant relation between the geographic environment and the consumption of the modern West, however,
is much more subtle than the simple preferences for the ob-

viously available products of a region, such as the cases of
building materials, foods, and textiles which we have mentioned. Indeed, this part of our subject deserves at least a
volume, and many volumes have been written upon it.

CULTURE AND CLIMATE

We will not linger on the subject of the relationship of
climate to our consumption. It is clear that climate reacts on
us in three ways: it affects the flora and fauna available for our
choices; it affects our physical needs; and it affects our energy,
just how subtly we cannot tell. Some writers consider climate
the most important of all geographic factors. Nor shall we
more than mention the factor of the physiographic and topo-
graphical features of a country, though some writers ascribe
the greatest importance to these. Dividing mountains, dividing or connecting seas, rivers, deserts, the presence or absence
of harbors, affect the form and stability of societies, their
extent, their isolation, their contacts, and hence indirectly
their cultures. It is claimed, too, though this is not so clear,
that the general aspects of nature, whether monotonous or
noble and awe-inspiring, react on the imagination and so
influence the type of thought of a people.

THE ECONOMIC VALUE OF NATURAL RESOURCES

What we do want to stress particularly here is the influence
of the economic value, the variety and the richness of natural
resources in general on the consumption of a people, and particularly on the consumption of the modern West in the twentieth century. There would be considerable grounds for an
argument that the trend of culture in the United States, England, and Western Europe today was ultimately to be explained by the presence of certain mineral deposits which
make factory manufacturing possible.

Three-fourths of the world's iron and two-thirds of the
world's coal comes from the eastern half of the United States,
England, and Western Europe. Where coal and iron are

found close together, conditions for manufacture are most favorable. Our modern Western civilization is based on coal and iron. A recent writer says:

"In these hundred years the output of pig-iron has increased 100 fold, of mineral fuels 75 fold, and of copper 63 fold. In the last fifty years the per capita consumption of minerals in the United States has multiplied 15 times. . . . The acceleration of the rate of mineral exploitation may be realized from the fact that the world has exploited more of its resources in the last twenty years than in all preceding history." [1]

This exploitation of mineral resources lies back of every one of the factory-made products entering into our consumption. Our daily food, our clothing, our homes and their furnishings, most of our recreation: all these things are dependent upon it.

The relationship between our achievements in industrial civilization and the fact we have had these mineral products to be exploited is striking. In the face of it, our common tendency to ascribe the progress in the United States and Western Europe to the superior abilities of the Nordic races seems simply amusing. Our author goes on: [2]

"In the past the leadership of the North Atlantic countries in mineral and power production has been regarded as a mere reflection of the initiative and energy of the North Atlantic races, and it has been more or less taken for granted that in time the development of other parts of the world would equalize the mineral situation; that, broadly speaking, one part of the world would yield to human effort about as well as another. . . . But the vastly increasing requirements of modern industrial civilization have brought a new perspective into the situation—new even to the special students in mineral resources."

A recent significant book which discusses the problem of large-scale manufacture from the point of view of the Far East [3] contains in the preface the following statement: [4]

[1] Leith, C. K., " Exploitation and World Progress." *Foreign Affairs*, October, 1927, p. 128.
[2] Ibid., p. 134.
[3] Bain, H. Foster, *Ores and Industry in the Far East*, New York, 1927.
[4] Pp. vi, vii. Preface is by Edwin F. Gay.

"Despite the recognition of cultural difficulties as an impediment to the rapid diffusion of Western industrialism, there has remained a fixed and general belief in the ultimate, if not immediate, effects of the supposed vast material resources of China, and especially of her potential mineral wealth. It was therefore with surprise, not unmixed with incredulity, that we have lately heard this belief challenged. The experts have announced, as the result of repeated explorations, that the Far East, estimated by Western standards, is seriously deficient in some of the most important minerals, and especially in iron, the basic metal of our civilization. . . .

"What is dubious for India is apparently certain for China and Japan. . . . Their supplies, indeed, are sufficient for the modest requirements of the immediate future, but they are entirely inadequate for the full growth of an Industrial Revolution of the type and stature the West has acceleratingly shown in the industrial growth of England, Germany and the United States."

This limitation in the Far East of minerals which are basic for our western type of manufacturing must not, however, be over-rated in importance. It means simply that the development of the Far East is hampered along our lines. If the Far East can produce other things more valuable than iron and coal the difficulty may be overcome; in that case it can get everything it needs through exchange. The question of developing an industrial civilization will ultimately resolve itself, then, into a question not of the kind, but of the economic value of natural resources.

Our conservationists, of course, are warning us that at our present rate of exploitation our own mineral resources will presently be exhausted, and we shall be in the same boat with those peoples who never had any. This raises two new questions: the question of making substitutions for the present approved industrial minerals; and the greater question of making a substitution for the industrial civilization itself. Into these questions it is not our province now to enter.

CHAPTER VII

THE HERITAGE OF BIRTH AND RACE

"The dearth of brains and the dearth of physique are the worst misfortunes that can befall a nation." KARL PEARSON, *National Life from the Standpoint of Science.*

The physical environment can do no more than furnish the field in which culture grows. It provides the raw materials and stops. Something else must furnish the incentive and intelligence to use these materials. This something else is obviously in man's own nature.

In discussions of the original development of cultures it is sometimes customary to contrast the geographical factors with the racial factors, or to be precise, with the biological factors. The term racial is legitimate only if we realize that race is frequently a convenient term used to cover many influences of diverse sorts. The term when used in connection with culture is not usually confined to the influence of physical inheritance, as for precision it should be.

At the same time there are certain biological influences of physical inheritance affecting culture that cannot be included under the term race at all.

The cultures of different groups vary much more than one would expect from the differences in the geographic environments among which the people live. This is perfectly plain. It is another thing to assume that merely biological differences in race account for these variations. A great deal depends on many other things. Yet biological race has an influence sometimes. Just what do we mean by race?

WHAT IS RACE?

The word race is used in ordinary conversation in several different ways. It is used to refer to the three major races or divisions of mankind, the Caucasian, the Negro, and the Mongolian. The Eskimo, the American Indian, and the Malay are treated as offshoots of the Mongolian race.

It is used also to refer to any group or sub-group of the three major races. We speak, for instance, of the Aryan and Semitic races, which are branches of the Caucasian; or of the Nordic and Mediterranean races, branches of the Aryan; or even of the English and Scandinavian as branches of the Nordic. Sometimes race is used to refer merely to the people of some special geographic area, or nation, if these people may be treated as biologically related.

RACE AND CULTURE

Many of the things which we formerly believed to be biologically a part of race we now know are due to social environment and culture. As the cultures of one group grow apart from that of another, if there is no diffusion, the cultures may have only the few most fundamental points in common. At the same time a physical differentiation and selection may take place, by which certain peculiar physical features become characteristic of this group, and others of that group. When the people of different groups have different interests and also different physical characteristics, who can tell which, if either, is cause, and which, if either, is effect? It is, as yet, an unjustified assumption to claim that physical differences are more than superficial as causes of culture; for all we know, they are the results of it.

We now know that outer physical differences do not argue anything at all as to native intelligence or desire and ability to learn. With regard to the three major races of mankind, we know that no one of them is biologically lower than any other in physical form. The Caucasian has the whitest skin but he is the most like the apes in having a hairy body and the longest limbs; the negro is like the apes in having the most projecting lower jaw; the negro's brain is smaller than the white man's, but the Eskimo's brain is the largest of all. These physical tests mean little or nothing, trustworthy evidence from mental tests is lacking, and the development of culture by these three races is really our only guide. The negro race shows to least advantage here; it has neither evolved a considerable culture of its own nor adopted the adjacent cultures of North Africa. On the other hand we must remember that the life of man on this globe has been very long, and that two thousand years ago most of the white race, including the Nordics, were apparently the rudest sort of savages—the Nordics were burrowing for bones on the banks of the Baltic, someone once observed. At the same time the culture of China has gone on for perhaps six thousand years. But to attempt to explain differences in culture by differences in race, and then to say that the only proofs of difference in racial capacity are differences in culture is to argue in a circle.

As a matter of fact there is no evidence that some races or important sub-races are 'naturally' or biologically naïve or suspicious, faithful or treacherous, clean or unclean, unworldly or materialistic. For all we know, it is cultural inheritance that accounts for this. Again and again the children of one race when adopted by the members of another have grown up as normal members of the new group with the same interests, attitudes, and mental characteristics as their foster-people; at least until they became aware that suspicion or misgiving was directed toward them because of their different origin. This is not to say that the race question is not important, but it is to say that certainly a good many of its problems are to be approached from a social and psychic, rather than from a biological, point of view.

There are, however, at least two factors affecting culture that are subject to biological inheritance and that apparently have had a causal effect in differentiating some large groups, if not races, of men. Intelligence is the first of these. Both intelligence, and the lack of intelligence, are certainly inheritable, although there is no agreement as to the extent of their inheritability. The second of the factors is the biological element in what psychologists term drive, or the native energy which man gives to his activities.

To what extent can sub-races or groups be distinguished from one another on the ground of superior native intelligence? Is there reason to suppose that some groups or races have selected themselves, or have been selected in the beginning, by superior qualities of intelligence? Of course that is possible. Probably the most outstanding example of this in the history of culture is the case of the Athenians of the classical period. The great anthropologist, Sir Francis Galton, held that this was the explanation of their superior culture. He believed that a few biologically very superior men happened, or in some other way came, to be gathered together in Athens. Perhaps superiority attracted superiority. We do not know, but it seems at any rate the simplest way to explain their great culture achievements. They had a superior energy probably, but their superior intelligence was even more surprising. By means of it they added to their culture certain interests which required an appreciation so far in advance of the degree of intelligence possessed by their neighbors that after the fall of the Athenian state, and the Roman state which borrowed from it, the Athenian culture fell into abeyance until the so-called Renaissance in the fifteenth century, and was even then only very partially revived.

In the same way, the great Renaissance itself was partly made possible because of the aggregation near Florence of another group of people of superior intelligence. Dante, Da Vinci, Michelangelo—was there ever gathered together, save in Periclean Athens, a group of men superior to these and their associates? We consider the contributions of the Greeks and the Florentines and their neighbors an integral part of our own culture today. Yet how many are there among us who are endowed with intellectual capacity sufficient for a true appreciation of them? Our own achievements as Americans are extraordinarily wide and various due to our superior energy and our superior conditions for its exercise, but our intellectual interests are relatively meagre and perhaps also our intellectual power.

Can we point out instances of groups whose culture is probably due to their superior mental energy? What about modern America? Would it not be the men of superior energy in various European stocks who would be the ones to set forth to the New World? Emigration, at least at first, selected the most courageous. And in so far as their superior energy had a biological basis, it would tend to remain in the new race being created in America. The fortunate circumstance of our rich natural resources has greatly contributed to our culture, but, more than this, our fathers were a group highly selected on the strength of their will to adventure, to endure, to strive, and to learn.

At the same time that very selective process which sent men of outstanding native psychic energy to new worlds may also have tended to keep in the mother country men of outstanding intelligence, for these would perhaps have been unwilling to live as pioneers must live, divorced from intellectual stimuli in a rude land. The American traveler in England is again and again impressed, on the one hand, by the relative richness of the intellectual culture, on the other hand by the relative apathy of the people who enjoy it. It would seem that the greatest minds remained in England while the most strenuous souls set out to the United States and England's over-seas dominions.

It is also possible to pick out some groups of low culture whose status is probably partly due to the fact that the whole group has or at some time had less than an average mental endowment. The Patagonians, the Indians living along the upper Amazon, the Bushmen, the now extinct Tasmanians, were peoples who perhaps because of some native lack could be pushed into undesirable physical environments. The relative poverty of their cultures is due in part to the undesirableness of their physical environment; but it may also be due to the fact that their groups were "selected" because of an original lack of intelligence or vigor. Thus they were pushed into or retained in these undesirable environments, and kept from getting out again into more favored regions.

In some cases it appears that such groups have been driven into apparently undesirable regions which nevertheless are potentially rich in natural resources. In such instances, as is the case in parts of Polynesia, the rich environment simply remains undeveloped.

Historically there have perhaps been many groups or even races selected either because of superior native endowment or the lack of it, but the matter is so complicated by other cultural influences that it is not easy to pick these groups out. Even when a people seems possessed by superior energy, its source may not be primarily biological. Religious enthusiasm or conviction, for instance, has been a potent factor in inducing migrations, and this often spurs on people who are biologically very ordinary to accomplish quite remarkable things. In the same way the lack of a vital morale in a people might work out in just the same way as a lack of biological vitality. Who knows in what was the real superiority of the Puritan founders of New England? Was their enthusiasm for education the result of real intellectual interests, or of ambitious energy, or of a conviction that education was right?

Mental energy, if not intelligence, is probably connected to some extent with the physical health of the body; not necessarily so, however. We know so little about the general health conditions of peoples in the past that we cannot cite examples of mental energy unaccompanied by physical energy, nor of physical energy unaccompanied by mental, among whole peoples. In the case of individuals it is common enough to see it. We all know individuals who enjoy excellent physical health and yet never seem to be interested or want to do anything. We also know people in poor health who have nevertheless a quality of psychic vitality which sets them distinctly apart from their fellows. Consider, for instance, the well-known cases of the three Scotchmen, the invalid

Stevenson, the dyspeptic Carlyle, and the delicate Sir Walter Scott—all of them possessed from birth with indefatigable mental energy.

Psychic energy and physical health are therefore two different manifestations, although it is probably true that psychic energy greatly influences physical health and it is of course obvious that physical health is an aid to the exercise of psychic energy. That healthy people and healthy groups have an advantage in culture, as in all other respects, is a point that does not need to be enlarged upon.

The Biological Inheritance of Individuals

We are now brought at last to the question of how his biological inheritance affects the number, variety, and type of interests of any individual—the part of our subject for which our evidence is the clearest; and probably, too, the most important part of our subject. "Differences between members of a herd of cattle are greater than differences between herds themselves," says a dairy husbandman. Differences between members of a group of people are ordinarily greater than differences between groups.

The biological inheritance of an individual which affects his interests can, as we have seen, be divided into two parts. The first is his intelligence, the second is the inheritable element in his mental vitality.

It is clear to us from our ordinary common observation that people vary greatly in aptitude, and we know that intelligence goes by families at least to a certain extent. At the lower end of the intelligence scale it has been proved that feeble-mindedness in its differing degrees is inheritable. To be feeble-minded means limited interests and limited culture. At the upper end of the scale various studies of families of genius lead us to presume that superior mental ability is also inheritable at least to some extent. Since mental ability has a physical basis in the convolutions of the brain, its inheritability would be expected.

Can anyone doubt that the extent of our intelligence is one of the most important factors affecting our interests? Our capacity for intelligence in the last analysis sets the limit to what and how many ideas we can take over from our group; and obviously it is only the most intelligent men who have original ideas and consequently who can conceive intelligent new interests to be introduced into society.

One of the most interesting and perhaps one of the most significant developments in modern psychology is the effort to measure native intelligence by means of mental tests. If we are able to do this successfully we shall know, of course, how much native aptitude varies and can draw correlations between aptitude and interests more accurately. Now we know hardly more than that there is such a correlation. The people who score highest in these tests usually are interested in the more difficult and complex aspects of life, and more deeply interested in them, than the people who score lowest. Any teacher can make that observation. There is, however, a middle group about whom it is not so easy to generalize.

Among students those most richly endowed with intelligence are those who try to find out the reasons for things, who cannot help but be interested in seeking profitable and in discarding foolish or wasteful interests. They may not, it is true, always act in accordance with their perceptions. Something more than aptitude is required for this.

Our tests to measure native aptitude are imperfect, but our tests to measure native mental energy are far more so. Here we must rely chiefly on our personal conclusions, but we can all make them. In any nation, any community, any business organization, and, indeed, in any class room, differences in the mental energy of individuals are outstanding. Among our acquaintances we easily recognize those who are interested widely. Such a one, we say, is interested in "everything." If she is a woman she tries all the new styles, all the new labor-saving devices, and belongs to half the clubs in town. If he is a man he is always getting and trying out marvellous new ideas for his business. These interests may not be very critically chosen, but there are many of them.

Some human beings are so possessed by this quality of their nature that it leads them long distances, spiritually or physically, to discover new elements of culture by which their society is ultimately enriched. At the lower end of the scale, other persons manifest it as merely a faint reaction of curiosity toward new objects to which their attention has been directed. How different the daily lives of the mentally energetic and the mentally apathetic groups! How different their cultural influences on the group of which they are members.

EUGENICS AND CULTURE

Although we do not know any too much about how biological inheritance reacts on culture, we do know enough to know that it is highly important. And biological inheritance is theoretically within our control.

The favored theory of inheritance today is that acquired characters cannot be transmitted biologically. This means, of course, that the only way to improve the native intelligence and native mental energy of men is through better breeding. This is a subject on which one can easily become excited. It presents possibilities, on the one hand, of the world at the cultural millennium; of the world as one vast feeble-minded colony, on the other.

The question of improving the breed of human life involves so many subtle ramifications that suggested ways of improvement must be viewed very cautiously, much as improvement itself is desired. The most extreme proposals ever made are perhaps those of Plato. He says that the end of union is the public good, and goes on: [1]

"It follows . . . that the best of both sexes ought to be brought together as often as possible, and the worst as seldom as possible, and that the issue of the former unions ought to be reared, and that of the latter abandoned, if the flock is to attain to first-rate excellence."

[1] *Republic.* Book V, 459. Translation of Davies and Vaughan, London, 1907.

In order that this latter may be effected easily, no mother is to know her own child. In this way "the children to be born may ever be more virtuous and more useful than their virtuous and useful parents."[1]

This is stern doctrine. In Plato's state, however, eugenics was not treated by itself. Improvement in eugenics was closely linked with general cultural improvement, and always was to lead directly to it. One could presumably suffer the means for the sake of a more glorious end concretely described and set before him.

Perhaps one reason that present-day proposals for improving the human breed have not met with wider sympathy has been that eugenics has been too narrowly discussed. Dean Inge asks somewhere if we are interested in breeding human mastiffs for policemen, human greyhounds for postmen. Plato's proposals were drastic but they were not narrow. The ordinary man or woman will not be interested in eugenics unless he or she is sure it is going to result not only in better biological specimens but in better culture. In a matter so complicated one must ask, how can we be sure that the obvious theoretical advantages of extreme eugenic measures will be actually secured? We get a breed capable of attaining a high culture, but we have disorganized many things to get it. What will be the net result?

These suggestions are only by way of explaining why, perhaps, our progress in eugenics is so slow. If we keep eugenics subordinate to culture we cannot put too much emphasis upon it.

[1] *Republic.* Book V, 461.

CHAPTER VIII

THE DIFFUSION OF CULTURE

"Sire, I am a citizen of the world. I have studied medicine in Bologna and philosophy in Heidelberg. . . . My tailor, as you see, keeps shop in Bond Street. Gastronomically my greatest fondness is for the more complicated curries of India. And as for my recreations, I prefer to take them in the Parisian style."— *Old Play.*

Did human culture begin in one place or in several places? Are the somewhat similar culture traits found all over the world the offspring of some one trait that has travelled far from its birthplace, or are they of independent origin? This is a question which perplexes anthropologists, and divides them into two main camps. One group emphasizes the importance of independent inventions of tools, utensils, religious rites, and so on. The other group visualizes an ancient culture home from which such traits once long ago set out on a journey to the ends of the earth. The swastika, for instance, is found among many widely separated peoples, literally from China to Peru. A sun worship similar to that of ancient Egypt seems to have prevailed in ancient Ireland and in ancient Mexico. What do we make out of that?

According to the strict interpretation of the second view, the bow and arrow, for instance, would have been invented only once. The fact that it has been found as a culture trait in so many widely scattered parts of the earth would indicate an original communication among the peoples using it. The other group of anthropologists would reply that the inventive faculty in man, though rare, is not so rare but that the same invention may conceivably be made independently two, three, or even more times.

We do not have to be able to answer these nice points in

72

order to be convinced that in any case diffusion is of very great importance.

THE MERGING OF WHOLE CULTURES

Sometimes diffusion takes place merely through the scattering of single culture traits. At other times whole cultures are merged. This merging of cultures has been effected both by the migrations of large groups or whole peoples and by the processes of war, conquest, military and political discipline.

We cannot know nearly so much as we should like about those migrations of peoples in prehistoric times by which cultures were merged. One of the most interesting studies that has been made of this subject is that of Ellsworth Huntington in *The Pulse of Asia;* wherein he describes the periodic changes of climate that caused great migrations of whole peoples in search of a more abundant food supply. North of China in the steppe regions the use of milk was developed and was carried with their culture by migrating tribes across Asia to Egypt and Mesopotamia, whence it spread to Europe and thence to the rest of the Western World; but China, by her Great Wall, kept out these nomads, and their culture with them, and up to this day the Chinese have not learned the use of milk.[1]

That other considerable migrations took place on the American continent, in Africa, and in Oceania, seems evident not only from a study of the cultures themselves, but also from the folklore of the people.

When pressure on the food supply grew too heavy in the cities of Greece, it was a very common practice to send colonies to some less populous region, and thus cultural contacts were spread. Rome did the same thing to some extent. A certain amount of colonization resulted from the Crusades, and the Germans sent some colonies among the Slavic peoples a little later.[2]

[1] See Wissler, *Man and Culture,* op. cit., pp. 238–240.
[2] See "Movements and Migrations of Peoples" in Vidal de la Blache, P., *Principles of Human Geography* (Bingham, M. T., trans.) New York, 1926, pp. 63–73.

The Western culture of the New World is of course a combination of contributions from many cultural sources. Although its basis is English in one part, Spanish or Portuguese in the other, both English and Spanish portions have been considerably affected by migration of groups of peoples of other cultures.

As for the question of the influence of war, conquest, etc., on the merging of cultures, we do not find much evidence of this in the more primitive societies. In truly primitive society there is apparently not a great deal of the real business of war-making, although feuds and sporadic fighting are common enough.[1] It requires a relatively high development of military and political discipline to put through and sustain a successful conquest. Of examples antedating the usual historic records, one of our best is apparently the case of the Incas of Peru who subdued and ruled with a rod of iron a weaker people. It is such a good illustration of conquest that it may not very well illustrate the blending of cultures. At any rate, we have no way of knowing how much of their original culture the conquered people retained.

In historic times we need only to mention the conquests of the Greeks, the Carthaginians, the Romans, and then the conquest of Rome by the barbaric hordes from the North. It is interesting to note that in these cases of conquest and consequent merging of cultures, it is usually the richer or sturdier or economically more advanced culture, whether that of victor or vanquished, that gets the upper hand in transfusion. The Romans imposed their own culture on the barbarians of Spain and Gaul, but when they conquered Greece it was Grecian culture that unconsciously imposed itself on them. So when the Germanic tribes descended on Rome and captured it, they furnished the means by which considerable portions of Roman culture were eventually transmitted to the whole Western world. There was, to be sure, an immediate destruction and great loss, but the years following the

---

[1] See Hobhouse, L. T., Wheeler, C. C., and Ginsberg, M., *Institutions and Material Culture of the Simpler Peoples*, London, 1915, p. 228.

fall of the Roman Empire were years of cultural diffusion to
an extent that has not generally been appreciated.

In the case of the Anglo-Saxon conquest of England it was
the Anglo-Saxon culture that took precedence over that of
the Britons. In the case of the Norman conquest, the Norman
culture became secondary to the Anglo-Saxon culture. The
Norman conquest added many elements of refinement and
changed the form of various institutions, but the every-day
life of the common people was not greatly affected. When
the Manchus conquered China they imposed their force on
the Chinese, but Chinese culture imposed itself on the Manchus.

Although we have spoken of war and conquest as resulting
in a fusion of cultures, as eventually it results in a fusion of
peoples,[1] occasionally the conquest is checked before there
is time for the cultures to be merged. In this case there is
merely a transfer of certain culture traits. For instance, the
conquests of the Arabs brought into Europe the beginnings
of certain kinds of scientific knowledge, and also a number of
important inventions from the East; but the Arabs were
driven out of Europe, and the cultures of the two were not
blended.

THE DIFFUSION OF SEPARATE TRAITS

Before efficient means of travel and transportation were invented, and especially in primitive society, one does not think
of much travel from group to group. Yet the amount has
usually been underestimated.[2] The motives or reasons leading
to these contacts might be various. Occasionally a man was

[1] If a people of superior material culture impose themselves on a people whose
culture is far inferior, it is hardly correct to speak of a fusion of cultures, and
there may be slight signs of a fusion of peoples for a long time, particularly if
the two peoples differ in race. Such cases, however,—the case of the whites
and the American Indians, for example—are hardly examples of war and conquest, but of domination. The culture of the conquerors is expanded in space
as their own numbers multiply, rather than diffused among another people.
In those parts of Latin America where the original Indian culture was highest,
however, there has been something resembling a merging of cultures. Cf. a
significant book, *Aspects Of Mexican Civilization*, by J. Vasconcelos and M.
Gamio, Chicago, 1926.

[2] Cf. Grierson, P. J. H., *The Silent Trade*, Edinburgh, 1903.

exiled from his own tribe and had to seek refuge with another.
Occasionally a man lost himself in the forest or his boat was
driven to some distant shore. More often, however, men and
groups of men set out deliberately to see other districts, fired
by a motive for adventure or by a desire to expand their experience. There was considerable travel from island to island
in Oceania. Travellers among Eskimo and among Australians
note that they both had a similar custom by which some
members set forth at intervals primarily to see the country.

It is of significance to observe that whereas a group may
take a hostile attitude to other groups it does not know, the
stranger who comes alone and unattended is usually welcomed
and treated as a friend.[1] Indeed that is so among ourselves;
a community which believes it has an antipathy to the Irish,
let us say, may make itself extremely cordial to the individual
Irishman who comes to visit or settle within it. The most
fascinating tales in the world are the tales of a traveller. The
information travellers bring stimulates new interests at once;
a stranger who settles among a distant people brings his customs with him, and is often a means of adding new elements
to the culture of those with whom he lives. A German woman
moved into a small New England village, and in three years
all the housewives were making *pfeffernüsse* at Christmas time.

The religious persecutions of the Middle Ages indirectly
reacted on culture through the exiles they effected. In particular we should mention the persecution of the Jews, people
generally closely in touch with the culture, and particularly
the material culture, of the regions where they lived. Driven
from one place to another, now here and now there, they
carried various culture traits with them and aided in bringing
European cultures more closely together.

The element of missionary zeal and endeavor in connection
with religion has been of considerable importance in diffusing
culture at some times and some places, for the missionary
brings with him not only his religious beliefs but his schools,

[1] Grierson, P. J. H., *The Silent Trade*, pp. 30–32.

his literature, his art, and, to a large extent, his material interests. Not all religions are missionary religions, but Christians, Mohammedans, and Buddhists have sent their representatives into distant parts. In the early days of Christiantity the zeal of its apostles had extensive results—the very names of the Epistles in the New Testament, the list of the churches mentioned in the Apocalypse, show us this—and along with the religion culture travelled too. One cannot estimate how much Christianity had to do with bringing the British Isles and the countries of Western Europe in touch with the general current of Mediterranean civilization. In mediaeval and modern times Christian mission work has been less aggressively pursued, but the various Christian mission posts scattered all over the world have considerable cultural influence today. In many a grass hut in the Congo dark-skinned babies are submitting to comb, brush, and soap in their anticipation of going to a phonograph party at the mission station.

With regard to Mohammedan missionary efforts we need only mention their effect on the culture of North Africa. Buddhist missionary zeal has probably had least effect on the general, and particularly on the material, culture of the peoples to whom it has been extended, since Buddhist practice is the least materialistic of the three.

The influence of trade on culture was relatively slight in primitive and in early historic society, but it has steadily been increasing, and today it seems to be undoubtedly the strongest of all influences on culture. So great is its present importance that we have given it a separate chapter.

DIFFUSION TODAY

The diffusion of culture traits today is proceeding more rapidly than ever before. Let us consider how our own daily lives are affected by it. We live in a house which may be Early American or "American Renaissance"; the chances are, however, its forebear was a Dutch colonial or an English cottage, a French château, a Spanish or an Italian villa.

Our public buildings are just as distinctly under foreign influence. From my window as I write I see ascending the slender towers of an East Indian palace on the club house of a college in the Middle West.

Men all over the world dress as London or New York advises. Paris dresses our own western world of women and now subtly insinuates its hardly recognizable touches into the costumes of China and Japan. Would Stockholm or Rio think of setting up their own criteria of fashion in dress? Certainly not. It must be Paris, and Paris is better late than never. One reads in a United States Department of Commerce circular to American clothing manufacturers that after styles of women's underwear originally emanating from Paris have become hopelessly out of date in Utica, New York, and St. Joseph, Missouri, they will still be eagerly purchased by the ladies of Montevideo and Santiago de Chile.

Our ideas of suitable types of commercial entertainment emanate chiefly from such great "pleasure centers" as Paris and New York. Certain styles of luxurious living learned in the hotels of Miami and Palm Beach creep into hundreds of modest suburbs. Scotch golf conquers the English-speaking world. Chinese Ma Jongh suddenly appears in New York City and baseball wins its ten thousand fans in Tokio.

What is the explanation of such diffusion as this? It is due to the great development of means of communication that has followed the Industrial Revolution: the development of means for diffusing the written or spoken word, and of means for making transportation more safe, more easy, more speedy, and more cheap.

Perhaps the most important of all these developments is the application of steam power to the printing press. Indirectly the printed page has furnished a means for bringing different groups into sympathy with one another, thus laying a foundation on which more direct communication could build. Directly, of course, it has been a means by which cultural interests originating in one group could be described and recommended to other members of that group, or to other groups. Nowadays the daily newspaper is a necessity of life in American homes. The great majority of homes receive at least one other periodical, and some receive many. Almost every American home has at least a few books of its own, and almost every community has a public library, or access to a travelling library. The distribution of printed literature throughout the United States is so great there is no need to dwell on the possibilities for spreading interests through the printed page. The wonder is, not that cultural traits travel fast, but that they do not travel faster.

The telephone, the telegraph, and the radio very obviously are other mechanical devices by means of which people have been brought closer together and interests have been spread. Today, by means of re-broadcasting, it is theoretically possible for everyone in the world to listen at the same time to what is going on in London or Calcutta or Timbuctoo. That grand-scale influencing of musical tastes which began with the phonograph is now proceeding on a scale still grander. A million people every Saturday night listen to what is essentially the same jazz band, or tune in to Walter Damrosch.

It would be hard to tell how much the potential benefits of devices for increasing communication by language fall short of realization because the languages of the world are so many, and few people are familiar with more than their own. This handicap, it appears, must continue to embarrass us for a long time to come. Attempts to get people to learn an artificial "universal" language such as Esperanto have not been successful, and no existing true language seems likely to be universally or even generally learned by the world's people. Hence interests of a group speaking one language reach the members of another group the more slowly because they must come by a second hand, or, in this case, by a second tongue, method.

The second group of inventions affecting our interests are those that have improved transportation. They began far

back in remote antiquity with the invention of the wheel and
the invention of the sail.   The principle of tacking, by which
a ship is enabled to sail against the wind, was known to the
Phoenicians, a thousand years before Christ, but from that
time on there was only slight improvement in means of communication for nearly three thousand years, or until the era
of the Industrial Revolution.

In the last hundred years as we know, things have happened
thick and fast.   The first true steamship crossed the Atlantic
in 1838—an event of the highest commercial and of the highest
romantic significance.   The first transcontinental train crossed
the United States in 1869, and the first successful effort to fly
around the world was in 1924.

Who today can estimate the importance for culture of that
travel which now forms a part of every liberal education?
High School boys and girls get up a trip to Washington.   College students go trooping abroad in thousands by the "Tourist
Third."   Their elders set off for the Lesser Antilles, or New
Zealand, or Thibet.   Those who travel in crowds of their own
countrymen and put up only at hotels where American comfort
prevails return, perhaps not much the wiser.   Yet they return
somewhat the wiser.   "Say!" exclaimed a certain lady coming
back from an all-expense, no care, no trouble trip around the
world.   "Say! I'm glad to get back to God's country! But
listen! I'm going to start one of those cute little Japanese
gardens.   And I'm going to try and find out how they do all
those mysterious things in India.   And I'm going to dress Jane
and Junior like those little French kiddies, and make them
behave like them too—if I can."

DIFFUSION AND DEMOCRACY

Within a country, the diffusion of culture traits is speediest
and most complete when democratic ideas prevail among the
people.   In countries where there are hereditary social classes,
as, above all, in India, some of the culture traits of the higher
classes may be regarded by everyone as a peculiar social privi-

lege. The culture trait, in other words, may come to have a social more than an economic significance. In certain countries of Europe the socially superior classes wear hats, the peasants never. Everyone agrees that the proper headgear for a peasant woman is a shawl. These same peasant women, if they emigrate to the United States, discard the shawl in about a month. In a month or two more they realize that they are socially free not only to wear hats, but to dress and act like senators and millionaires if they like; and they do so. Europeans who come to new countries from Europe are continually impressed by the fact that everyone does the same thing.

Political democracy may prevail, of course, where social democracy does not. An English village woman once said to the author: "I'd like a bit of fruit for breakfast now and then, but our neighbors would think we were putting on airs. You see it's the gentry who eat fruit in the morning."

It must be said, however, that while there cannot be too much democracy so far as diffusion is concerned, a complete dead-levelism in society is a very bad thing for stimulating new interests. Where there are no distinctions whatever a stimulus is lacking. The writer would compare two small towns with which she is familiar, one in New England, the other in the Middle West. In the Middle Western town there are practically no social distinctions of any sort, and the consumption of all the people is alike: the same houses, the same food, the same clothes, the same books, the same recreations. Young people of superior abilities in that town usually become unhappy and long to get to Chicago or New York. They do not know what is wrong, but the fact is there is no stimulus for them there.

In the other small town some slight social distinctions prevail. A few families attempt to carry on some old aristocratic traditions. They feel they must keep in contact with the best that is going on in the world. They travel and collect old books and works of art. One of these families has never been able to afford a car, but it has given the town a town hall planned by the best architect in the country. They are continually introducing into the town new culture traits. These pass completely over the heads of the families at the bottom of the social scale, who are socially ignored. The most able of the townspeople, however, copy the new traits. Abstract conditions for diffusion are not so favorable as in the other town; the amount of diffusion is just about the same, because there is more to diffuse.

The ideal social condition for diffusion is a democracy that encourages individuality and discourages artificial social distinctions.[1]

[1] For an excellent treatment of social effects of communication see Cooley, C. H., *Social Organization*, New York, 1916, pp. 66-103.

CHAPTER IX

TRADE AND CULTURE

"I went to the market—what did I behold?—
Strange stuffs from the Indies, and spices and gold.
Oh, long will I labor and late will I spin
And far will I journey, such treasures to win."
                                        —*Nursery Rhyme.*

In the preceding chapter we said that expansion of culture through the development of markets was so important a part of diffusion as to deserve a chapter to itself. Of all the many influences affecting consumption at the present time, undoubtedly the most important is the aggressive effort of business men to dispose of their wares. Wherever business men have penetrated—and today that means the whole world—they have tremendously affected both the amount and the kind of consumption. This influence on consumption was not nearly so important in early days as it is today; yet who can tell to how great an extent even in early days the consumption of the peoples of the globe was enriched by exchange?

We can draw a romantic picture of the trader in the past, a man in outlandish garb who enters a market place, laden with strange and curious things. He spreads out his wares. Children gather around him and then the older people approach. They bring their native products to give for the new goods and the stranger goes away, perhaps never to return. His wares, too, may lose their novelty before their use is discovered, and be discarded. But perhaps the new goods will find a genuine welcome. Perhaps the trader will return, he or another, and offer the same things again. In such ways are new tastes quickened, new interests aroused, new goods introduced into society.

The motives that inspire the trader's efforts are not necessarily economic. Business success may be desired for its own sake, or for emulation, or as a good excuse for adventure. This is true even of twentieth-century business men. One has only to read their biographies to appreciate to what extent they have taken money-making as a challenge to their abilities, rather than a thing to be sought for itself.[1]

Whether or not business men, ancient or modern, have been interested in money-making chiefly for its own sake, however, it is clear that if they are to win any distinction, other people must exchange with them. Other people must buy what business men are trying to dispose of. Whether the motives are primarily economic or non-economic, they are accomplishing economic results.

HISTORY OF THE MARKET

Exchange may and does exercise some influence on consumption long before it is aggressively practiced, but its great influence begins when it becomes a business for the creation of demand. In primitive society we have very few examples of the deliberate creation of demand. Natural products were exchanged and occasionally primitive manufacture was spasmodically practiced by individuals. Such organized exchange as we find in primitive society, however, is usually accompanied and frequently overshadowed by diverse social and ceremonial observances, which interfere with the development of economic motives in the traders. Much early exchange was very similar to gift giving and receiving.[2] But as it is a long step from gift exchange to the beginnings of commercial exchange, it is likewise a long step from the beginning of commercial exchange to the deliberate creation of markets, to the deliberate effort to awaken new demands for goods.

There was little indeed of this deliberate creation of markets for new goods or for new extensions of old goods before the

---

[1] See Taussig. F. W., *Inventors and Money Makers*, New York, 1915. *My Life and Work*, by Henry Ford in collaboration with Samuel Crowther, is a good example. Garden City, 1922.

[2] See Hoyt, E. E., *Primitive Trade*, London, 1926, Ch. VII.

classical period. In ancient Egypt we find there were trading voyages and buying and selling in the cities, but little evidence of attempts to develop new markets for new goods or old ones. For one thing, there was very little large-scale manufacture to produce the goods to sell, although there seem to have been factories for making pottery in Greece and some fairly large-scale manufacturing establishments in or near Rome. Even without large-scale manufacture, however, some enterprising traders did gather together from many sources the products of a district and seek to sell them in other places. During the classical period their ships did a picturesque though irregular business among various Mediterranean ports. In the days of the Roman empire there was even a trade with China. These adventurous traders were the first entrepreneurs, and from what we know of their lives we may conclude that they loved risk and danger more than they loved trade. Even after the Elizabethan period in England, the chief body of organized foreign traders bore the name of Merchant Adventurers.

The creation of organized markets was more or less incidental in the early days of trade, although it became of prime importance as time went on. Because of the activities of traders, wealthy people in all parts of the known world came to enlarge and extend their interests, and luxuries were introduced into far corners of the globe. The trade carried on between cities was largely the exchange of luxuries. Outlying provinces sent corn and wine to Athens, Corinth, and Rome and received some of the refinements of life in exchange.

To a slight extent in Egypt and Mesopotamia, to some extent in Greece, and to a far greater extent in the Roman Empire, we find indications of the existence of a new class of people, bankers and money-lenders, who were interested in developing trade while they themselves remained snugly and safely at home. These people equipped ships or loaned money for the equipment of ships, and sent traders forth to extend trade for their own profit. With their advent on the scene, the development of the market begins to look deliberate.

These bankers and money-lenders of Rome were the forerunners of the famous banking houses of the Middle Ages, which developed and, in fact, did much to create the commercial prosperity of the Northern Italian cities. We know of the many trade routes by sea and by land of the mediaeval period. It is rightly claimed that the blocking by the Ottomans of the three main trade routes from Europe to Asia furnished the immediate incentive for the voyages of Columbus and the other explorers of the fifteenth and sixteenth centuries, and thus indirectly opened up the markets of a whole new world.

The organization of trading companies in England and on the Continent, immensely stimulated by the discovery of America, proceeded on increasingly deliberate and business-like lines. England, the Netherlands, France, Spain, and Portugal contended for the new markets of the West, and their efforts went through a process of evolution from warlike and adventurous to the more effective methods of calculated business.[1]

All the foregoing has reference chiefly to the opening of new markets in an extensive sense, the development of trade in distant or new portions of the globe, the creation and diffusion of new interests among alien peoples. This is the more spectacular aspect of the development of new markets and the aspect more easily traced. It is probably, too, for the ancient and mediaeval periods, the more important phase of the growth of the market.

We are also interested, of course, in the growth of domestic markets from within, the creation and diffusion of new interests by a trader within his own country. What was done along this line during the ancient and mediaeval periods? Were new goods of domestic make introduced as well as new foreign goods? Relatively very few. An increase in domestic consumption was certainly not cultivated as an increase in foreign

[1] For a picture of the history of trade, see Knight, M. M., *Economic History of Europe to the End of the Middle Ages*, Boston, 1926; and Weber, Max, *General Economic History* (Knight, F. H., trans.), New York, 1927, especially Ch. XVI.

consumption was. All through the ancient, mediaeval, and early modern periods the new goods introduced into a society came in chiefly through importations, not through new home manufactures. From these importations, moreover, it was chiefly the wealthy classes who profited; the poor and middle-class families were scarcely better off at the beginning of modern times than they were in the classical period. They were too poor to buy expensive imported luxuries, and, without improvements in manufacturing processes, home-made goods could not be offered them at prices they could afford.

The great change in consumption affecting the masses of the people and affecting them at home as well as abroad, was brought about, of course, by the Industrial Revolution. The economies in manufacturing processes made possible by machinery decreased the price of necessities and raised real wages, so that nearly everyone could extend his consumption beyond what had formerly been the necessities of life. With the advent of the factory system, the most significant person in extending consumption ceased to be the trader or the banker financing the trader, and became the manufacturer. The large-scale manufacturer was of course entirely dependent for his maximum success on selling his product as widely as possible. If he was making a new good he must create a desire for it, if an old familiar good he must create a desire for more of it. Sales methods began to be scientifically cultivated, and the many and varied products of the new manufacture met on the market in a contest to which each producer eventually found he must bring his utmost intelligence and art.

It would be hard to over-estimate the effect of these new intensive efforts on increasing and on changing the character of consumption both in foreign and domestic trade. So far as domestic trade is concerned, we do not need so much to emphasize these facts of change as the precise methods by which they were effected, and this we shall do in Chapter X and Chapter XI. Foreign trade, however, deserves special attention here.

CONTRIBUTIONS FROM ABROAD TO AMERICAN CONSUMPTION

In Table II are given the principal commodities entering into foreign trade in the United States.[1] From the import column it is seen that our greatest single import is 412 million dollars' worth of raw silk. Probably every woman and girl in the United States gets a bit of it. We import also 42 million dollars' worth of silk manufactures. We should note also that we import nearly a hundred and fifty million dollars' worth of wool and mohair and their manufactures, a hundred million dollars' worth of cotton and its manufactures, a hundred million dollars' worth of hides and skins, and nearly fifty million dollars' worth of flax and hemp, all of which go to keep us in garments, shoes, and hats. Former Secretary Redfield once said that if all the articles we wore should speak at once in the native tongue of their country of origin the confusion would be worse than the tower of Babel.

TABLE II

FOREIGN TRADE OF THE UNITED STATES—LEADING IMPORTS AND EXPORTS FOR THE FISCAL YEAR ENDED JUNE 30, 1927. (Figures in millions.)

(United States Department of Commerce)

Imports		Exports	
Raw silk	$412.5	Raw cotton	$866.9
Crude rubber	368.5	Petroleum and products	536.7
Coffee	293.4	Machinery	408.1
Cane sugar	254.8	Automobiles, parts, accessories	359.6
Paper	144.0	Wheat and flour	318.1
Furs and manufactures	138.4	Packing-house products	219.0
Paper base stocks	118.6	Coal and coke	207.4
Petroleum and products	118.5	Iron and steel mill products	178.1
Tin	105.5	Copper, ore and manufactures	147.1
Copper, ore and manufactures	96.9	Leaf tobacco	135.8

[1] Figures compiled from United States Department of Commerce, Bureau of Foreign and Domestic Commerce, *Monthly Summary of Foreign Commerce of the United States*, June, 1927, pp. 118–141.

Imports		*Exports*	
Hides and skins	$95.1	Fruits and nuts	$129.7
Fruits and nuts	87.2	Cotton manufactures and	
Wool and mohair	83.7	semi-manufactures	123.8
Burlaps and bagging	82.0	Sawmill products	101.0
Leaf tobacco	76.7	Iron and steel, advanced	
		manufactures	76.1
		Chemicals	73.0
Oil seeds	70.8	Rubber and manufactures	63.5
Sawmill products	70.6	Leather	49.8
Vegetable oils	66.6	Naval stores	38.3
Cotton manufactures and		Wood manufactures	38.2
semi-manufactures	64.3	Oil cake and meal	28.6
Wool manufactures	61.6		
Diamonds	57.5	Paper and products	27.3
Art works	56.4	Rye and flour	24.7
Chemicals	56.2	Furs and manufactures	23.6
Fertilizers	53.3	Books and printed matter	22.7
Cocoa beans	50.8	Fish	22.6
Flax and hemp products	49.0	Vegetables and preparations	21.7
Silk manufactures	41.9	Fertilizers and materials	20.2
Dairy products	38.9	Pigments, paints and var-	
Vegetables and preparations	38.7	nishes	19.8
Raw cotton	37.2	Tobacco manufactures	19.0
		Photographic goods	18.8

Our next greatest import after raw silk is 368 million dollars worth of crude rubber, on which our automobile industry depends. We use three-fourths of all that is produced in the world, but as yet we do not control the production of a single ton.

Of our foods, coffee, cane sugar, fruits and nuts, vegetable oils, and vegetables are our most important imports. Mr. Redfield says: [1]

"On a single day in April, 1922, the New York wholesale market received among other supplies of the kind 800 crates of honey-dew melons from South Africa, 4000 crates of vegetables and a shipment of lima beans from Cuba, 10,000 packages of vegetables and 1700 barrels of potatoes from Bermuda, 4000 crates of onions from Chile, and 18,000 bags of onions from Egypt."

Other important consumers' goods are tobacco, diamonds, and art works. We must remember, however, that consumers

[1] *Dependent America*, Boston, 1926, p. 95.

just as truly consume our imports of metals, chemicals, fertilizers, and so on, for producers' goods are desired only because they help make possible consumers' goods in the future.

EXPANSION OF MARKETS OVER THE WORLD

When we are considering American imports we are dealing for the most part with commodities which Americans desire and have gone out to seek. When we are dealing with American exports we are dealing not only with commodities which other nations have come out to seek from us, but with commodities for which we are trying to create a demand abroad. Our greatest export is raw cotton, a practical necessity of life all over the world and demanded by all nations. But our business men on their search for profits are trying to make other countries demand more of it and its products than they otherwise would demand. Our next greatest export is petroleum and its products. It is said that an American oil company gave every family in a certain part of China a kerosene lamp so as to create a greater demand for kerosene. No business men are more aggressive in teaching new wants to the rest of the world than are our automobile manufacturers. They would like to see every Eskimo and every Hottentot riding in a car of his own. Automobiles, parts and accessories, are our fourth greatest export.

It would be hard to over-estimate the effect of intensive sales efforts by American business men and the business men of other countries in changing and in increasing consumption in foreign lands. Cultures all over the world have been extended and enriched (and in a few cases unfortunately undermined) by the aggressive efforts of business men since the Industrial Revolution. The total value of the import trade of 72 countries in 1926 is estimated by the Department of Commerce to be nearly thirty-one billion dollars.[1] And since,

[1] Information furnished directly by the Division of Statistical Research of the Department. The most careful study of this subject is the League of Nations' Memorandum on Balance of Payments and Foreign Trade Balances, 1910–1923, Geneva, 1924.

as we shall see when we come to Chapter XXVI, the present per capita consumption in most countries is far below that in the United States, we can believe that the potentialities in foreign trade are as yet hardly recognized; the surface is now no more than scratched. The commerce-laden argosies of magic sails envisaged by the poet have hardly begun to float across the blue.

Foreign markets are developed by business men in countries of similar culture to theirs—as in the case of English or German markets for American goods and vice versa. But business men are now extremely active also in developing markets in countries whose cultures are very different from their own. The appearance of Ingersoll watches in Liberia and of Bovril in Samoa is, of course, the result of just one thing: the efforts of traders to sell their wares. The agency of the trader is often perhaps the only agency, and it is now usually the most powerful agency, introducing the culture traits of Western civilization to primitive or backward peoples. This is not the place for us to discuss the injurious culture traits which are introduced along with, or sometimes unfortunately to the exclusion of, the good ones: the development of a taste for strong drink among American Indians, the cultivation of the opium habit in Siam. Neither are we concerned here with the fact that imperialism has too often fallen wide of its professed mark and the efforts of traders have been abortive.[1] We are emphasizing only the fact that trade at present is the most powerful agent in introducing new culture traits, whatever they may be. If the traders have their way, there will soon be no cultures undeveloped in a material sense.

The current literature of foreign trade is written almost exclusively for the benefit of producers, but from it one may easily deduce what changes in consumption are taking place through the aggressive development of markets in foreign lands. Books advising business methods, on the basis of

---

[1] Note Moon, Parker T., *Imperialism and World Politics*, New York, 1927, especially Chapter V: "Clothes, Culture and Caoutchouc in Congo."

past experience, are coming out continually.[1] The foreign
trade departments of large firms are recognizing there is a real
art of foreign selling, requiring methods different from those
used at home. Now the more progressive houses are making
organized efforts to round up all possible consumers in every
nation under the sun. The first great material bond of the
human family will probably be its common consumption of
Brownie Soap or Moonshine Biscuits!

The best statistical evidence as to the extent to which foreign
trade is affecting consumption is afforded by figures showing
the per capita imports of the different countries of the world.
In 1924 the average per capita imports for all countries
amounted to $17.13. Imports to the United States were $30.96;
to Canada, $86.47 per capita. For some countries the figure
was very small: Guatemala, $8.36; Haiti, $7.19; Ecuador, $5.26;
British India, $3.14; China, $2.12, for instance. The countries
with imports averaging over a hundred dollars in value per
capita are countries of limited general production which have
enjoyed a relatively high standard of living for some time:
such are Denmark, Switzerland, the United Kingdom, and
New Zealand. It is interesting to observe, however, that
some countries that we customarily think of as backward or
as having recently been backward in an economic sense are
now consuming very considerable importations: British Hon-
duras, $86.53; Cuba, $86.03; Malay Federated States, $36.11;
Panama, $30.87.[2] A part of these importations, of course,
are consumed by foreigners in these countries, not by the
nationals themselves. Nevertheless the figures are significant.

EFFORTS OF THE UNITED STATES DEPARTMENT OF COMMERCE

The United States Government, through the Bureau of
Foreign and Domestic Commerce of the Department of Com-

[1] See for instance, Cooper, Clayton S., *Foreign Trade: Markets and Methods*,
New York, 1922; Hough, B. O., *Practical Exporting*, New York, 1921; *The
Export Executive*, Scranton, 1925.

[2] United States Department of Commerce, Bureau of Foreign and Domestic
Commerce, *Statistical Abstract of the United States, 1925*, Washington, 1926,
pp. 814, 816.

merce, now maintains foreign offices as an aid to the development of American markets in forty-five foreign cities from Alexandria, Athens, Barcelona, and Batavia to Tokio, Toronto, Vienna, and Warsaw, and has special commodity divisions for fifteen general classes of commodities. In the year ended June 30, 1927, the Bureau rendered nearly two and one-half million trade promotive services to American business men.[1]

What sort of work does it do? The following examples speak for themselves.[2]

"After the field representative of a Detroit automobile manufacturer had paid unsuccessful visits to Batavia, Dutch East Indies, over a period of two years, the American trade commissioner obtained for him a local dealer who is now buying cars to the value of $10,000 a month.

· · · · · · · · · · · ·

"Through a connection established by the Buenos Aires office, a San Francisco fruit-exporting firm was able to do $100,000 worth of business with Argentina in a three-month period.

· · · · · · · · · · · ·

"An agency for American cigarettes, placed through the efforts of the bureau's Calcutta office, netted $25,000 worth of business in the first 10 months of its existence."

The Bureau publishes an annual yearbook of about 700 pages and weekly commerce reports, as well as other periodical material, and in October, 1927, had issued over a thousand bulletins dealing with various aspects of foreign trade, including such subjects as the following: Furniture Markets of Argentina, Uraguay, Paraguay, and Brazil; Leather and Boots and Shoes in European Markets; Cotton Fabrics in British India and the Philippines; Cuban Market for Paper and Paper Products; Turkish Markets for American Hardware; and Chinese Market for American Foodstuffs. A little imagination, and such titles make us see Windsor chairs and gate-leg tables

[1] United States Department of Commerce, Annual Report of the Director of the Bureau of Foreign and Domestic Commerce to the Secretary of Commerce, Washington, 1927, pp. ii, 1.
[2] Ibid., pp. 11, 12.

from Grand Rapids adorning the drawing-room of some ranch-er's wife on the pampas; we see the trim feet of Norwegian girls, Greek girls, and Russian girls tripping along in the same distinguished footgear that excites our admiration on Fifth Avenue; we see a Chinese family gathered together by the fragrance of Virginia corn pone and Gloucester herrings.

The efforts of export houses and of government agencies instituted to serve them go in part, of course, to help fill de-mands already existing in foreign countries. Their effect in creating and stimulating demand is nevertheless directly and indirectly of great importance.

SOCIAL AND POLITICAL EFFECTS OF FOREIGN TRADE

It may be well to consider what are the social and political effects of this great economic expansion. The point we have been emphasizing is, of course, the material extension and enriching of cultures which normally follows it, although oc-casionally traders introduce culture traits appealing injuriously to the physical appetites, and peoples undisciplined in such tastes have sometimes fallen victims before they could develop the necessary protective morale. On the whole, however, the effects of foreign trade have been in the direction of a fuller and richer material culture. Indirectly through foreign trade, moreover, certain contributions along lines of art, literature, and philosophy have been made by the less advanced material cultures to those more advanced in material lines. We, for instance, have taught China the advantage of kerosene oil and incidentally have ourselves learned something about Chinese art.

But what are the effects of this foreign trade on the general field of international relations? [1] Is peace the "natural effect" of trade, as Montesquieu declared? It is easy to see the af-firmative arguments. In the first place, trade leads directly to mutual understanding, and indirectly as enlarging cultures

[1] For several suggestions in what follows, see Young, Allyn A., " Economics and War," *Economic Problems New and Old*, Boston, 1927, pp. 1–21.

become more similar, other peoples seem less strange to us.
That increase in international understanding may be small
which is made possible by mutual appreciation of grapefruit,
sweet potatoes, and Ford cars, or by Wedgwood pottery or by
Thuringian wood carving; but there is undoubtedly something
in it. "I'd like them better if they didn't wear such queer
clothes," said an American housewife of her foreign neighbors.
"Frog-eating Frenchman" is a phrase with which more than
once a man has been dismissed from consideration as a possible
comrade. It is only another illustration of the working of
association in one's mind: questionable consumption, questionable consumers.

In the second place, trade leads to common interests which
we must protect in common, and hence to the growth of organizations which are independent of political boundaries.
Such are the international organizations already functioning
in the field of shipping and transport.

It is impossible, however, to shut our eyes to the fact that
struggle for markets has had and is now very obviously having
a disturbing effect on peaceful international relations. "Commerce, which ought naturally to be among nations as among
individuals, a bond of union and friendship has become the
most fertile source of discord and animosity"—thus Adam
Smith. Why so? International trade leads to rivalries for
the furtherance of selfish interests. Methods considered un-
fair in domestic trade are used as a matter of course in foreign.
Compare our own Webb-Pomerene Act. Nationals of one
country gain control of extensive properties in another country
and then appeal to their own country for its military protection
in domestic disturbances in the foreign land. Occasions for
conflict are many and citizens of one country are always alive
to any real or fancied injury that one of their number may
receive under another flag. They are quick to perceive the
faintest shadow cast on their own country's prestige. "Uncle
Sam will show them where to get off" is or was the sentiment
of many an old-fashioned home-brewed patriot engaged in

exploiting resources on a foreign shore. Understanding the purport of such sentiments, we can appreciate the feelings of the soldiers of Martinique with their popular song: "Uncle Sam is all right for an uncle but we don't want him for a father."

Contact with economic goods, the discipline of economic measures, however, though they may not be instigated by rationality are good teachers of it. The chief reason why trade in so many cases now results in social and political conflict is not because we are so economically minded, but because we are still in the early stages of international contacts: we are not yet economically minded enough.

CHAPTER X

AGGRESSIVE METHODS OF SALES-MAKING

"The strange wild whisper of waters curling on the beach; the peacock glow of a sea of jade and azure; the sharp tang of fresh salt air. How thrilling and how beautiful! Such sensations this pattern brings to you! At the same time you know that by its use you are proving yourself a member of that rare company of discriminating souls who draw to themselves the finest, the choicest and the best."—*Current advertisement for a bath towel.*

In the preceding chapter we have been dealing with the growth of markets over the whole earth. We took up the development of markets very largely from the point of view of their extension in space: the opening of new trade channels, the creation of new trade contacts. These channels and contacts, even when made by one particular firm alone, for one particular product alone, impress us, nevertheless, as fundamentally a contribution toward the general movement for closer economic relationships with foreign countries along many lines. In other words, in the earlier stages of trade, contacts between countries, the activities of the General Motors Export Company, let us say, are of importance not only in selling motors, but in laying foundations on which many other firms, exporting other products, will later build. From a broad point of view, then, the development of a foreign market for one particular product may have indirect economic effects on opening a way for other products and be more important in the long run than the sale of that one product itself.

When we come to the further development of a market already flourishing, however, the ground is already well tilled and fertilized, and the business man has only to drop his seed. The indirect results of his activity are usually not nearly so great as the direct results—the sale of his particular product. Hence the intensive viewpoint, the precise manner by which sales are effected, is the aspect of most importance here.

In the present chapter, then, we shall approach the consideration of sales-making from the point of view of the means by which a business man creates a market for his own particular product. We are concerned with the methods by which consumers are approached, and flattered, cajoled, or even threatened into buying. In particular, how and to what an extent do the aggressive methods of sellers influence our consumption at present? Is this influence ultimately a social gain or a social waste?

It is unnecessary to spend much time in emphasizing what a large part aggressive sales methods have come to play in modern business. A man makes an article. His task is only begun. He must go out into the highways and byways and attract attention to his product, interest in it, effective demand for it. Practically all firms have an aggressive sales policy of one sort or another. If they do not have it, no matter how excellent their product, their aggressive competitors are likely to get their market away. The modern business man does not retire to his office and patiently wait for trade to come knocking at his door. Along with his organizations for producing he is developing an organization for selling his product. In some lines it takes more money and more effort to get people to buy the thing produced than it does to invent and manufacture the thing in the first place.

There are several kinds of advertising: the local retail advertising done by stores; the advertising of new stock and bond issues by financial houses; national advertising of "standard" products by their producers; and other types. The national advertising of standard products by their producers, ordinary magazine advertising, is the type of advertising most often attacked [1] and the type which is by far the most costly.

---

[1] It is attacked not only by consumers but by retail merchants and their representatives. See Borsodi, Ralph, *The Distribution Age*, New York, 1927.

Local retail advertising and financial advertising are largely if not chiefly informative, but the national advertising of standard products is distinctly aggressive and is hence the type of advertising dealt with in this chapter.

The "Science" of Selling

There are various ways by which the business man works his will on the consumer, of which salesmanship and advertising are the most important. The existing literature on salesmanship and advertising is enormous. College courses, and indeed whole schools, are devoted to teaching the "science" of advertising and salesmanship. This so-called science consists in the application of various principles of the science of psychology to the business of selling. Sometimes this application is so far-fetched as to be amusing. It is frequently assumed that the potential consumer is either without defenses or should not be permitted to exercise his defenses, and the great end of making a sale is exalted above the most ordinary common sense.

Of late, however, a more intelligent apprehension of the methods and potentialities of selling has been gained, and more and more, in the literature of sales methods, we find emphasis on the real or imagined services of such methods to the consumer.

Recognition and Creation of Demand

The phrases recognition of demand, creation of demand, are familiar to all advertisers. Recognition of demand takes place when a producer endeavors to fill an already existing want. Creation of demand occurs when the producer makes people want for the first time his own new product.

So far as the recognition of expressed or unexpressed demand is concerned, it is clear that the producer has a very useful part to play. A wise producer keeps his ear to the ground. He knows that marketing possibilities sometimes appear almost in the twinkling of an eye; in particular, a potential market for one thing may suddenly appear as the result of the consumption of another; they are complementary goods, in the term of the economist. The most progressive firms are beginning to employ research workers to make painstaking studies of potential markets both at home and abroad. In this way they are able to make use at once of general changes in the habits of consumers which might possibly react to their own advantage. For instance, a recent book dealing with the cotton industry points out that the invention and widespread use of the radio is keeping women at home more than formerly; this suggests that wide-awake manufacturers of cotton yard goods may sell large quantities of materials for house-dresses. In the same way, the almost universal use of the automobile has had a depressing effect on sales of white dress goods and has made possible the success of campaigns for colored fabrics suitable for wear in motoring.[1] The fabric manufacturers first to sense this situation would be in a strategic position to deflect the rising demand for colored motoring fabrics to their own product: pushing their own fabric, silk, rayon, or cotton, into the limelight. An intensive campaign at the psychological moment may determine the interests of consumers, at least for the immediate future.

Most actual recognition of demand, however, is not the recognition of a new want and the attempt to fill it with a new product, but rather the attempt to fill an old want with some particular brand. For instance, everyone uses soap, and people would make it at home if it could not be bought. They do not keep themselves cleaner because of soap advertisements. The manufacturer's recognition of demand for soap is simply his effort to make people buy his brand instead of his competitors'. In this case, the producer's recognition of demand is for his own, not for the consumer's advantage.

All this has to do with recognition of demand; but again

[1] Bader, Louis, *World Developments in the Cotton Industry*, New York, 1925, p. 138.

and again, in our discussion of foreign markets, we have referred
to the creation of demand.   Occasionally someone claims
that there is no such thing as a creation of demand by business
men; there is only, he says, the provision of means to gratify
existing wants and desires.   Our early consideration of the
development of interests, under the head of the Psychology
of Consumption, has shown us clearly that this is not true.
Man is not a bundle of unsatisfied interests; on the contrary,
he has to learn his interests, and usually he learns hard; but
if he has a teacher he learns more readily than he learns by
himself.   The business man who wants to sell his product becomes perforce a teacher.   He is engaged in the process of
teaching interests.   To be sure he will be most successful if,
other things equal, the interest he tries to teach serves some
purpose, or leads out of an already existent interest, or is associated with things with which the prospective consumer is
already familiar.   Almost all creation of demand has made
use of some such aids as these; but it is true to say, nevertheless, that in almost every case, if a man puts a new good
on the market, he has to do something himself to create a
demand for it before it will sell, and certainly before it will
sell quickly.

In the case of many products, creation of demand and
recognition of demand run along together.   Let us say that
a pioneer producer induces people to buy canned beans for
the first time.   He creates demand.   But a dozen others following him know that people already use canned beans and
aim not so much perhaps at creating demand as at deflecting
demand to beans of their own.   They do not emphasize so
strongly the merits of canned beans in general as they emphasize the merits of their own make.   Yet, although the
pioneer producer of canned beans does the initial work of
creating a demand, his competitors help develop it until—
if this has ever happened—the entire potential demand has
been permanently aroused.   As time goes on the producer's
effort, if he is a good business man, passes more and more

from demand creation to so-called consumer recognition or acceptance, but the element of demand creation probably always to some extent remains.

We see then that there are real changes in human wants which arise from salesmanship and advertising. Through recognition of demand by the producer, the process of consumption may be sped up; through creation of demand by the producer, consumption is varied or increased.

To the question, how greatly do aggressive sales methods affect consumption, we cannot give an entirely satisfactory answer for obvious reasons. In fact, nobody knows. There are other influences beside selling efforts affecting demand: general social tendencies, changes in demand for complementary goods, frequently an improvement in the product itself. There is no doubt, however, that in some cases the speeding-up process due to advertising is huge. The late great increase in the demand for raisins in the United States has undoubtedly been due very largely to the efforts of the California Raisin Growers' Association, and the increasing consumption of citrus fruits has been effected in considerable part by the advertising of the California Fruit Growers' Exchange. The demand for automobiles and radios is due to many factors: advertising and salesmanship is an important one. It is probable that the increasing consumption of many new luxuries of the toilet is chargeable almost entirely to advertising. High-pressure salesmanship of domestic electric equipment has probably been the chief factor so far in introducing the electric washing machine and vacuum cleaner into American homes. "It pays to advertise" has become a slogan on every one's lips and expenses in the United States for national advertising alone are estimated to average nearly ten dollars for every man, woman, and child in the country. We are told that the Wrigley Company pays $108,000 a year for the electricity consumed in one advertising sign in New York City. The cost of the advertising in each issue of *The Saturday Evening Post* is nearly a million dollars.

Aggressive Sales Methods as Social Gain

The arguments as to the social advantages of aggressive sales methods are various, of which two are most important. The first emphasizes the direct effect on the consumer. Through advertising he is stimulated to want more and better things than he would otherwise have wanted. At the same time, in order to be able to buy the things he wants, he is stimulated to greater production, a good thing in itself. The second argument emphasizes the effect of advertising on price: as demand increases through advertising, it is possible by mass production to reduce the price of goods.

The first of these arguments is undoubtedly substantial. Aggressive methods of sales-making are educational agencies of great potential influence. They hasten the introduction of new goods, and new types of old goods: beautiful bath towels, for instance. It is true enough that artistic production is stimulated by efforts to make sales.

We must not, however, lose sight of the fact that in practice aggressive methods educate wrongly as well as rightly. To take two cases to which we have referred: the advertising campaigns for citrus fruits have educated us to the fact that such fruits are rich in Vitamin C; but the campaign for raisins has implied that raisins are rich in iron—which they are not. We have had the advantage of frequent brushing of teeth stressed by advertisements, but we also have been alarmed by an unsubstantial terror that four out of five of us were doomed to pyorrhea. In short, the argument about the directly educational value of advertising must at present be taken with a generous pinch of salt.

Even when aggressive sales methods are not directly educational, however, a good deal must be said for their great power to create and enlarge interests. Let us picture a small and economically backward community off the main lines of travel. There is here, let us say, no window decorating, no high-powered salesmanship and nobody here subscribes to any periodicals. Then let us suppose that some one gives to every household half a dozen popular periodicals full of advertisements. Whether these advertisements carry educational matter or not, they will undoubtedly be educational in the sense that they will have the effect of increasing the desires of the people.

Such desires would not amount to much if there were no means to gratify them. But they may in themselves provide the drive for their satisfaction. Certainly in some cases, new desires stimulate a person to harder work so he can actually fulfill these awakened desires.

Of course all new interests are not necessarily good ones. Sometimes they impair life or upset it. More usually, however, they are not actually injurious, and serve a man better than the negative state of having no interests at all. Moreover, by the long process of trial and error the least satisfactory interests will in time be eliminated. It must be said, however, that this trial and error method is certainly not highly intelligent, though it may be the most effective method we have at present.

The second argument usually advanced in favor of aggressive sales methods is that by increasing demand they make possible greater production and so lead to decreasing costs. This is true in some cases, but it is by no means so true in practice as in theory it appears to be. The price of Ford and other cars has undoubtedly fallen in part as a result of advertising. Two large manufacturers of canned soups have given the author substantial evidence that mass production made possible by advertising has reduced the price of their product. The same facts could probably be shown in the case of other manufactured products which are not luxuries.

In other cases advertising has very little effect on price one way or the other. We should not expect the prices of agricultural products to be subject to decreasing costs of production as manufactured products are. We have the figures of annual sales by carloads of the California Fruit Growers' Exchange and its predecessor from 1896 to 1925.[1] Their extensive advertising campaign was inaugurated in 1907. Its effects on price were slight. One fruit market man observes: "The advertising of apples or oranges cannot reduce the retail price, but is resorted to to create a demand for the ever-increased production of these commodities."[2]

A good deal of intensive sales effort, however, leads to increases in prices. It is not directed to increasing demand as such, but to increasing demand at a price, and usually at a price that enables the producer to pocket a large margin. This is particularly true of luxuries; where the cost of advertising is added (and sometimes many times added) to the cost of the product. It would be interesting to see what would happen if manufacturers of electrical household equipment should now let up on their high-pressured and high-priced salesmanship and put down the prices of their wares in proportion to the savings thus indicated. They might find they would make more sales and have greater profits. A little advertising and a low price may be more effective than much advertising and a high price.

Aggressive Sales Methods as Social Waste

We are thus brought to the negative statement of the argument, for which we shall take up more in detail some points we have already raised. First, aggressive sales methods stimulate and create interests which are sometimes harmful, often useless, and practically never the best. Second, the cost of such methods is altogether excessive.

A large body of illustrative material as to the harmfulness and uselessness of advertised goods has been presented by Stuart Chase in his *Tragedy of Waste*, and by Stuart Chase and F. J. Schlink in *Your Money's Worth*. The field of adulteration, misrepresentation, and quackery is huge, although the federal

---

[1] Compiled in Vanderblue, H. B., *Economic Principles, A Case Book*, Chicago, 1927, p. 76.

[2] Quoted in ibid., pp. 77–78.

Pure Food and Drugs Act and various state laws, together
with the efforts of such scientific bodies as the American Medical
Association, are doing very much to protect the consumer
here; but much also remains to be done. No agency, however, but his own common sense has as yet been able to preserve
the consumer from the advertisements that for a price promise
to endow him or her with intelligence and personality, the
ability to speak French or play Beethoven in ten days, to develop strength and loveliness, or to defeat the advancing years.

But a greater case can be made out against the cost of aggressive sales methods. The total yearly expenditure in the
United States for national advertising alone is estimated
to be over a billion dollars, or, as we have said, ten dollars
for each man, woman, and child in the country. Who pay
the billion dollars? Of course, the consumer pays it. He
gets some of it back, to be sure, in so far as increased demand
results in increased production, which leads to a decreased cost
of production and a fall in price, but, as we have seen, this
very often does not happen. A large amount of advertising,
probably over one half, has for one aim the creation of a prestige
value for the product; and for this prestige the consumer is
certainly expected to pay. A manufacturer of plated silver-
ware, for instance, describes his product in terms of distinction
and sells it at twice the price that unadvertised plate of the
same quality demands on the market. Economists are familiar
with "class price," that is the setting of various prices to
appeal to different classes on what is essentially the same
product. The woman who must have the best soap thus pays
fifty cents a cake for the same product (in a less distinctive
wrapper) that her more canny neighbor buys for five cents.
Stuart Chase and F. J. Schlink found many cases in which the
same product was offered at widely varying prices, sometimes
by the same company; or where a superior product, not advertised, could be bought at considerably less than the cost
of an advertised inferior product. The long-run equalization
with which students of economics are familiar proves in this

case a very long run indeed: not so much because competition is slow as because consumers are so easily played with. There is even a sense in which some consumers undoubtedly enjoy being played with. P. T. Barnum made the famous statement: "The people like to be humbugged;" and some advertising writers make a great point of the additional satisfactions consumers derive from what critics call the "fictitious values" of high prices and pretence. If a person gets the idea he is elegant, aristocratic, and superior by paying a dollar for a bottle of lavender bath salts, the materials of which are worth three cents, then, say such writers, your advertisement has done him a real service.

But by no means all the people like to be humbugged, especially not in matters of price; and even in the case of those that do like it, such wasteful prestige selling may on broad social grounds be condemned as appealing to and developing one of the least worthy sides of human nature.

There is still another aspect of unnecessary cost in aggressive sales methods. We have seen that the potential demand for an article may never be finally developed, but often it is very nearly developed. Then, when few more sales, consequently few more economies in production, can be expected, competitors go on advertising, each trying to draw the already awakened demand away from the others. A glance through the advertising pages of any popular periodical will show how very extensive is the amount of chiefly competitive advertising, a part of which must be added to price. In fairness, however, it must be granted that all sensible competitors are trying to draw trade not merely by advertising, but to some extent also by improving their product. Where competitors are making exactly the same thing there is some tendency for them to combine, or at least to come to an agreement by which competitive costs will be lessened. Unfortunately, however, few competing manufacturers of consumers' goods are making what they would concede to be exactly the same thing.

A Specific Illustration of Advertising as It Is

Our points will be clearer if we illustrate them specifically. Let us select at random a copy of the great advertising medium, *The Saturday Evening Post*, which has the largest circulation of any periodical in the United States and is read by many classes of readers. We have said that the advertising in one number costs nearly a million dollars. *The Saturday Evening Post* is a "high-class" advertising medium. It does not carry advertisements for cigarettes, real estate promotion enterprises, proprietary medicines, remedial dentifrices, dandruff cures, face clays, wrinkle eradicators, photoplay correspondence schools, and other goods and services believed to be in themselves objectionable.[1]

In this issue which we choose, that of January 28, 1928, there are seventy-three full pages of advertisements. Ten of these pages advertise goods which may be more properly classed, not as consumers', but as producers' goods—trucks, steel fences, and so on. We shall cast these out.

Of the remaining full-page and half-page advertisements, fifty-nine in all, four call attention to relatively new goods: window glass admitting ultra-violet rays, straws to sip milk through, colored plumbing fixtures, and a new type of felt rug. Eleven call attention to goods not new but the consumption of which might be considerably increased: peanuts and lubricating oil are examples. The remaining forty-four call attention to goods already used very generally if not universally: automobiles, watches, hats, canned vegetables, soap. They emphasize the brand of some particular producer.

The subject matter of the advertisements tells us practically nothing about the products to distinguish them from other brands of the same thing. The advertisements do, indeed, use such phrases as "everything is now done in the white light of science"—without telling us how or what; "dazzling performance;" "silence, comfort, and stability;" "integrity;" "fine

---

[1] Information furnished by the Advertising Department of the Curtis Publishing Company.

appearance;" and so on. We are told also that a certain pen is "almost self-writing," whatever that means; and that you can throw it into the Colorado Canyon without breaking it. We are told that in a certain coat "snow-storms become a sheer delight." But what is there educational or helpful to us about such statements as these?[1]

Now the consumer may be perfectly willing to pay well for his new knowledge of the ultra-violet-ray window glass, his new incentive to eat peanuts, and his general stimulation and thrill from the advertisements as a whole. He may be willing to pay considerably over half a million dollars for a single appearance of these advertisements. They may be worth it. We cannot tell, for we do not know the cost of alternatives. But on the face it seems a rather expensive proposition, even taking into account the fact that as a result of this advertising we get *The Saturday Evening Post* for five cents!

THE WAY OUT

Advertising and salesmanship are doing us a service. There is no doubt about that. Such criticisms as we make are made in the full consciousness that, with conditions as they are, probably no substitute for commercial advertising could so efficiently take its place at the present moment. We are not offered a choice between the present competitive system of advertising and salesmanship, on the one hand, and on the other hand, an ideal organization for educating consumers' demand. We must face facts as they are.

Whose fault is it that advertising costs so much and is, with certain exceptions, so unintelligent? Is it the fault of the magazines? the advertising agencies? the producers? Partly. Chiefly, however, the fault rests on your head and on mine for

---

[1] Professor Rosamund Cook, of the University of Cincinnati, who is well-known for her efforts to standardize textiles, collected a dozen advertisements of four different brands of sheets from several magazines and cut out the brand name from each advertisement. It was then evident that all the advertisements made exactly the same points; smooth texture, whiteness, long wear, etc. She asked a member of the firm producing one of these brands to identify his own product from the advertisements. He was unable to do it.

allowing ourselves to be hoodwinked by nonsense. Our first problem is not to devise some system better than our present system of advertising, but to convince ourselves that we need a better system. The ordinary man as yet doesn't care because he doesn't know. Such phrases as "made in the white light of science" sound very good to him.

The great criticism of advertising is not that some of it is fraudulent and dishonest. Everyone, even including most advertisers, is opposed to dishonesty. To attack dishonesty is a small problem compared to attacking stupidity and inertia. The consumer's greatest loss comes, not from the deliberate fraud of advertisers, but from his own failure to apply the common sense he really has. The huge wastes of competitive advertising would not take place if the consumer used his head. It would no longer pay to run the merely competitive advertisement.

It would not be true to say, however, that the problem of advertising would be solved merely by the application of the consumer's common sense. In some cases actual fraud still remains to be dealt with. In a larger number of other cases, the consumer needs more information with regard to the actual qualities of products. He suffers from a lack of standardization, over which his control is partial and remote. This subject, however, belongs more properly to a later chapter on a more intelligent technology for the guidance of consumers. The point we wish to emphasize in this chapter is how great is our lethargy and how high a price we pay for the services rendered us by aggressive methods of sales-making.

CHAPTER XI

PRODUCTION AND CONSUMPTION

"And so, yielding to his importunities, I released the genie from
the bottle, whereupon he raised so great a smoke and became so
terrible to behold that I was fain to cover my eyes and grovel before him; but, restraining myself by a mighty effort, I called out
in a loud voice: 'Hold! Are you the Master or am I?'"—*Arabian
Fairy Tale.*

When in 1619 a young Oxford graduate named Dudley took
control of his father's foundry and tried to smelt iron with coal
—and secured, as the price of his partial success, the jealousy
of neighboring iron-masters—he little realized that he was taking one of the first important steps in a series of changes that
was going to inaugurate a new era for the world. Nor could
James Watt have dreamed, when he went out to walk on a fine
Sunday afternoon in 1765, that on that walk would come to
him an idea that would be one of the chief means of revolu-
tionizing the world's production and consumption—the idea of
a separate condensing chamber which for the first time made
possible the invention of a true steam engine. They never knew
the importance of these ideas. In fact, we are only just now
beginning to realize to what extent our everyday lives are lived
under the domination of the various inventions used in power
machinery. These inventions are, to a certain extent, our
servants. To a certain extent they are our masters.

Of course there has always been a direct relationship between
the state of the productive arts and the amount and type of
consumption. In early times, however, and in fact up to the
period of the Industrial Revolution, it would seem that the
consumer had more control of the producer's hand than he has
today. Today certainly the producer tries to direct the preferences of the consumer. "See this," said the producer, "and
this; and this; and this. I made them for you. Take them, try

them. Now I'll think up something else for you." The consumer is so confused by the multitude of offerings that he rarely conceives anything new himself. The incentive of use is usually a slow incentive compared to the incentive of profits. The desire for conspicuous rewards to be won from profits in production gives the producer a flying start. Whatever can be made by the use of power machinery, that the producer tries to make. Then he sets about to teach the consumer to want it.

SOME PICTURES OF CONSUMPTION AT VARIOUS STAGES OF PRODUCTION

The most primitive men, such as those we talked about in our second chapter, lived in a state sometimes known as direct appropriation. That is to say, they directly appropriated for their use the products of the earth and waters without doing anything to modify or increase the yield. They had no organized production at all. They ate fruits, nuts, and berries, or such animals as could most easily be caught, and lived in natural shelters, or in such shelters as could be erected from simple materials with the least trouble. And of course, at the beginning, having no means to get clothing, they wore no clothing. Some of them presently discovered more efficient methods of hunting and hence were able to secure meat in great quantity. The catching of animals made possible the use of animals' skins for clothing, for shelters, and for utensils, although not all peoples utilized skins. Along with the development of hunting went the development of fishing. In this stage it is hard to think of the producer as leading the consumer into unfamiliar ways. Every man was of course his own producer. The two functions of production and consumption were not so sharply set against each other as is the case with us.

The course next taken by production and its accompanying consumption varied with the people and their geographic environment. Almost all peoples learned to tame animals very early. The dog was man's first ally, as we have seen. In lands where grazing conditions were favorable, but where the soil was not well adapted to agriculture, the domestication of cattle became of great economic importance. A cow, captured alive and kept to be killed later, gives birth to a calf. This is the beginning of animal husbandry. Over grazing lands the people led a nomadic life, wandering with their flocks and herds from one place to another. Their food consumption was very largely meat, fresh, smoked, or dried. They drank milk and learned to make butter and cheese. They wore skin clothing and also spun the wool into garments and rugs. Their homes were very frequently tents made of skins. They made ornaments and utensils from the teeth, the bones, and the horns of animals— as the drinking horn reminds us.

For other peoples, direct appropriation was directly succeeded by agriculture. Domestic animals might be kept in this stage, too, but the emphasis here is rather to be placed on settled homes and gardens. In this stage we have the use of cultivated grains and vegetables, and later of cultivated fruit. Since grains are usually cooked before being eaten we have a considerable development of the art of cookery. Wool is spun and, depending on the geographic environment, garments are made also of cotton, linen, or silk. The important fact that homes are settled means that possessions can accumulate—a great incentive to consumption. The homes are furnished, and various utensils are used for cooking and for storing foods.

So far there has been very little division of labor except for the primary division of labor between the sexes. The first division of labor among males, after the professional occupations of chief and priest or shaman, has to do with facilitating the making of production goods rather than of consumption goods. Among many people we have the office of blacksmith or tool-maker as the first industrial occupation. For the most part every family makes its own consumption goods.

Historically the next stage of development is that of specialized handicraft. Here we have more division of labor and, in consequence, the number of consumption goods available begins to increase rapidly. In this handicraft stage men specialized in their homes, or, more rarely, in large establishments, such as the factories for the production of pottery, the ruins of which have been found in Greece. The classical civilizations were civilizations made up of a combination of agricultural and handicraft stages. The early modern period in Europe was a handicraft period. Modern China is a combination of agricultural, handicraft, and industrial stages.

In the era of handicraft, people normally have more goods than in the pastoral or agricultural stages because of the economy of specialization. Each group during this stage specializes in some particular form or forms of production, as the Greeks specialized in fine arts, the early modern English in woolen textiles, the Chinese in paper and pottery. After specialization within a group begins, the consumption of its members—even its poorest members—is to some extent enriched. Even the members who do not themselves specialize profit by being able to buy certain goods at prices lower than formerly.

Although the pictures we have given are substantially correct as far as past history is concerned, it does not follow that all peoples must today go through these stages. Today men could pass from the stage of direct appropriation immediately to the industrial stage, if the change were made slowly and carefully.

This final industrial stage of production of which we spoke at the beginning, is of course the stage of large-scale power manufacture. Specialization of human labor continues, but there is even more specialization by machines, and as a result of this it is possible to produce many more goods far more cheaply and far more quickly than before. In the first years of adjustment to the new system in England, the handicraft workers were thrown out of employment and the manufacturers were able to get these dispossessed workers for the merest pittance. Thus the manufacturers were the first to profit by the new system and the standard of living of factory operatives did not rise at once except as they could purchase the new goods cheaply. Gradually, however, the workers came to appreciate their importance to production and by organization were able to hasten the process of securing higher wages. So the consumption of everyone was eventually greatly increased by the new economies of the factory system.

It is hard to over-estimate the importance of the great changes of the Industrial Revolution as they affect our consumption. Consider the miserable homes of the common people in England just prior to that period. At best they had only two or three rooms with no glass in the windows, damp and imperfectly heated by open fires. In the evening they sat by firelight or candle-light, if they had any light at all. Their furniture was of the roughest. They were fortunate if they had sheets for their beds. Their food consisted chiefly of bread, turnips, cabbage, a little meat, perhaps a little honey; later potatoes introduced from the New World, tea imported from China. Their cooking utensils were two or three iron pots and pans, their dishes of heavy earthenware, their knives and spoons of iron. Their costumes never gave them any variety of style: one suit for every day, made to last several years; one suit—if they were fortunate—for Sunday wear. They had the roughest shoes. The children went barefooted except in winter. The people wore home-made hats or caps and had no umbrellas. There were no dry cleaners in those days, and it must indeed have been difficult to keep heavy woolen garments in a sanitary condition. Only a few could read. They had no magazines or newspapers. None of them travelled, except on foot and rarely on horseback. If they were sick there were no facilities for caring for them. They could buy nothing in the way of relaxation or amusement. There were no comforts for the aged; for the children there was only the poorest schooling.

Two hundred years later the descendants of the same people, men and women of English ancestry in the United States, are enjoying here in this country[1] four and five room homes, with

[1] It must be granted that the standards of living of workers in England and in the United States are different. A less glowing picture than this must be drawn for the semi-skilled English industrial employee; and still less glowing for the English agricultural laborer.

bathrooms in the towns and cities, dry, well-heated, comfortable. Electricity brightens their evenings, perhaps cooks their food, and is beginning to do the washing, ironing, cleaning, sewing, and refrigerating of even the more moderately circumstanced. All have plenty of furniture—probably not beautiful, but that because of poor taste rather than lack of money. There are few who do not sleep between white sheets. It is the normal thing to have several articles of food to a meal, different dinners every day in the week, and between meals amazing quantities of ice cream, candy, peanuts, gum, and pop. It is the normal thing for them to have their cupboards full of shining cooking utensils, of table-ware at least semi-porcelain, and of knives, forks, and spoons of silver-plate. Their clothing changes in fashion with every season, and even so they must have a variety of colors, fabrics, and styles at any one time. Everyone has several coats and several hats. Children no longer cry for shoes. They cry to go barefooted.

At a very mediocre American standard of living, all families have a daily paper, most have magazines, all have free access to books. All have travelled somewhat, some to other countries; and many, even of the poorest, have their own cars. Those who wish them have pianos, phonographs, radios. The street-cleaner and the scrub-woman are not too poor to wear a watch and carry a fountain pen. On account of the multitude of interests no one with his faculties has an excuse for feeling old; and as for the children, they above all others are having material facilities for instruction and enjoyment showered on them from all directions.

THE STATE OF PRODUCTION AND QUALITY OF CONSUMPTION

There has been then a gradual if not a continuous increase in amount and type of consumption as production has improved. To show, however, the very obvious relationship of amount and type of production to amount and type of consumption is quite a different thing from correlating amount and type of production with quality of consumption, or with quality of civilization. This is a thing we are liable to overlook. Just because production is extensive and varied is in itself no guarantee that it serves men well. The goods produced in number and variety may be wasteful or even injurious.

It is true there is a presumption in favor of a highly-developed state of production against its opposite, since even with a hit or miss production, in the long run injurious and useless consumption goods tend to drop out through the trial and error method of experience. When production is highly developed all kinds of new things get introduced and they may find a hearing chiefly because they are new and different. Fads belong to this class of goods. But a thing which has virtue simply because it is new and different does not stay after it has become an old story. Nobody wants it any more. In the same way various sorts of more or less serviceable goods are continually being replaced by something better. Useless things are always passing out, and the less useful are always being succeeded by the more useful. We see ourselves that such articles as nose rings, bric-a-brac, and kewpies have left us after a period of trial longer or shorter. The only trouble is that the trial period is so often longer. Production does indeed lead to intelligent consumption by the very round-about process of trial and error, a process, so to speak, of letting one's heels save one's head.

Such being the case, we should not be surprised if we found, in history, cases of highly developed production with very little intelligence in consumption yet achieved; neither, on the other hand, should we be surprised to find a state of high intelligence in consumption with but a moderate development of the productive arts.

There is a possibility that we in the United States today are ourselves an illustration of the first point suggested, highly developed production with little intelligence in consumption as yet; or at least very little compared with the potentialities of our high degree of control over processes of large-scale manufacture. Certainly we are criticized from this point of view, and it might be well for us to take to heart the criticism as seriously as we are able.

As for a case of high intelligence in consumption and a state of production but little developed there is no more outstanding an example than Athens in the classical period. We find in Athens in the age of Pericles an appreciation along intellectual and aesthetic lines as great as, and probably exceeding, anything that has been achieved since. Certainly we ourselves today often find it hard to enter, even partially, into so refined an attitude toward human affairs, so pure an appreciation of the beautiful. Yet the Athenians had made only meagre progress in production.

"We must imagine houses without drains, beds without sheets or springs, rooms as cold, or as hot, as the open air, only draughtier, meals that began and ended with pudding. . . . We must learn to tell time without watches, to cross rivers without bridges, and seas without a compass, to fasten our clothes (or rather our two pieces of cloth) with two pins instead of rows of buttons, to wear our shoes and sandals without stockings, to warm ourselves over a pot of ashes, . . . to study poetry without books, geography without maps, and politics without newspapers. In a word we must learn how to be civilized without being comfortable. Or rather we must learn to enjoy the society of people for whom comfort meant something very different from motor-cars and armchairs, who, although or because they lived plainly and austerely and sat at the table of life without expecting any dessert, saw more of the use and beauty and goodness of the few things which were vouchsafed them—their minds, their bodies, and Nature outside and around them. Greek literature, like the Gospels, 'is a great protest against the modern view that the really important thing is to be comfortable. The Comfort promised by the Gospels' (and that enjoyed by the Greeks, whether the same, or somewhat different) 'and the comfort assured by modern inventions and appliances are as different as ideals can be.' (Burkitt, F. C., *Essays on Some Biblical Questions of the Day*, Cambridge, 1909, pp. 208–9.)" [1]

Does Production Bring Us What Is Best for Us?

From this discussion of the state of the productive arts and the quality of consumption we are led naturally to ask, to what

[1] Zimmern, A. E., *The Greek Commonwealth*, Oxford, 1922, p. 215.

extent does modern production bring us what is best for us? The answer is already indicated. John A. Hobson makes the following charges against our present productive system.[1]

"The fact that the monetary profit of producers is the principal determinant of most changes in the nature of consumables and the standards of consumption is one of the most serious sources of danger in the evolution of a healthy social economy. The present excessive control by the producer injures and distorts the art of consumption in three ways. 1. It imposes, maintains and fosters definitely injurious forms of consumption, the articles of 'illth.' 2. It degrades or diminishes by adulteration, or by the substitute of inferior materials or workmanship, the utility of many articles of consumption used to satisfy a genuine need. 3. It stimulates the satisfaction of some human wants and depresses the satisfaction of others, not according to their true utility, but according to the more or less profitable character of the several trades which supply these wants."

Modern production is a hit or miss method. The modern producer studies the consumer not as a human being but as a prospective purchaser, and takes a chance. Other things equal, the goods with the most superficial appeal and the most rapid sales prospects are most likely to be produced. Few of today's producers would risk years of waiting to educate consumers to some good thing that might begin to pay a hundred years hence. That is one reason why governments must take a hand in providing such things as museums and great parks for the people. They might eventually pay for themselves and make the producer or entrepreneur a profit, but no entrepreneur will wait several generations for his returns to come in.

The fact that production does not keep pace with the potentialities of consumers' welfare has led some thoughtful people to suggest that we should have, either in connection with the government or apart from it, an organization to study consumers' welfare and direct or advise production. The chief difficulty with the suggestion is, where are the people wise enough to do this? It is indeed hard to tell where they are, if they are anywhere. Governments are, however, already exer-

[1] *Work and Wealth*, New York, 1914, p. 112.

cising some discretion in these matters, and if intelligently
directed they might do more. Our greatest hope, of course, lies
in the better education of consumers' demand.

Does Production Bring Us What We Want?

But if producers do not give us what is best for us, do they
at least give us what we want? Do they perceive our demands
as they arise? As soon as consumers will hasten to buy a
product, does someone put it on the market? For the most part,
probably yes. In the long run and on the whole producers keep
pace with consumers' demands when they know what they are.
The "spread" between a potential effective demand and a
supply is not usually very great. The many failures of business
men testify, in part, to their efforts to meet potential demands
too soon. To be sure we can perhaps all of us, by hard thinking,
name half a dozen things that we wish someone would invent
or produce, but the fact we have to exert so much effort to name
even two or three shows that we do not feel the lack of them
very greatly. As a matter of fact, as we have seen, we learn
to want things largely by using them or seeing others use them.
Most of us don't know that we want a thing until we have a look
at it. As we have seen, consumers do not know what they want
and producers do not know either, so the whole matter of
awakening new interests is left to chance. Once in a while some
producer strikes it right, and on such lucky accidents our
progress is for the most part based.

The complaints we so frequently hear, that the sturdy textiles
of our grandmothers' day are no longer offered on the market,
are partly ill-founded. If we really wanted silk that would
wear sixty years someone would undoubtedly find it to his
advantage to supply it. With rapid changes in styles there is
less and less demand for the substantial. But the case must not
be over-stated. This argument does not carry so well in the
case of household textiles such as sheets and towels, things not
greatly subject to style. In these lines consumers are now
putting up a demand for standardization and producers are

getting uncomfortable. This demand for standardization may be applied to other consumers' goods also. Consumers are at last taking an initiative in these matters. This subject is further discussed in Chapter XVII.

Neither should we over-state the case with regard to the speed and facility with which producers offer us needed new inventions. In the first place, after an invention is produced, there is a tendency among some producers to try to make a few sales at a high price rather than to set the economies of large-scale production going and make more sales at a lower price. Henry Ford tells of the opposition he received when he started to make a car "for the great multitude. . . . It will be constructed of the best materials, by the best men to be hired, after the simplest designs that modern engineering can devise. But it will be so low in price that no man making a good salary will be unable to own one."

"How soon will Ford blow up? " was the question asked by his competitors and selling agents. Mr. Ford declares:

> "They thought that our production was good enough as it was and there was a very decided opinion that lowering the sales price would hurt sales, that the people who wanted quality would be driven away and that there would be none to replace them. There was very little conception of the motor industry." [1]

In another place he says:

> "In automobiles there was not much concern as to what happened to the car once it had been sold. How much gasoline it used per mile was of no great moment; how much service it actually gave did not matter; and if it broke down and had to have parts replaced, then that was just hard luck for the owner. It was considered good business to sell parts at the highest possible price on the theory that, since the man had already bought the car, he simply had to have the part and would be willing to pay for it." [2]

The motor industry is very largely on a different basis now, but some other industries still cling to the idea of large profits

[1] *My Life and Work*, in collaboration with Samuel Crowther, Garden City, 1922, pp. 72, 73.
[2] Ibid., p. 38.

at the price of small sales or even at the price of poor service. This is particularly true in the field of new inventions and equipment. In the field of electrical devices for the home it is said that the manufacturing cost of a piece of equipment is sometimes only one-fourth or one-sixth of the selling price. The rest is charged to high-pressure salesmanship or "sales-resistance"—a vicious circle, for the price has a good deal to do with the resistance. One investigator found that a certain piece of equipment, a pressure cooker, was offered by the manufacturer at twenty dollars, but precisely the same model was sold through a mail-order house for eleven dollars.

In the second place, some things that might profitably be produced are not produced. A professor in a home economics college perceived the need of change in design in certain household equipment to make housework more efficient, and suggested the change to certain manufacturers. That demand should come from consumers or consumers' agents was a new idea to them. They ignored the request and went on with their own man-designed and imperfect models. This was, to be sure, bad business on their part, but not all modern business is efficient business, even in the United States.

We can only repeat that producers keep pace with consumers' actual demands in the long run and on the whole. At any given time or for any given thing they may not be doing it. Business men have their own prejudices and their own restricting mores and even the powerful profit motive is not always strong enough to break these down.

CHAPTER XII

THE REIGN OF THE PRICE SYSTEM

"But the Boy was disappointed. 'I asked you,' he said, 'concerning the Nature of the Creature, and you reply by showing me a Skeleton.'
"'Softly, my Son, softly,' cried the Old Man. 'Consider well the Skeleton, for it hath a Virtue and indeed at times as it were an Animation of its own.'"—*Eastern Fable.*

The price system is the mechanism, or we may say the skeleton, by means of which consumers are brought into contact with producers. As such it performs a service to both sides. Its service to consumers is by way of simplifying their problems of making choices and of securing goods. In the early days of human society when barter was spasmodic and there was no price system at all, consumption was very limited indeed: partly because consumers could not easily get what they wanted but much more fundamentally because consumers had not learned relative values, nor even what to want. With the development of trade and, finally, with the institution of money, a common measure of value and a medium of exchange, their problem was simplified. Through the price system they were provided with a measure of value. Before the introduction of the price system the economic value of apples, let us say, had always to be separately determined in eggs or coon skins or nails or in whatever else the apple grower happened to want. This was a nuisance and hindered exchange. How much more convenient to know that the economic value of a bushel of apples was fifty cents, that eggs were twenty-five cents a dozen, coon skins a dollar apiece, and nails five cents a pound.

At the same time the price system furnished a medium of exchange, which was a tremendous convenience. In the modern department store, money or checks in the hands of consumers

123

are much more welcome than their apples or eggs, and the consumer has good reason to be glad of it. In the past, the price system sped up the whole process of exchange; and now the better the mechanism becomes, the more easy it is for consumers to know what they want and to get it.

The study of the interplay of the forces of demand and the forces of supply belongs as a whole to value theory rather than to consumption, but the price system has nevertheless certain special influences on consumers' choices which should be mentioned. There is its service as a convenience in speeding up consumption, to which we have just referred, a service becoming more valuable as the price system becomes perfected. This service ought today to be examined with particular care in respect to one aspect of the price system which has come recently into prominence—instalment buying.

Along with the price system and closely related to it, if not precisely a part of it, go cyclical changes in prices. Business cycles exert their own special influence on consumption which, as we shall see, is different from the influence of constant prices, or of prices steadily rising or steadily falling.

In the third place, the price system has certain unforeseen and apparently perverse reactions on consumers. According to orthodox value theory we should expect consumers to be more likely to buy at a low price than at a high one, but for some consumers there seems, indeed, to be a fatal attraction in high prices and a repelling power in low ones. This aspect of the price system must also be examined with respect to its peculiar influence on consumption.

General Credit and Instalment Buying

The rather widespread practice of credit buying by consumers, and especially instalment-credit buying, merits our special attention. This appears to furnish not only a convenience in buying but, as a result, to exert a direct influence on the amount and kind of consumption, probably stimulating consumption as a whole, and certainly stimulating it for those

goods for which consumers' credit is available. The effects
of lump-sum credit on consumers' demand are probably not so
important as the effects of instalment credit. Lump-sum credit
is granted usually only for short periods and as a convenience—
as in the case of the monthly payment of department store,
grocery, electric light, and telephone bills. Instalment credit,
on the other hand, has been developed with the idea of directly
stimulating consumption.

The extent of instalment buying is discussed by Professor
Seligman in his classic treatment of the subject, *The Economics
of Instalment Selling*.[1] He concludes that [2]

> "Instalment sales, in the case of the durable consumption goods
> to which the system is primarily applied, amounted at the end of 1926
> to about four and a half billion dollars out of total retail sales of about
> thirty-eight billions."

Automobiles and furniture account for about three-fourths of
all instalment sales to consumers. The estimates of Professor
Seligman, based on a revision of an estimate by M. V. Ayres,
are given in Table III.[3]

TABLE III
TOTAL SELLING PRICES OF CONSUMERS' GOODS SOLD ON INSTALMENT CREDIT
(Seligman and Ayres)

Goods	Price in Millions of Dollars
Automobiles, total	2,734
Furniture	850
Clothing	275
Pianos	189
Radios	169
Washing machines	95
Sewing machines	90
Vacuum cleaners	51
Jewelry	50.75
Phonographs	33.4
Gas stoves	25
Refrigerators	14
Total	4,576.15

[1] New York, 1927.
[2] Pp. 331–332.
[3] Pp. 117, 118. By permission of the publishers, Harper and Brothers.

Jeremiads against consumers' instalment buying have been one of the popular methods by which social critics express their dissatisfaction with the present order. As Professor Seligman points out, there have been abuses in the system, more particularly as it has been worked by high-pressure salesmen against low-paid and relatively uneducated wage-earners. Its faults, however, are largely the faults of any new method of doing business and are not inherent in the system. Criticism is merited more by the methods used by the salesmen than by the system itself as such.

But what precisely is the effect of instalment credit on the character of consumers' demand? First let us consider its effect on deflecting demand to the goods for which instalment credit is offered. In times of rising incomes, the tendency of consumers is to spend their new money rather recklessly. They are trained neither in educated spending nor in saving, and the thing that catches their eye is the thing with the greatest superficial appeal. In times of rising income the first new demand comes for ephemeral goods; the consumption of spirits increases, if spirits are available; showy clothing, amusements, and similar luxuries appeal first to the uneducated taste.

The offering of instalment credit for buying durable consumption goods tends to offset this tendency at such times and proves at any time a gentle means of educating the consumer. It may be too much to expect him to save until he has the money to buy a car, but if he can buy it by instalments he will buy it and he will be made to save to meet his payments. It is sometimes said that instalment credit for consumers has an adverse effect on their saving; there is as much claim for arguing it has a beneficial effect. In the latter case they save, not before they use, which they might never do; but while they are using, which they must do.

In the second place, instalment credit not only deflects particular demands, but probably stimulates demand as a whole, as it furnishes a more satisfactory buying mechanism or technique. As we have seen earlier in the chapter, the institution of the price system itself increased demand because it decreased the amount of energy required for the mere mechanics of effecting an exchange. Improvements in the mechanism of the price system would naturally have the same effect. Professor Seligman further argues that by the privilege of instalment buying the consumer secures goods sooner than he otherwise would be able to do and hence by wise consumption he is able to increase his production earlier also; thus his purchasing power should be augmented.[1]

As conditions are in the United States today, the whole point of the argument about instalment credit for consumers would seem to hinge on the question of whether or not it is wisely administered, and what wise administration is. Of its theoretical advantages there can be no doubt.

Closely related to the instalment buying under discussion is, of course, the credit financing of home building and the instalment buying of house lots and of homes. Building and loan associations in the United States are a success, and almost everyone agrees that their policies are a good thing for consumers. It is the case *par excellence* of the encouragement of consumers to buy a consumption good both durable and necessary, and one productive of long-time satisfactions. Without credit facilities and the possibility of instalment payments, home ownership would never be undertaken by most consumers.

THE EFFECT OF BUSINESS CYCLES ON CONSUMERS' DEMAND

Business cycles have never been explained in a way that everyone considers satisfactory and a discussion of this point is not fundamental to our purpose. Whatever their ultimate cause, however, they are intimately bound up with the price system. The characteristics of business cycles are first a gradually increasing period of prosperity until a peak is reached; then a decline at first usually sharp, finally more gradual; eventually a rise of prosperity again. No state of prosperity

[1] Op. cit., pp. 279–283.

or depression is constant. We are always at some point in the course of a business cycle, although both the period of rise and the period of decline may be not steady but fluctuating. The period of length of business cycles varies greatly, and indeed authorities sometimes disagree as to the time of beginning and ending of any particular one. A cycle may last only a year or two, or it may be seven or more years long. There are even cycles within cycles, which confuse the issue.[1] Producers are much more conscious of business cycles than consumers are, and the consumer is, indeed, usually a more or less passive participant in the cycle.

Consumption, however, is affected by the cycle in at least two ways. The cycle brings about changes in the prices of consumers' goods and it brings about changes in the money incomes of consumers.

The first of these influences is probably the least important to consumers and it is the one for which we have the least concrete evidence. One of the characteristics of a business cycle is maladjusted production—too much production of a certain kind of goods, so that, when decline begins, the price of these goods must be reduced below cost in order to get rid of them. If the particular goods over-produced and consequently marked down in price happen to be consumers' goods, the consumers get a chance to try out something new, perhaps, that they would otherwise not have been able to afford. In such ways new tastes and interests may be implanted.

The consumer, however, as a worker or even as a capitalist, shares in the prosperity or depression of business, though it affects him less than the producer and it affects him late. The rate of wages and the extent of unemployment are directly correlated with the cycle. A recent book, *Social Aspects of the Business Cycle*,[2] shows among other things how business

---

[1] The student is referred to Mitchell, Wesley C., *Business Cycles*, New York, 1927. On page 343 he concludes that during recent years in the United States the modal length of business cycles has been from three to three and one-half years.

[2] Thomas, Dorothy Swaine, New York, 1928.

cycles in the United Kingdom have affected the consumption
of beer and of spirits.   The consumption of beer, which is
regarded almost as a necessity by the working men of England,
was somewhat affected; the consumption of spirits, which for
most men are a luxury, showed a notably high positive correlation with the cycle. The author makes a significant comment [1]:

> "The close connexion between the consumption of spirits and pros-
> perity offers an interesting suggestion as to the relative effect of psy-
> chological and economic factors upon such a phenomenon. Theoretically
> the greatest psychological need for drunkenness would arise at the
> time of the greatest misery. But, however sordid the surroundings and
> however intense the desire to escape from them, the ability to make
> such an escape is a function of the ability to purchase. The ability to
> purchase varies directly with the degree of prosperity and acts as a
> limiting factor to the consumption of spirits (or beer) during a business
> depression. Furthermore, once prosperity obtains, the condition of
> those who suffered from the preceding depression is not improved at
> a stroke. Escape from the reality of miserable surroundings through
> drink is often easier than a definite attempt to reconstruct and improve
> those surroundings."

Although we cannot present statistical evidence of the correlation of the consumption of other luxuries with the business
cycle, it is a matter of common knowledge that in times of
prosperity all types of expenditure do not increase with equal
step. Expenditures for luxuries, especially more showy luxuries, take on unwonted importance and continue in importance
until the consumer has time to develop his tastes. The physical
appetites and the taste for emulation, however, do not have to
be cultivated. Our war-time experience illustrates this. With
increase in wages, the apportionment of expenditures changed
greatly. For some time people remained living in the same sort
of houses and sought no better education for their children.
But what greatly increased expenditures for fur coats, automobiles, amusements, jewelry!

The relation between cost of living and money incomes of

---

[1] *Social Aspects of the Business Cycle*, pp. 129–130.

factory workers during the ten years 1914 to 1924 is shown in the following chart.[1]

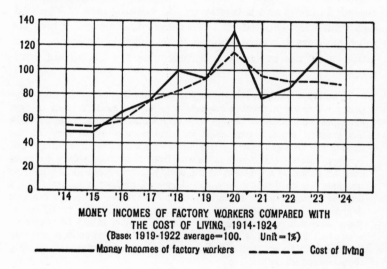

MONEY INCOMES OF FACTORY WORKERS COMPARED WITH
THE COST OF LIVING, 1914-1924
(Base: 1919-1922 average=100.   Unit = 1%)

—————— Money incomes of factory workers   — — — — Cost of living

During the war and post-war years there was at some times a very wide spread between cost of living and money incomes. But changes in cost of living and money incomes practically never exactly coincide.

If there is suffering on the downward curve of the business cycle as it affects consumers, the upward curve of the business cycle is a time for the implanting of new desires. Neither the amount nor the type of consumption remains on a level. The consumer denies himself in periods of hardship and makes new experiments in periods of prosperity. Many of the effects of business cycles are unfortunate, but they offer the consumer an experience of expansive living he would not otherwise obtain, and so permanently change his tastes.

[1] Compiled from various sources by Berridge, W. A., in Berridge, W. A., Winslow, E. A., and Flynn, R. A., *Purchasing Power of the Consumer*, Chicago, 1925, p. 41.

INCREASE OF DEMAND WITH INCREASE IN PRICE

If the price system worked as we should naturally expect it to work, demand would increase as prices fall and would decrease as prices rise. Ordinarily we expect that cheapness in price is an inducement to buy, and vice versa. The amount of the rise or of the fall would depend, of course, on the elasticity of the demand, or the importance of the good to consumers. Such doctrine is familiar to all students of elementary economics. A rise or fall in the price of quinine would probably have little effect on demand, one way or another. If you are ill with fever you will pay ten dollars a gram for quinine; if you are not ill, a price of a penny a ton will not induce you to buy it. In the case of most things, however, the price exercises an important influence on the amount of demand: the general demand for luxuries usually rises or falls sharply in inverse relation to price, and even the demand for bread, salt, and water though not usually elastic, has been shown under certain conditions to vary considerably as price varies.[1]

The consumer, however, is a difficult person to deal with, for he sometimes acts in an unexpected and unaccountable way. He—or more likely she—sometimes shows a perverse disposition to buy more when the price is high and buy less when the price is low. The psychology behind this is, of course, the consumer's belief that high price is an indication of quality, or sometimes her more illogical conviction that the payment of a high price gives her a certain prestige. This failure of the consumer to act as the economist expects her to act cannot be shown to affect the demand for large classes of goods, such as food, clothing, luxuries, in the long run; but it can be shown to affect the short-time demand for many special classes of goods, particularly the demand of a limited class of consumers. The attraction of high prices will not apply when people are living close to the standard of necessaries or decencies required by

[1] Marshall, Alfred, *Principles of Economics*, London, 1920, Book III, Chapter IV, paragraphs 1–5.

their class, but it applies strongly to that class of consumers whose money incomes are running ahead of their education in buying and consuming.

It is unfortunate that we do not have more statistics to show the extent of the influence of a high price on increasing sales. We can, however, collect many particular instances of this from the experiences of individual dealers.

It is said that a certain breakfast food, selling for ten cents a package, had very small sales. A "go-getter" became sales-manager, and first of all put up the price to fifteen cents. The product began to move, and eventually the success of the food became tremendous. In this particular case an advertising campaign helped things along very considerably. In other cases, there is no advertising at all. A certain shoe dealer exhibited in his window some women's shoes bought at a job-lot sale and marked them two dollars a pair. No one asked to see them. He changed the sign to six dollars a pair—approximately the normal price—and closed them out in a day or two. Books which teach commercial advertising make much of the point that a consumer has a certain price in mind as the proper price below which it is unsafe to buy. If the usual price for breakfast food in a package of a certain size is not less than fifteen cents, the housewife is afraid a ten-cent package will contain sawdust. If six dollars is the price a woman usually pays for shoes, she suspects two-dollar shoes of having paper soles.

The converse of these cases—high prices attracting large sales—is seen most frequently in the case of style and luxury goods. The most extreme example is diamonds and other jewels, to the demand for which pecuniary emulation contributes. No one expects to get a Paris model for twenty-five dollars, but put a price of two hundred dollars on a model from Newark, New Jersey, and somebody will probably order it. An ordinary "high-class" drug store will not be able to sell face powder at ten cents a box. The more some women pay for face powder and perfume the better they think it is. Says a druggist: "I got a big shipment of perfume which I decided to offer as a special at thirty-nine cents an ounce. Could I sell it? Nothing doing. Then I made a big sign saying *La Romance* and marked it five dollars an ounce and got rid of it. What was in it? Well, for all I know, skunk cabbage."

The number of college girls who confess themselves positively attracted by high prices, for some things at any rate, runs, according to the author's experience, at about 90%. In the case of the *nouveaux riches* the percentage is probably nearer a hundred and the number of things included much larger. Yet we should not from this conclude that the perverse influence of price on consumption is very important in the long run and for consumers and commodities as a whole. Books on sales-making are likely to give a false impression of its importance, for most of them deal particularly with relatively "high-class" goods. Not all shopping is done on Fifth Avenue. The Beehive, the Boston Store, the Racket, and the Fair attract customers to whom a high price is no inducement whatever. Somebody is glad to get perfumes and powders for ten cents, as anyone can observe by walking through a Woolworth store. The attraction of normal and of high prices must, however, be recognized as an influence on certain types of consumers for certain types of goods. When high prices are combined with advertising they may have a very considerable, if temporary, effect on consumers' demand.

CHAPTER XIII

THE DISTRIBUTION OF INCOME

"There were two who sat in a great gold chariot with purple cushions. They visited only the very fine booths and would not look at less than silver. In the end they said there was nothing fit to be bought at the fair. The buying, in fact, was mostly done by people who had come on the backs of nags or ponies. The children saw them, some sad and some merry, loading their saddlebags with boots and cotton stuffs, and fastening to the saddle dishes of pewter and shining tin. Some poor souls, who had come on foot, bought nothing, but feasted their eyes on the display of the rest."—*Fairy Tale.*

Although the limits of consumption are set by production, the satisfactions received from production are dependent not only on the type and quality of production, as we have seen, but also on the proportions in which the values produced are distributed among men. If most of the purchasing power goes to a few very wealthy people, that is quite a different thing from having it distributed equally among all. And not only does the total amount of satisfaction vary with the distribution, but the kind of goods and services consumed varies too. A million dollars going to a rich man means, perhaps, a yacht, a greenhouse, and an under-butler. A million dollars divided among a million poor men means, perhaps, more chewing gum, ginger ale, and cigarettes. So we must study in what proportions purchasing power is divided among people before we can understand consumption as a whole.

DISTINCTION BETWEEN WEALTH AND INCOME

The distribution of wealth is a somewhat different problem from the distribution of income. Wealth is an accumulation of economic goods or claims to goods or services, from which an income in money or satisfactions may be received. Income

134

is a flow of money or of means to satisfactions. Wealth is a reservoir, income a stream.

It will be seen that anyone with wealth may have an income. A man who refuses to invest his money because he is afraid of banks, stocks, and bonds has wealth without income, but he may have income if he wishes. Possessions that cannot yield an income of any sort either in money or satisfaction are not wealth at all. Occasionally, of course, wealth may skip its regular dividends for a time, but when it has no prospect of ever yielding dividends it has ceased to be wealth.

But though everyone with wealth should have an income, not everyone with an income has wealth. By far the largest part of incomes in the United States are received as wages, salaries, and business men's profits, none of which issue from wealth in the economic sense. In the United States many people have considerable incomes with very little wealth; we all know people who spend lavishly, but who have never accumulated any property. At the same time, since it is customary for all men in the United States to have some pecuniary employment, no matter how wealthy they may be, few families are limited to incomes from accumulated wealth alone. Thus most families with considerable wealth have also considerable incomes. In England, where wealthy men more frequently turn to leisure or pursuits that yield no income, many families have no income but that received from wealth.

From the point of view of consumption, the distribution of wealth is important chiefly as it results in distribution of income. We shall confine our chapter to the latter.

FACTS OF INEQUALITY OF INCOMES

In very simple societies where everyone must gain his own means of livelihood with his own hands there is not a great deal of inequality of income. Just as soon, however, as any considerable division of labor arises we find inequality. The first very large differences in income, however, are brought about in most cases by division of the people into the rulers and the ruled. Inequality greatly increases as labor divides itself into functions of manual labor and oversight and organization. Up to a certain point, at least, it appears to be still more enhanced as the function of the capitalist increases in importance.

The reason that one man earns more than another is not necessarily that the one is abler than the other. As we know from simple value theory, on the market it is not so important to be able to do a thing well as it is to be able to do a thing that is wanted at the time it is wanted. A man who is a very good poet may not be able to manage a baking-powder factory, and if it is baking powder that the world thinks it wants the poet is economically out of luck. The market has a rough and ready scale of values, sometimes quite mistaken so far as welfare is concerned. While the world is making the baking-powder man a millionaire, the baking powder may be giving everybody dyspepsia. It is the same trial and error, fumble and failure process of learning with which we are already familiar.

In ancient and mediaeval society there were, broadly speaking, only two great divisions of the people important enough to be called social or economic classes: the small upper class who enjoyed many luxuries, and the large lower class who were confined to the merest necessities of existence. The lower class consisted not only of slaves, serfs, or villeins but of free men as well. In ancient and mediaeval literature we find that men frequently preferred slavehood or villenage to freedom, since a greater economic insecurity was often its price. The serf was taken care of; the freeman had to fend for his own barley-cake and sheepskin coat.

Towards the end of the middle ages, however, we observe the appearance of a new class, the middle class, the bourgeoisie, who gained their ascendancy not through allying themselves with political rulers, but through dominating the rising new commerce and industry. The rulers, the aristocracy, began to decline as an economic class; though they continued, and still continue in old countries such as England, to hold the greatest social prestige and some economic importance. In countries such as the United States the only economic inequalities of consequence are those connected with the industrial system.

It is hard to compare inequalities of income today with inequalities in ancient and mediaeval times, since we lack statistics for the earlier period. Generalizing, one might say there was a far greater gulf between the upper and the lower groups in earlier civilized times than now. Today in the industrial society of the United States the greater number of the people, while they are nearer those popularly called poor than they are to those popularly called rich, are massed in between these two classes.

The latest figures of the National Bureau of Economic Research give us a total national income of $89,682,000,000 in 1926, or an average of $770 per capita, an average of $2,010 per person gainfully employed.[1] The actual distribution is, of course, quite different. The latest estimate of that is the Bureau's study of distribution of incomes in 1918, which is given in Table IV.[2]

TABLE IV

PROPORTIONS OF RICHEST AND POOREST INCOME RECEIVERS IN THE
UNITED STATES AND THE PERCENTAGE OF THE TOTAL NATIONAL INCOME
RECEIVED BY THEM IN 1918; TOGETHER WITH THE RANGE OF THEIR
INCOMES

(National Bureau of Economic Research)

Proportion of Income Receivers	Percentage of Total Income	Range of Income
Richest 1 per cent	15 per cent	$8,000 to over $1,000,000
" 5 " "	26 " "	over $3,300
" 10 " "	35 " "	over $2,300
" 20 " "	47 " "	over $1,700
Poorest 10 " "	2 " "	less than $700

From another point of view the inequality of incomes may be stated as follows. The arithmetical average income in 1918 was $1,543. The median income, however, or that halfway between the lowest and the highest, was $1,140. This indicates a very

[1] News Bulletin of the National Bureau of Economic Research, No. 23, p. 1.
[2] Income in the United States, Vol. I, New York, 1921, pp. 134–135.

uneven distribution. Three-fourths of the people received less
than $1,574, that is to say nearly three-fourths of the people
received less than the average income.[1]

PERSONAL CONSUMPTION IS LESS UNEQUAL THAN INCOMES

The fact, however, that incomes are so unequal does not
necessarily mean that the narrow personal consumption of
individuals or families is unequal in the same degree. Money
received is one thing. Money spent is another. The reasons
for this are at least four.

In the first place, a considerable part of large incomes is not
spent but saved for investment or re-investment in business.
Thus it serves society indirectly by increasing the supply of
capital and decreasing the interest rate, hence decreasing costs
of production.

In the second place, an appreciable part of some large incomes
is directly or indirectly spent for or invested in projects aimed
to benefit society. Most organized charities are chiefly supported from greater-than-average incomes. Philanthropic and
private educational enterprises are also supported mainly by
the more wealthy. From the wealthy come many contributions to education, medical research, scientific expeditions, art
museums, community orchestras, and other social services of
like nature.

In the third place, as we shall see in the next chapter, the
taxation of the United States is to a small degree progressive,
and thus large income receivers pay relatively a greater proportion of the costs of government.

Finally, as we shall see in Chapter XX, a part of the purchasable satisfactions that people enjoy are not bought directly
from their own incomes but from the revenue of the government.
The roads, education, parks and playgrounds, are open equally
to all without distinction of income. This is a means by which
a greater equality of satisfactions is presumably brought about.

[1] Op. cit., p. 132.

Results of Unequal Distribution from Point of View of Greatest Satisfactions at Any Given Time

Does income unequally distributed result in as great a sum total of satisfactions as if it were distributed equally? For any given time the answer is probably in the negative.

From the law of diminishing utility we know that the more one has of a thing, the less satisfaction he gains from each successive unit of it, other conditions remaining constant. The reasoning applies to purchasing power. Provided no change takes place in capacity for appreciation, the utility of each increment decreases. Hence it follows that if all men were able to appreciate equally, the greatest sum total of satisfactions, at any given time and under any given conditions, would be reached by dividing the means of satisfactions equally. Ten thousand dollars, in other words, would bring more satisfaction if divided among one hundred poor men, giving them one hundred dollars apiece, than if divided among two of them, or than if given to one of them. A hundred two-weeks' vacations will give more pleasure than one de luxe trip around the world.

This reasoning assumes that capacities for appreciation are equal. But how far are they equal? We know, as a matter of fact, that in actual life men's abilities to enjoy satisfaction vary a great deal, not only because of differences in education but because of differences in natural aptitude. The ideal distribution of means for satisfaction would not then be an exactly equal division. It would be a distribution according to capacity to utilize or to enjoy satisfactions.

Does our present unequal distribution in any way favorably correlate with this unequal potential capacity to utilize? To what is our unequal distribution due? In the United States today, differences in income are due to several causes: on the one hand, to good fortune, to privilege or inheritance, to different standards of business ethics among competitors; on the other hand, to ability. The last, of course, is significant for our purpose, though it is doubtful if it is the chief cause for differences in income.[1]

But is business ability at all the same thing as ability to appreciate? Is it an index to ability along other lines, including ability to consume? Are those who are most able to acquire goods those also most able to use them intelligently? One cannot answer this off-hand, and the answer is further complicated by the fact that it is not necessarily the earner of the money who does the spending of it. More usually it is his wife, his sons, and his daughters. The typical American business man slaves at his desk and can hardly be persuaded to take a vacation, while his wife and his children make away with the fruits of his toil.

At best there are definite limitations to positive correlations between ability to produce and to consume with intelligence. The correlations hold better in comparisons for the middle of the income scale than they do at either the higher or the lower end. So far as the higher end is concerned, whatever advantages there may be to large incomes, their advantages in increasing individual satisfactions are relatively slight. Five thousand dollars may bring more satisfaction to one highly intelligent man than an extra thousand apiece may bring to five unintelligent people; but no man, whatever his ability, can increase his consumptive satisfactions much by being able to raise his income from one million to two million dollars. The extra million would bring far more immediate satisfaction if divided among many. There may have been times and countries where some men could profitably consume more than any man could produce, but it is not true today in the United States. Incomes from profits run up to a million dollars, but no one knows enough to spend advantageously a million dollars a year on himself. Men of great income who have the reputation of being wise spenders

---

[1] Further studies of the correlation of general aptitude quotients with occupations, and success in occupations, will be of interest. A fairly close correlation between measurable ability and occupational grouping is suggested in Kornhauser, Arthur W., " Intelligence Test Ratings of Occupational Groups,". *American Economic Review Supplement*, March, 1925, pp. 110–122.

are usually spending a good deal in a semi-social way, as by making collections which sometime the public will probably enjoy.

At the lower end of the income scale, too, with social conditions as they are at present, there are some persons who are lacking the physical necessities of life. A deprivation of physical necessities should, and as a matter of fact usually does, cause more acute suffering than a deprivation of conventional necessities or luxuries: in other words, though our ability to produce as measured by money may be almost nothing, the very fact of our being alive gives us needs or a fundamental ability to consume. A zero of productive ability never correlates with a zero of consumptive ability, for even the helpless man wants to live. Such a consideration from a broad social point of view gives force to the maxim: Necessities for all before luxuries for any. It is an argument for intelligent social legislation, and is one of the strongest points made in favor of Socialism.

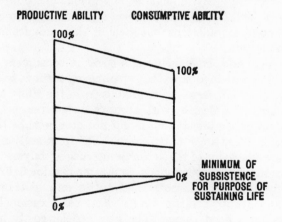

The figure shows that even if productive ability and ability to use were essentially related, their correlation would be least at the minimum and at the maximum extremes of ability; it shows that productive ability as measured in money would vary more than consumptive ability measured the same way; and that though ability to use might increase with income, it would increase at a diminishing rate.

THE LONG-RUN EFFECT OF UNEQUAL DISTRIBUTION ON CHARACTER OF INTERESTS

In the preceding section we considered the effect of unequal distribution on satisfactions at any given time. From the point of view of satisfactions at any given time we saw little or no social justification for very large incomes. By noting, however, that the large income receivers were generally the large savers, the large givers, and the large taxpayers we left a way open for showing that certain indirect benefits may arise from large incomes.

Now we are faced with another question: are there any long-run beneficial results from the spending of large incomes, results that do not appear from an analysis of satisfactions at any given time? An analysis made at any given time does not, as a matter of fact, tell the whole story: a given situation may be poor in actual satisfactions but rich in the seeds from which satisfactions grow.

As we have said, huge incomes, if spent in consumers' goods, bring so little satisfaction to the person using them as to appear very largely social waste. But producers, in the effort to meet the pleasure of the wealthy with profit to themselves, cast about to introduce new interests that might not otherwise be thought of. Some of these are simply foolish. The front section of one well-known magazine of the better group runs a "buyers' guide" which in one issue recommends an Easter egg for $10.50, the ugliest conceivable "mascot," half turtle and half bird, for $20.00, and a baby's rattle for $30.00. Yet occasionally producers strike a good thing. The new article, costly at first, may meet with an immediate and wide response: then more will be produced and, with decreasing expense, the price declines. So goods that start out as luxuries for the few sometimes end by being necessities for the many. The automobile is one example of this, the fountain pen and even perhaps the bathtub are others.

From an historical point of view, too, we can see a social advantage in the wealthy aristocracy of ancient and mediaeval times. Their actual and potential demands stimulated the foreign trade of their periods and this was indirectly and in the long run the means of bringing about great improvements for civilization as a whole. Had income been equally distributed, or distributed on the basis of ability to use well at any given time, there would have been little opportunity for costly experiments such as these. So huge incomes, which do not have much significance in satisfactions for the wealthy, indirectly may serve us all.

Such considerations are not by any means to be considered as arguments for the retention of the existing inequality of distribution in so far as it is not justified by conditions at a given time. We are doubtless intelligent enough to devise means for social experimentation in unknown fields. So far, however, we see that such experiments have been left to the hit or miss method of trial and error on the market; and inequalities of distribution of income have greatly contributed to make such experiments effective.

In the long run, then, there is a sense in which unequal distribution to a certain extent defeats its own inequality. Great incomes do little service to the rich who do not know how to spend them. The very rich man casts madly about to dispose of his income, and whatever he may be as a producer, as a consumer he is likely to be pathetic. He has the form but not the substance of satisfactions. At the same time all society profits from great incomes indirectly. But their wastes are great.

CHAPTER XIV

TAXATION AND TARIFFS

"Each for himself and the devil take the hindmost."—*Proverb.*

Taxation and tariffs are complicated economic questions. All we can hope to do with them in the space of a single chapter is to cast on them a consumers' point of view, for they have direct and positive reactions on consumption. We have heard a good deal about the effects of taxation on producers, but the consumers' point of view has in the past been rather neglected, partly because of our general ignorance of consumption. The consumer, the man most deeply concerned in legislation on these matters, has been unaggressive, ignorant, and dumb.

Taxation in the United States and in most other countries has a sad tale to tell. We all know that the government must be supported, but no system for doing it meets with everyone's approval, and one of the prevailing principles or canons of taxation is for legislators to choose whatever methods they can get away with most successfully; in Montesquieu's phrase, to pluck the goose with the least squawking.

One reason why our principles and practice of taxation have not made more progress is that the principles and practice of consumption have been so little understood. Taxation is in large measure a consumers' problem. Many tax payments come from consumers' margins which would otherwise be available to spend for other things; but even tax payments made by producers often affect consumers indirectly.

Systems of taxation may react on consumers intelligently or unintelligently. In the first place, the consumption of particular goods and services may be discouraged by specific taxes placed upon them, or encouraged by specific taxes placed upon competing goods and services. In the second place, the sum

144

total of satisfactions enjoyed by the people as a whole may be decreased or augmented according to the way taxation deals with the unequal distribution of wealth and income.

At the outset we must say a word as to how the burden of taxation in the United States is actually met today. Our federal revenue from taxation and tariffs is about seven-eighths of our total federal revenue. It amounts to about three and one-half billion dollars. Of this, income taxes on individuals and corporations are over two billion, miscellaneous internal revenue and tariffs over half a billion each. The exact figures of our federal revenue are given in Table V.[1]

TABLE V

TAXATION AND TARIFFS (ORDINARY RECEIPTS) OF THE UNITED STATES GOVERNMENT FOR THE FISCAL YEAR ENDED JUNE 30, 1927

(United States Department of the Treasury)

Internal Revenue
  Income tax
      Corporation...............................$1,308,012,533
      Individual................................. 911,939,911
  Miscellaneous
      Estate tax................................. 100,339,852
      Alcoholic spirits, etc...................... 21,195,552
      Tobacco manufactures...................... 376,170,205
      Admissions and dues...................... 28,376,657
      Automobiles and motorcycles.................. 66,437,881
      Pistols and revolvers....................... 192,539
      Cereal beverages........................... 198,611
      Yachts and motor boats (use)................. 7,967
      Corporation capital stock tax................. 8,970,231
      Stamp taxes, including playing cards........... 37,345,552
      Oleomargarine, process butter, etc............. 3,185,297
      Miscellaneous, including prohibition and narcotic
        taxes, etc................................. 3,310,341
      Total internal revenue....................... 2,865,683,130
Customs... 605,499,983
      Total internal revenue and customs............ 3,471,183,113

Over one-half of total taxes received are paid to state and local governments, and do not appear in this table. The practices of state and local governments vary, but it is estimated

[1] Internal revenue figures (by sources) from United States Department of the Treasury, Annual Report of the Collector of Internal Revenue, 1927, pp. 75-76. Customs figures (by daily Treasury statements unrevised) from United States Department of the Treasury, Annual Report of the Secretary of the Treasury on the State of the Finances, 1927, p. 6.

that about-three fourths of their tax receipts come from the so-called general property tax. This is in theory a tax on real estate, personal property, stocks, bonds, mortgages, and other evidences of the control of wealth. In practice it is a tax chiefly on real estate, since neither personal property nor intangibles are customarily discovered by the assessors; if they are discovered, they are likely to be taxed considerably below their value. Some of the states have inheritance taxes. A dozen, including New York and Massachusetts, have income taxes.

The total taxes of federal, state, and local governments were estimated by the National Industrial Conference Board to amount to $7,716,000,000 in 1923, or an average of $69.72 per capita.[1] These figures do not include tariffs.

Taxes on Specific Goods

The simplest taxes to study from the point of view of consumption are excise taxes, or taxes on the production or sale of some particular commodity. About 15% of the total revenue of the federal government from taxation and tariffs comes from them. It is clear that unless the goods taxed are produced by a monopoly the excise taxes are paid by the consumer. If the demand for the goods is inelastic, if the consumer insists on having the goods in spite of the tax, the government will profit at the expense of the consumer. If, however, the demand for the goods is elastic, the consumer may refuse to buy at the increased price. The problem of such taxes is complicated by the laws of increasing and decreasing cost, with which the student of elementary economics is familiar. Excise taxes may be and frequently have been used deliberately to discourage the consumption of some particular thing.

By far the most important excise tax in the United States today is that on tobacco. It will be seen from Table V that about 11% of all federal revenues received from taxation and tariffs comes from taxes on tobacco. Such taxes pay the gov-

[1] National Industrial Conference Board, *Tax Burdens and Public Expenditures*, New York, 1925, p. 12.

ernment 60% as much as all customs receipts together. We have no way of knowing how much they discourage the use of tobacco. Cigarettes are taxed more highly than other forms of tobacco, so the taxes put a premium on pipe smoking.

Before the passage of the Volstead Act a significant amount of revenue was derived by the federal government from taxes on liquors, and by local governments from licenses to saloon-keepers. These taxes doubtless had some small effect in keeping down the consumption of drink.

We have also in the United States a rather peculiar tax on oleomargarine, secured by butter manufacturers who wished to discourage the use of a product which competed with their own. There are taxes also on adulterated and renovated butter and filled cheese. The federal government places a 3% tax on automobiles and motorcycles, presumably for revenue purposes only; and a 10% tax on pistols and revolvers, presumably to discourage their use.

During the war the federal government taxed admissions to entertainments, dues to clubs and associations, jewelry, soft drinks, and chewing gum, not, however, to discourage the use of these goods and services, but on the assumption that they were luxuries and a tax upon them was an easy way of getting money.

State governments have their own special taxes on certain things. Gasoline taxes and licenses for motor cars and motor-car drivers are the most conspicuous examples. A considerable revenue is received from these taxes, but their cost to the individual consumer is so small a part of the total cost of operating his car that such taxes probably do not materially discourage the use of motor vehicles in the United States. In England, where these taxes are much higher, they definitely interfere with ownership and operation of cars.

The local dog-tax undoubtedly keeps down the number of dogs, though the government here has in mind not the welfare of the consumer or owner, but the welfare of the body social.

In so far as the general property tax is enforced on personal property, it tends to discourage the ownership of jewelry, automobiles, pianos, radios, fine furniture, and other expensive consumers' goods. Its actual effects on consumption, however, are probably slight.

PROGRESSIVE TAXATION

Though the relationship of taxation and consumption is important in the field of special taxes on particular consumers' goods, there is a more fundamental if less tangible relationship in the way taxes react on the distribution of wealth and income. If men are taxed equally, that means one thing; if they are taxed in proportion to their wealth or income, that means another thing; if they are taxed progressively, that means something else.

Progressive taxation is taxation wherein the *rate* increases progressively as the income increases. A man has to pay more not only proportionately but progressively as his means to pay increase: a rate of 1% on a thousand dollars, or ten dollars, might change to 2% on two thousand dollars, or forty dollars and so on.

From Chapter XIII we have seen that other things being equal, the satisfactions received from income do not increase proportionately as income increases. After a certain point, the increase of satisfactions is regressive, or subject to diminishing utility. We saw for instance, that an extra hundred dollars would ordinarily mean much more to a poor man than to a rich one. Hence we concluded the sum of satisfactions enjoyed by society would be increased if incomes were more equal than they are.

A policy of making incomes exactly equal would, of course, be bad even from the point of view of immediate consumption, and it would be worse from the point of view of stimulating production; nevertheless, from any point of view, incomes could safely be made more equal than they are, if we had a legitimate means of doing it. One legitimate means is afforded by progressive taxation. Progressive taxation rightly applied becomes, therefore, not only a means for securing revenues for the government, but a means for securing these revenues at a minimum of social cost. Ideally it demands of men equal sacrifices based on equal ability to pay: a dollar from a farm laborer may represent to him the sacrifice that ten thousand dollars represents to a captain of finance.

Progressive taxation to be rightly applied demands, of course, some means of measurement of satisfactions, which is at present lacking.[1] The field is open for experimentation, however, and out of this we may hope to arrive at rough standards for practice.

Progressive taxation is a product of modern times which is receiving increasingly wider recognition. The most thorough-going application of the principle of progressive taxation in the United States was the income tax law of 1919. The expenses of the war demanded greatly increased federal revenues, and the moderate rates of taxation then prevailing were greatly increased and exemptions lowered. Taxable incomes over a million dollars were required to pay 77%. As a matter of fact, however, large incomes are customarily invested in great part in tax-exempt securities, so the income tax they actually pay is much smaller than would otherwise be the case. It should be noted, however, that what a person gains from owning tax-exempt bonds should be largely cancelled through the lower interest rate which such bonds would normally carry.

In 1924 and again in 1926 the income-tax law was changed and is now not so progressive as the 1919 law. According to the law of 1926, after certain possible deductions, the taxpayer pays:

$1\frac{1}{2}\%$ on the first $4,000
3 % on the next $4,000
5 % on all above $8,000

---

[1] See, however, Fisher, Irving, "A Statistical Method for Measuring 'Marginal Utility' and Testing the Justice of a Progressive Income Tax," in *Economic Essays Contributed in Honor of John Bates Clark*, New York, 1927. Professor Fisher in a letter refers to Frisch, Ragnar, *Sur un problème d'économie pure*, Norsk Mathematisk Forenings Skifter, Serie 1, Nr. 16, 1926: " Dr. Frisch not only devised a method but applied it to obtain definite statistical estimates with which my own tentative and unpublished figures are, at least, consistent."

There is in addition a surtax based on the net income without deductions. This begins with a tax of 1% on the part of the net income from $10,000 to $14,000 inclusive and ends with a tax of 20% on the part of the net income in excess of $100,000. Such rates of tax and surtax for large incomes would seem from the point of view of consumptive satisfactions to be very moderate.

In summing up the relationship to consumption of taxation federal, state, and local the following table is presented as an approximate picture of the situation.[1]

TABLE VI

PERCENTAGE OF TOTAL TAXATION, FEDERAL, STATE, AND LOCAL, OBTAINED FROM VARIOUS SOURCES.   (Not including tariffs)

(Author's Estimates on Data as Indicated in Text)

Taxes on specific goods and services, federal, state, and local......................	10%
Progressive taxes on incomes of individuals..	16%
General property taxes.....................	44%
Corporation taxes and miscellaneous........	30%

Thus it appears that the point of view of consumers is taken into account in some way in 26% of all taxes, those on specific goods and progressive taxes.

The taxes on specific goods, 10% of all, tend to discourage the consumption of the specific goods taxed. Whether the net results of such taxation are good or bad depends on what the specific goods are. Tobacco accounts for more than half of these taxes.

Progressive taxes on incomes of individuals account for 16% of all taxes, and these taxes, as we have seen, are based on recognition of the law of diminishing utility.

The 44% of taxes derived from general property is at best proportional and not progressive. These taxes are supposed to cover unearned increments in land values. For the most part, however, the general property tax, though paid largely by

[1] These percentages are derived from Table V and the conclusions of the National Industrial Conference Board, op. cit.

consumers, represents a theory of taxation which, whatever its merits, has nothing to contribute directly to their welfare.

Corporation and miscellaneous taxes, 30% of all, are not paid directly by consumers. We shall not attempt to evaluate them, for they would involve us in problems exceedingly complex.

THE TARIFF

The tariff pays into the federal treasury about 17% of the total amount received from tariff and taxation together.

If it is difficult to deal fairly with the effects of taxation on consumption, it is even more difficult to deal fairly with the effects of tariffs. There is probably no economic subject on which the opinions of theoretical economists are so much at variance with business practice. The subject is usually not discussed as a problem specifically for consumers, but it may nevertheless be reduced to that. To think of it as a consumers' problem is to take one step to clarifying it.

In the first place, let us distinguish between tariffs for revenue and tariffs for the protection of industry. Tariffs for revenue are simply another form of taxation, and, so far as the consumer is concerned, have the same immediate effect as excise taxes, or taxes on goods produced within the country. They normally raise the price of the goods to the consumer by the amount of the tariff. If the demand for imported articles is elastic, the effect of a tariff is to discourage their use.

Practically all consumers' goods are dutiable: the only significant exceptions are certain leather goods, including boots and shoes, coffee, tea, and bananas. Even spices and most tropical fruits, where there is no question of protection, must pay to cross the customs barriers. It would take pages to discuss the discouragements to consumption in the tariff schedules; a shorter approach is to ask why the consumption of certain things should be singled out for exception. We can see by what logic Bibles are placed on the free list, but why particularly do we by a process of elimination so signally encourage the consumption of chestnuts, palm leaf fans, and darning needles?

In general, duties on manufactured goods are higher than duties on raw products. According to the Tariff Act of 1922, duties on cotton, wool, and silk goods range ordinarily from 30 to 90%; on food products, from 20 to 35%; on furniture, $33\frac{1}{3}$ to 60%; and on china, from 60 to 70%. What the precise ad valorem duties shall be is in the hands of the President, who has power to change classifications upon the recommendations of the Tariff Commission.

Most of these tariffs were devised for the protection of American industries. Such tariffs are extremely difficult to evaluate. The theory, well known to students of elementary economics, is that the government by putting a duty on an import, let us say silk, and by raising the price to the consumer as a consequence of the duty, encourages the development of the silk industry within the United States. The silk industry is protected from competition so that it can get on its own feet. The tariff raises the price of imported silk goods to such a point that the native silk manufacturers can afford to face the vicissitudes of a struggling industry, for, owing to protection, they will still come out on top. In the end, it is claimed, when the industry is really standing on its feet, the law of decreasing costs comes into effect and the need for the tariff disappears. Competition among manufacturers finally reduces the artificially protected price of silk, and in the end the consumer is better off because producers have been encouraged to become efficient. For our purposes, the whole question is simply: Is the consumer benefited?

We may distinguish three points of view from which the effects of tariffs are estimated. There is the immediate or short-time point of view; the longer-time point of view, the effects of the tariff over a period of, let us say, one, two, or three generations; and the long-time or secular point of view.

From the short-time point of view, the effects of protective tariffs seem to be only harmful. Other things equal, their short-time effect is simply to put up the price. The American traveller who arrives from Europe with a trunkful of purchases

curses the tariff that makes him pay to the customs officials on
the dock perhaps nearly as much again as he paid abroad.
"Why," he storms, "must I pay ten dollars and seventy-five
cents on my watch? If the Swiss can make good watches
cheaply, why should Americans be taxed for it?" And his
wife exclaims: "Ninety per cent on my dresses! What's the
sense of having such skillful Parisian dressmakers if the American government takes away all I thought I saved by shopping
in Paris? "

If a manufacturer is standing on the dock he will be moved
to expostulate with these over-hasty citizens, and will give
them a longer-time point of view. "My good friends," he will
say, "I pay my duties with enthusiasm because I know the
government is interested only in our welfare. We consumers
pay somewhat more now, but before we die it will all come back;
or at least our children or grandchildren will be grateful for it.
We must have these duties to encourage American watch
manufacturers and American dressmakers. You know how
clever the Swiss and the Parisians are. We could never compete
with them on equal terms. But give us a good start of them and
you'll see how smart we turn out. Why, fifty years from now
watches will be so cheap in America that we will have a different
watch for every costume."

While our friends are weighing the advantages of this prospect
against their present inconveniences, let them hear a word from
a philosopher who has arrived with them, and who is presumably unprejudiced because he is too poor to have investments in industry or even to have any dutiable goods. "These
government barriers," he will say, "seem to me, in the long
run, artificial. As consumers we are not primarily citizens
but ordinary men and women. In the long run we are just as
much interested in encouraging the industry of Switzerland and
Paris as we are our own industry. When we were a weak and
struggling country it was all very well to protect ourselves in
this way, but now it seems to me there is no merit in trying to
make all things all at once in the United States. There are

plenty of new industries shouting to be developed. If it is going to pay us to compete with Paris modistes, that will appear in due time. Oh, of course I have nothing to say to you as producers and patriots—I was regarding you as consumers."

This conversation on the dock has assumed that tariffs are what they claim to be, honest, if sometimes mistaken, efforts to serve the people. It is only just to say, however, that they frequently are not this. They are too often subject to corruption. Political pressure is brought to bear to increase or continue tariffs for the immediate benefit of the producers in some one industry. It is so difficult to get the truth in connection with tariffs that almost any aggressive group of producers may for a time, often for a long time, deceive themselves and the legislators about the facts. Professor Alfred Marshall observes that a protective policy in fact is a very different thing from a protective policy as painted by sanguine economists, and concludes that the corruption which accompanies it may well outweigh its theoretical benefits.[1]

It is difficult to draw trustworthy conclusions about the tariff from the experience of different nations with free trade or protection. In every case so many factors other than tariff policy contribute to the progress or regression of production, wages, and cost and standards of living that it needs great wisdom to evaluate any particular tariff or free trade experience. Our remarks have presumed only to indicate that in this complex question it helps to keep throughout the point of view of the person ultimately interested in tariff policies, the consumer.[2]

[1] *Money Credit and Commerce*, London, 1923, pp. 219–220.
[2] It is perhaps needless to add that the subject of international trade has other and still more complicated ramifications affecting the consumer. The reader is referred to Taussig, F. W., *International Trade*, New York, 1927, especially Chapter XIII.

PART IV

CONSUMPTION DELIBERATELY CONTROLLED
BY THE CONSUMER

CHAPTER XV

INTELLIGENCE CHALLENGES THE CONSUMER

"What is the hardest thing in the world?—to think."—R. W. EMERSON, *Journals*.

In the preceding nine chapters we have been discussing how the consumer is influenced, more or less unconsciously, by forces that play upon him from without. The geographic environment wherein he lives, his biological inheritance, all the various social and economic aspects of life about him, these leave their marks upon the consumer, in the shape of the interests they awaken in his mind. Out of the possibilities they offer he makes his own selection, it is true. But in the last nine chapters we have studied, the consumer has taken no initiative. Is this always the case? Does the consumer ever take an initiative of his own? Can he?

He can and to some extent he does, as is shown by the long story of our struggle to discover and to apply scientific principles in our living. Of late a new word has been coined, euthenics, which means good environment, as supplementing eugenics, good birth. Euthenics is the study of the control of the environment to serve human purposes best. It represents the challenge to the consumer of his own capacity for intelligence. Though the word is new, the idea is very old, as we shall see. Old as it is, however, up to the last few years it exercised relatively little power over human life.

We must recognize that the cultures of today are superior to the cultures of the past, not because we as men and women are superior to our forefathers, but because we have the benefit of their culture plus all that has come since. Our cultures are not our original inventions; they represent rather the composite experiments and efforts of many preceding generations. Our

155

true capital is the accumulated wisdom of all who have gone before us. If the presence and memory of our culture could be taken away from us, we should have to begin all over again; even we, the highly developed men and women of the twentieth century. We should have to spend a few hundred thousand years discovering by processes painfully slow the use of fire, a cutting instrument, string. This is what is meant by the cumulative nature of culture. It has accumulated outside of us; it is not born with us. If the children of the greatest among us were left in infancy on an uninhabited island they would, of course, die at once; but if we could imagine them fostered by animals, they would grow up like animal children, without any more culture than wolves and bears. Herodotus tells a story that someone wanted to find out what was the "natural" human language; he segregated some children so that they could never hear a human voice. What then turned out to be their "natural" tongue? They had none.

Now in the past, as we have said, our culture has been built up of experiences in which deliberately exercised intelligence played a very minor part. The test of actual trial and error has been its basis. A girl was asked to carry some dishes from the second floor to the kitchen. She went downstairs again and again, carrying one dish each time. "Take them on a tray," said her grandmother. "Let your head save your heels." She answered: "I'd rather let my heels save my head." The girl's position is that of the ordinary consumer. He chooses with the least immediate effort. He is acted upon by inheritance and by his environment, but he does not himself act on them.

THE PAINFULNESS OF THOUGHT

In the very beginning, choices are made by chance, and are, as we have said, confirmed or discarded by the trial and error method of experience. If there is a problem to be solved, the man tries now this and now that, until he hits upon something that works. Let us say that he is cold. The environment offers a cave, a brush heap, and a snow bank. He tries the brush heap and finds the wind penetrates it, he tries the snow bank and finds it damp, and finally he turns to the cave and discovers it is the most satisfactory of the three. From this he forms the habit of living in caves, his associates imitate him, and cave-dwelling becomes a part of the culture of his group.

This process is the same as that followed by animals when they are confronted by a new situation demanding solution. A mouse in a puzzle box runs here, there, and everywhere in its effort to find the means of getting the cheese which is just out of its reach. When it has once found the means of getting it, it does not rush about so much the second time and after a certain number of experiences it goes and gets the cheese directly.

It is easy to see that although a culture might be built up by the trial and error method of experience, its progress would be very slow. Every new interest coming within human ken would have to be tried out at least once by the person who introduced it, and the only way for other people to test the worth of this new interest would be to experiment with its alternatives for themselves. Time and experience are good teachers but their pupils always die on their hands.

At the present day, although we are applying intelligence directly to our wants to some extent, there is a vast field in which trial and error by experience is still the dominant selective force at work. This is true in the huge range of interests introduced and fostered by fad and fashion, where emulation rather than reason is the motive power in choice. It is true also of a very large number of the new interests which the profit motive of business men is forcing on our attention. In the case of fad and fashion interests, we leave ultimate survival to the test of experience because we do not care: we are not seeking what is ultimately useful, all we want is to be in the mode. In the case of some interests introduced for the profit of business men, however, we do care. We wish we knew what was best, but experience is frequently our only means of finding out.

When thinking begins, a little extra energy at the beginning

saves a tremendous amount later. Let us return to the mouse
in the puzzle box, which ran thither and yon until chance re-
vealed to it the way of getting the cheese. We said that a man
would do the same thing if the situation was altogether new to
his experience. If, however, there is anything at all familiar
in the situation, an intelligent man sits still and goes over in
his mind in advance the probable effects of running here and
there, until he has arrived at some basis for action; he is letting
his head save his heels. The man turns over one by one situations and possibilities which he can visualize either directly or
on the basis of similar experience in the past. By the expenditure of a little brain-power he saves a great deal of power in his
muscles. So if our man who is hesitating for shelter before a
cave, a brush heap, and a snow bank has ever climbed a tree
he may remember how the wind whistled through its branches,
and he will pass by the brush heap without even trying it out.
If he has ever got any real idea of what snow is like he will pass
by the snow bank, too, and go to the cave directly.

Thinking, however, is painful: we cannot deny it. "The mind
starts working only under compulsion," said Seneca. The
immediate initial effort of using our heads is often so great that
we avoid it. The pain cost of thinking may be tremendous
at the outset; a barrier must be crossed and we require all sorts
of stimuli to get us started.[1]

Thinking in order to solve problems is not, however, the
highest type of thinking: the highest type is thinking in order
to get the problems to begin with. The transition from trial
and error through the imagination to creative thought may be
psychologically a difference of degree rather than of kind, but
in many cases of the actual exercise of the two we can see a
sharp practical distinction. The man in the puzzle box makes
a choice among already existing alternatives and seeks a solution to a problem which he recognizes as a problem. But the
solution arrived at in this way is by no means necessarily the

[1] Cf. James, William, " The Energies of Men," in *Memories and Studies*,
London, 1911.

best possible solution, for all possible alternatives may not have been at hand. All the trial and error method can do is to point out the best of alternatives actually offered. In the same way, the trial and error method solves problems, but offers no guidance as to what men's problems had best be. Let us illustrate this. Fifty years ago, an intelligent physician might tell his patient whether medicine or diet would do him more good, but he could not prescribe treatment by the ultra-violet ray, which might be better than either. Fifty years ago the trial and error method applied in solving problems was leading to the rapid improvement of the telephone; but in itself it did not and never could suggest the desirability of speech without wires at all. The ultra-violet ray and the radio, are, as we say, new ideas. They are ideas, to be sure, for which men are greatly indebted to suggestions in the environment, and toward the working out of which experience gained in other ways has greatly contributed; but no merely classificatory system of thought would ever have produced them.

The genius takes over a suggestion offered by the environment and creates a new interest for his fellows. He shows them something that may have been present all the time but which no one had been able to see. Such was the fact undoubtedly in the case of men's first practical interests—fire, a cutting instrument, string—which we have already discussed; and it has been true in the case of all new interests ever since.

We have said that intelligent thought of the trial and error, problem-solving variety is difficult, but the difficulties of creative thought are so great they can hardly be judged at all. When a man has a problem to solve he has at least the stimulation of an objective to be reached, by which he may compute his progress. He knows, moreover, that there is a certain reward at the end, if he succeeds. In the case of creative thought he must make his own objective and his only sustenance is the vitality of his creative impulse.

The Culture Hero and the Culture Heroine

Folklore is full of stories of culture heroes, men who introduced or made effective new and better ways of living. Hiawatha was one of these. In the footprints of such as he, the crowd moved forward. The lower ranks of culture heroes were those merely who thought a little more and a little harder than their fellows. The upper ranks were the inventors and teachers of the new. Outstanding personalities are of high significance in all stages of culture, though the chief fields of their service have varied from period to period and age to age.

As the means of living grow more complex the service of culture heroes and culture heroines, great and small, is not necessarily the introduction of more new culture traits. With the increase in means of living, in things and services to be consumed, there is also an ever-growing necessity for the perception of new and significant relationships between culture traits, and for the recognition of those combinations of interests and modes of living which will at once emancipate and enlighten the group and the race. And the culture hero and heroine serve, too, in taking the lead in applying what is known but not yet applied, in setting their intelligence against the mores.

Anyone, in fact, may be to some degree a culture hero. In a small country village in Maine nearly a hundred years ago a penniless young man borrowed from the local doctor a book on health and became convinced that most people lived on a faulty diet. The knowledge was nothing new, but it was new to find anyone at that time applying it. In this young man's home no greasy foods were eaten, no fat pork, and the bread was made from whole grain flour—the village grocer had to put in a special order for the family. This poor family led the dietary standards of the United States by about seventy-five years, on an endowment of nothing but common sense. Their neighbors got the point and followed, and the town became progressive in health lines. In Europe people still laugh at the man who drinks milk. Not long ago they laughed here at the girl who wore low-heeled shoes and no corsets. A little culture-pioneering can put a laugh on the other side of the mouth. We want to know that someone else is doing it and then we ourselves will have the courage to do likewise.

Special Obstacles in Applying Intelligence to Consumption

There are, however, some special obstacles in applying intelligence to consumption: obstacles which stand in the way of both the discovery of truth and of its application when discovered. In Chapter I we stated that the development of consumption was dependent on the development of certain sciences, particularly psychology, anthropology, and the sciences which treat of the welfare of the body. The fact is, however, that consumers themselves have not furnished much impetus for these new discoveries. The impetus has come largely from abstract thinkers, crank geniuses, long-haired philosophers, and "mad" scientists. And the consumer has not only failed to furnish impetus; he, or she, has been very slow to make use of what was discovered.

Why is this? Most of the consuming of the world is done through the agency of the household. The home as an institution is regarded as more or less sacred and after the manner of sacred institutions it looks for its guidance to the past rather than to the present. "I want my home to be a haven of peace," says the tired business man. "I don't want to live in a laboratory for trying out new ideas—I've got to have my car and my radio of course, but I want the kind of home mother (or grandmother) used to make." And the tired business man's wife is very much of the same mind. She doesn't want to run a laboratory either. She sits and sings:

> "I want to be an old-fashioned wife,
> In the good old-fashioned way,"

or else she gets out and finds a "real" job outside the home altogether. Nobody, it seems, wants to stay in the home and be progressive inside its four walls. The words "progressive home " are almost an anomaly.

The Industrial Revolution, as we know, changed completely the productive processes of the home, but the home has not adapted itself to these changes, and the energy and money saved has been spent to a large degree in luxurious by-products along the old lines rather than in more intelligent ways of living along new ones. It has gone into velvet overdrapes with tassels, into ship-models concealing radios, into bedroom-lamps disguised as dolls, and into hand-painted silk pillows that shout "heads off " to the weary head.

It is said that nine-tenths of all buying is done by women. It is certain they buy the food of the household, the furniture and furnishings, usually choose the house, pick out most of the clothing including some of their husbands', and have a very large influence in the family's expenditures for recreation. What is more, they decide on how much money will be spent for each item in the family's living expenses. In some homes the woman's chief function is to spend what her lord produces.

The business man in making his purchases for his business has always before him the incentive of money profits. If a new thing seems to be the best for his business he will try it out at once. He does not wait for his neighbors or his competitors; he hopes he can get ahead of them. But his wife in her buying waits until everybody else is doing it, which is likely to be a long time. By the side of money profits, welfare is a poor incentive. It cannot be so easily tested; when achieved it cannot be so easily displayed. The business man is not naturally more intelligent than his wife. She has the more exacting job.

The business man's job, however, is not only the less exacting; he is trained for it. But very few people are trained for consumption or for even the technicalities of household buying, partly, of course, because we have not known how to train them. The housewife

"is not selected for her efficiency as a manager, is not dismissed for inefficiency, and has small chance of extending her sway over other households if she proves capable. She must buy so many different kinds of goods that she cannot become a good judge of qualities and prices, like the buyers for business houses. She is usually a manual laborer in several crafts, as well as a manager—a combination of functions not conducive to efficiency." [1]

When schools of home economics began they spent a good deal of their energy, perhaps necessarily, on the old-fashioned wife's pound cake, mysterious icings, and bric-a-brac; but now their point of view is changing. They have a great opportunity to give practical instruction in consumption.

Intelligence may be applied to consumption through scientific knowledge of what contributes to welfare. Physiology and psychology help us here. Intelligence may be applied also in helping consumers to buy efficiently and economically. We need a technology of buying as well as a welfare science of consumption. In the third place, intelligence may be applied in making consumption an art. Science does not tell us everything; the technique of buying is but a mechanism serving other ends; we need in addition a glorified and enlightened common sense.

[1] Mitchell, Wesley C., *Business Cycles*, op. cit., p. 65.

CHAPTER XVI

THE SCIENCE OF CONSUMPTION FOR WELFARE

"There seems scarcely any limit to what could be done in the way of producing a good world, if only men would use science wisely."—BERTRAND RUSSELL, *What I Believe.*

"A man is but what he knoweth," said Lord Bacon. Yet intelligent thought is rare. We have emphasized that again and again. Dreams come first, speculations second, experiments third. The philosopher's study precedes the laboratory. Men are loth to go to the trouble of checking their conclusions by experience and experiment. Since science depends on this check of experience and experiment it develops later than philosophy, and consequently the material and immediately practical applications of intelligence are delayed. Science is, in fact, very largely a product of the last hundred and fifty years.

The complete history of science has yet to be written.[1] Curiosity about the universe is as old as man, but in early days men seem to have given more of their energy to abstract than to immediately useful matters. With the exception of some pressing practical problems of healing, it was such sciences as the movements of the stars, mathematics, and physics that received the most attention at the beginning; and in so far as practical applications of these were made at all, they were made to production rather than to consumption.

In the *Works and Days* of the Greek epic poet Hesiod, written probably in the eighth century before Christ, we find, along with various pieces of advice to the husbandman and warnings against unlucky days, some instructions looking

[1] Consult, however, for mediaeval science, Haskins, C. H., *Studies in the History of Mediaeval Science*, Cambridge, 1924; and Thorndike, Lynn, *History of Magic and Experimental Science*, New York, 1923.

toward a science of consumption. He tells, for instance, what weaves and what types of garment will best keep off cold and wet; he notes that men need more food in cold weather; for hot weather he advises light food and plenty of liquid: [1]

> "Then at last be thine the rocky shade, the Biblian wine, a light well-baked cake, the milk of goats, . . . and the flesh of a heifer . . . which has not yet calved, and of first-born kids . . . and the ever-running and forth-gushing spring, which is untroubled by mud. Pour in three cups of water first, and add the fourth of wine."

The great father of science, Aristotle, discusses, among other things, the properties of milk. He declared the function of the stomach was to cook foods and, according to the amount of cooking, to transform them into blood or phlegm.

Pliny the Elder, who lost his life while pursuing his scientific studies at the great eruption of Vesuvius in 79A.D., tells us in his *Natural History* of the nourishing qualities of cheese. You will put on weight, he says, if you eat sweets and fats.[2] He advises what type of cistern is best for filtering drinking water [3] and he gives, often correctly, the assumed properties of a large number of vegetables and fruits.[4] A little later Galen, physician to Commodus, wrote three books entitled *The Properties of Foods*.

The surprising thing is not how much these men knew but how little they knew compared to the generally wide range of their interests and the quality of their thinking. Their capacities were immensely in advance of their knowledge of such practical things.

SCIENCE AND LENGTH OF LIFE

The most striking single accomplishment of science applied to consumption has been in lengthening the average duration of life. In the Middle Ages the average length of life seems to have been about eighteen or nineteen years. In 1841–1850 the

[1] §§ 536–600. Translation by Banks, Rev. J., Bohn's Classical Library, London, 1876.
[2] Bk. XI, 96, 97, 118.
[3] Bk. XXXVI, 52.
[4] Bks. XIX–XXIII.

average duration of life for males in London was 35 years, in
1920–1922 it was 54 years.[1] In 1901 in the registration area
of the United States the expectation of life at birth for white
males was 48 years, in 1910 in the same area it was 50 years,
and in 1919–1920 it was 54 years.[2] A large part of the gain has
come through improving the conditions surrounding the lives
of infants.   In the United States the infant mortality rate fell
nearly one-fifth in the six years 1915–1921 and is now about
70 per thousand.   We should contrast this with a rate in 1922
of 42 per thousand in New Zealand and a rate of 240 per thousand in Chile.[3] No infant mortality statistics are available
for the countries most backward in hygiene, but it is said that
in China not more than half the children survive the first year
of life; the claim is made that in some sections of large cities,
as Canton, not one child in five is able to live.

How has this great increase in life been made possible? By
improvement in medical science and in hygiene applied to consumption.

The first considerable beginnings of science as affecting consumption came in connection with medicine. Human suffering
cried out for attention. It is obvious that men must have been
stimulated very early to find some means of combating pain,
disease, and death. The occupation of medicine man among
primitive peoples is one of the first occupations to be specialized.
Yet there was very little true reasoning from cause to effect
in these early treatments of disease. Disease was closely connected with demons and witchcraft. There was often, indeed,
an attempt to reason from cause to effect, but it was usually of
a superficial nature: heart-shaped leaves cure pain near the
heart, and so on.[4] If the remedies applied were efficacious,

---

[1] Newman, Sir George, *Lancet*, July 25, 1925, p. 165.
[2] United States Department of Commerce, Bureau of the Census, *United
States Life Tables, 1890–1910*, Washington, 1921, pp. 64, 70; *United States
Abridged Life Tables, 1919–20*, Washington, 1923, pp. 24, 26.
[3] Woodbury, R. M., *Infant Mortality and Its Causes*, Baltimore, 1926, p. 8.
[4] As late as 1872 in Philadelphia a book was published—*The Complete Herbal-
ist: or the People their own Physician*—which applies this same reasoning by
superficial analogy or association.

as often they were, it was usually either because of mental suggestion or because a good remedy had been discovered by accident and then retained. In some cases men learned by following the example of animals, who know enough to eat certain herbs when they are ailing.

It is said that a Chinese emperor wrote a treatise on medicine about 2800 B.C. The Egyptians, the Persians, the East Indians, and of course the Greeks and Romans devoted considerable attention to these matters. It is hard to tell, however, how much of the scientific knowledge of medicine of ancient and mediaeval times was the result of discoveries by trial and error and how much was the result of application of a direct scientific method. A great deal of it was undoubtedly the former; progress in one science may considerably precede progress in another, it is true, yet scientific methodology itself does not develop for one alone long before it develops for others. Hence the discoveries of medicine which had been of real help to mankind at the beginning of modern times came not so much because physicians had a more scientific spirit than other men but because, owing to continuous pressure for the treatment of disease, they had a larger body of experience from which to draw.

The actual dissection of bodies was not carried on until the Renaissance, and Harvey's discovery of the circulation of blood came in 1616. It was not until the second half of the last century, however, that modern medicine really began. Shortly after the middle of the century the germ theory of disease was expounded, and the principle of antisepsis shortly followed. The essential control of tuberculosis has come within twenty-five years, and almost every day now brings an account of new progress made toward the solution of some hitherto baffling problem of disease.

Yet preventive medicine and the science of public health are quite as important as remedial medicine, in lengthening the average duration of life, and here also the greatest progress has come in the last few years, following the discovery of the microscope and the development of bacteriology. When drainage, drinking water, milk, and mosquitoes are under control, we may thank God and take courage. Some of the most outstanding illustrations of the success of sanitary science in controlling the environment are afforded by the recent sharp decline in typhoid fever cases in the United States, the great decrease in cases of malaria, yellow fever, and plague in the Canal Zone during the digging of the Panama Canal, and, probably, the disappearance of such diseases as the Black Death, which periodically used to carry off large proportions of the population.

The Physical Joy of Living

But length of days in itself is not necessarily a blessing. To be able to survive to old age is only half the battle of life. We may say with Stevenson that it may be better to go out like a comet at fifty, than to trickle miserably to an end in sandy deltas at ninety-nine. The healthy young people of today, who scorn to be ill, have little appreciation of the weary days endured by preceding generations.

It is true that science is now keeping alive, perhaps for a miserable existence, some who would otherwise have died, but those who would have lived anyway are living the better for what science has done. Along with typhoid fever, malaria, yellow fever, and plague a host of minor ailments are leaving us. Nervousness and headaches are something to be ashamed of. A certain amount of ill health used to be considered a necessary evil, but it is now out of fashion. How well our literature reflects the changed situation. No modern writer would dare give us for a heroine the frail and delicate creature beloved by early Victorians. "Man is born to trouble as the sparks fly upward," exclaimed Job, and it has been left to the science of the nineteenth and twentieth centuries to disprove it.

How has science accomplished this? First it has come through preventive medicine, second through nutrition, third through housing and dressing according to sanitary standards. Of preventive medicine and the science of public health we have spoken already.

Closely akin to the science of public health is the science of nutrition. "Tell me what you eat and I will tell you what you are," runs a proverb. Give a man the proper food, and not only does he lose his dyspepsia, but he walks with a brighter eye and a firmer tread. He enjoys the taste of his dinner and he sees the sunset, he smells the lilac, he hears the bluebird, and feels the breath of spring on his cheek.

Ancient physicians had recognized that some men ate too much, or were insufficiently nourished, but there was no recognition of the different types of nutritive substances and the functions of each until the beginning of the last century. In 1834 William Prout declared that foodstuffs were of three sorts— saccharine, oleose, and albuminous; Magendie a little later was the first to distinguish the unlike nutritive values of the three. The importance of the proteins was first emphasized by Liebig about the middle of the century. The significance of the various minerals necessary to the body and the part played by each was not brought out until considerably later. A theory that something more than chemical compounds was necessary for nutrition was suggested by Voit in 1881, but the vitamin hypothesis did not receive general recognition until 1912 and 1913.

Much work remains to be done in the field of nutrition. We still do not know exactly the optimum caloric requirements of people of different sex, age, and type engaged in different occupations. We still do not know the optimum combinations of proteins, carbohydrates, and fats in the diet, nor to what an extent one group of chemical compounds may be substituted for another. The exact amount of minerals required is not known, and the nature and functions of vitamins is still only partly understood. Nevertheless our progress in this field has been very fast and the large amount of research now going on in physiological chemistry is advancing this progress yet more rapidly.

Another factor contributing to physical vigor is the sanitation of buildings with regard to light, heat, humidity, and ventilation.   Inquiries here have been carried furthest for public buildings and factories, and most states have their sanitary codes covering construction and provision of fresh air, at least for school buildings.   There is still, it is true, a great deal of disagreement as to what good air is and how much should be provided,[1] but the significant thing is that the importance of the problem is at last recognized.

So far as the private home is concerned, minimum health standards have been formulated by the United States Bureau of Industrial Housing for the houses of industrial workers to be built under the direction of the Bureau.   The British Government likewise has instituted standards for the cottages of agricultural laborers.   It is true that we do not know definitely what such standards should be from the point of view of health alone, but it is significant that we are trying to find out all we can about it.   The modern architect is planning homes quite differently from the way they were planned twenty-five years ago; sleeping rooms must be larger and be provided with cross draughts if possible; the living rooms must have suitable exposure to the sun.   Window glass admitting ultra-violet rays is already being used.   Artificial ventilators and humidifiers are finding their way into many private homes.

In progressive schools, desks and chairs are adjusted to the height and size of the children using them.   The same principle is at last creeping into the provision of furniture and equipment for the home.   A commercial manufacturer of beds amuses us by advertising "beds built for sleep," but after all, why not? For years we stood in need of living rooms in which there was space to live; we are still needing kitchens where the equipment is suitable for proper performance of the work.   Long ago some carpenter said that thirty inches was the proper height for a

[1] Cf., New York State Commission on Ventilation, *Ventilation*, New York, 1923, and Winslow, C. E. A., *Fresh Air and Ventilation*, New York, 1926.

sink, and a million housewives in consequence have had back-aches from that day to this.

Scientific investigation has brought out the advantage of certain fabrics, certain weaves, or certain colors of clothing materials for specific purposes, and has taught us what forms of clothing best supply warmth while they are least encumbering or restricting to the body. Unfortunately, however, such researches seem to have little direct effect upon our manner of dressing. The fashion by which women came to dispense with the encumbering garments they had worn for so many generations was doubtless initiated, as so many other fashions have been, by emulation. This particular fashion, however, has been confirmed by comfort, if not by a recognition of its service to health, and for some time there have been no great changes in modes. Paul Poiret, indeed, is already complaining that the end of modes has come. This, however, is too much to believe. High heels have again succeeded in forcing an entrance into the house of fashion.

There are, however, some encouraging signs of deliberately intelligent attention to healthfulness in matters of dressing. Whether because of the teachings of science or not, weaves which provide means of more fully ventilating the skin have of late been more widely adopted for underwear, particularly men's underwear. The initiative here seems to have been taken rather by the producer than by the consumer. The study of infant hygiene, however, which has been prosecuted so energetically in late years, has certainly effected substantial changes in the manner of dressing young children. Twenty-five years ago a mother thought she must adorn her baby with long and often heavily embroidered garments, but today's progressive mother does not let her vanity weigh one grain against the physical welfare of her child. Whatever Paris modistes may say, little children at least are to wear garments warm, well-ventilated, light in weight, and unencumbering to the limbs. Such signs are encouraging. In time we may deliberately apply the same principles to children of a larger growth.

Consumption and Mental Hygiene

So far all our discussion of scientific consumption has been confined to that which directly affects the physical body, and that is natural, for physical means and effects are those most easily measurable, hence most amenable to scientific method. We have had, nevertheless, in the last few years the beginnings of an effort to determine the conditions most favorable for sane mental life.

As our knowledge of physical health began with the study of disease, so the study of mental life received originally a great impetus from the existence of abnormal mental conditions, for which a cure was sought. Now the attention of psychologists and psychiatrists has turned in some measure toward serving and securing the fullest development of the normal.[1]

The relationship of consumption to the development of a sane and full mental life is just as close as, though it is certainly more complicated than, its relationship to physical health. In the first place, it is through the study of mental capacity, as measured, for instance, by intelligence quotients and by determination of special aptitudes, that we are able to obtain some idea of and to what extent a man is able to use and to appreciate economic goods and services, both general and particular. In the second place, knowledge of mental health is beginning to point out to us, a certain capacity being given, how fast we can profitably proceed in our consumption and to what an extent it is desirable or undesirable that our consumption be varied, in order to obviate as far as possible the action of the law of diminishing utility, and hence to secure maximum development and maximum satisfactions.

A little later we shall have occasion to refer to the idea that a standard of living is, or should be, "organic." The goods and services we consume should be looked upon not as things-in-themselves but as things contributory to the end of a better

[1] Cf., for instance, Burnham, W. H., *The Normal Mind*, New York, 1924; Overstreet, H. A., *About Ourselves*, New York, 1927.

rounded life. A friend writes: "Whenever I feel myself going down hill mentally I pull myself up by giving myself some pleasure that will revive my spirits: a box of chocolates, a play, a new garment, or even a trip somewhere." To the intelligent individual a box of chocolates is, indeed, not a mere box of chocolates but a box of potential service or disservice to a good life. In discussions of consumption there used to be considerable confusion over whether or not it was justifiable to consume luxuries. Looked at from the point of view of the individual consumer himself, the question resolves itself merely into a question of the definition of luxury. If the thing under consideration—no matter what it is—contributes to a more complete life, consume it. If it does not, cast it aside. It is not the thing but the circumstances that determine one's answer to the question.

The subject is, of course, extremely difficult. Our knowledge has, nevertheless, gone far enough so that an individual may already make some applications of benefit in his own life. In particular, parents may be guided by this knowledge in the education of their children.

SCIENCE AND AESTHETICS

Depending on one's point of view, the question of aesthetic satisfactions may be considered as a part of the development of mental life, or it may be considered as another and separate question. Aesthetic satisfactions are very frequently, and perhaps even generally, achieved without conscious knowledge or study of science. This is true alike of music, of poetry, of the fine arts, and of course in the same way of the arts applied to economic goods of common consumption, houses, furniture, clothing, and so on. At the present day the creation and appreciation of the beautiful is not usually taught or studied as in the domain of scientific law. The modern artist, architect, or draftsman may be instructed in a few elementary principles of design and color, but these carry him only a limited way; for the rest he must rely on his own taste or skill,—hence we speak

of an artist's intuition, rather than of his science. Only a few
have the intuition which yields satisfaction, hence the majority
of the things we look at are more or less unsatisfactory from an
aesthetic point of view.

None the less we know absolutely that certain of the sources
of aesthetic satisfaction spring from exact mathematical relationships which give variety and at the same time economize
energy. Pythagoras, who is believed to have been the first
person to discover the numerical relationship of the notes in the
scale, declared that number was the basis of all things. The
Greeks, the masters of aesthetic creation and appreciation, appear to have known its mathematical basis as well as, if not
better than, we do.

The fact that the aesthetic satisfaction obtained from certain
simple forms can be proved to lie in mathematically measurable
proportions suggests that more complex expressions of beauty
could be reduced to exact scientific law if we only knew the
proper weight to be ascribed to each constituent element of an
aesthetic unit. In this way, of course, the principles of artistic
creation could be accurately taught and not left to chance or
skill, and so the common articles of consumption in everyday
life, our houses, our furniture, our automobiles, our clothing,
and our bathtubs, would yield us the maximum variety of
interest with the maximum economy of energy, hence the
greatest possible aesthetic satisfaction.[1]

Some one asks if artistic appreciation will not flag if everything can be exactly tailored to fit it. Surely it would, if such
aesthetic discoveries should limit the expression of the artist,
but there seems to be no reason why the forms of beauty may
not be as innumerable as the changes in a kaleidoscope.

It is true, of course, that even the little we do know about the

[1] Two recent writers attack this problem, Jay Hambidge in *Dynamic Sym-
metry*, New Haven, 1920, where the mathematical principles believed to un-
derlie Greek art are set forth; and Claude Bragdon in *The Beautiful Necessity*,
New York, 1922. Says the latter in his preface, p. ii, "Art is an expression
of the *world order* and is therefore orderly, organic; subject to mathematical
law and susceptible of mathematical analysis."

scientific basis of aesthetics is not always applied, due to our inertia, nor appreciated even when applied, due to our falsely educated tastes. This is perhaps the most delicate and difficult of all the possible applications of science to consumption, and the American people are far behind the ancient Greeks and probably far behind the modern Chinese and Japanese in a comprehension of what aesthetic gratification may mean. Our present status with regard to aesthetics may be compared to the status of Aristotle and Pliny and their fellow Greeks and Romans with regard to nutrition. Exact science has moved since then. It is still moving.

CHAPTER XVII

THE TECHNOLOGY OF CONSUMPTION

"'I have brought no money,' cried Moses again. 'I have laid it all out in a bargain, and here it is,' pulling out a bundle from his breast; 'here they are; a gross of green spectacles, with silver rims, and shagreen cases. . . . I had them at a dead bargain, or I should not have bought them. The silver rims alone will sell for double the money.'

"'A fig for the silver rims,' cried my wife in a passion; 'I dare swear they won't sell for above half the money, at the rate of broken silver, five shillings an ounce.'

"'You need be under no uneasiness,' cried I, 'about selling the rims, for they are not worth sixpence, for I perceive they are only copper varnished over.' . . . .

"'And so,' returned she, 'we have parted with the colt, and have only got a gross of green spectacles with copper rims, and shagreen cases! A murrain take such trumpery.'"—OLIVER GOLD-SMITH, *The Vicar of Wakefield.*

The intelligent direction of consumption may be approached from two points of view: the first is, What is best for us? That is the aspect of the problem discussed in our preceding chapter, The Science of Consumption for Welfare. The second point of view is, How can we get what we want and get it best?

The second point of view does not lead us to attempt to pass judgment on the character of our wants but is concerned only with how we can most economically gratify them. We call it, therefore, a technology of consumption rather than a science of welfare. It leads us to consider such questions as how we may recognize what we want, how we may get the best qualities for the least money, how we may be informed as to the suitability and serviceability for various purposes of the articles we buy. In other words, the broad field of the intelligent direction of consumption leads us to consider not only what we ought to want, but how to get what we want, whatever it is. That is the point of view to which we turn in this chapter. It takes a certain standard of living for granted. It is not concerned with telling you whether or not you should eat canned soup, or have a radio; but if you want the soup and must have the radio it will help you recognize the best for your purpose. A large part of the subject matter of the technology of getting what we want might be approached under the name of standardization.

POINTS TO BE COVERED BY A TECHNOLOGY OF CONSUMPTION

A technology for consumption should cover three fields. First, it should protect us from misrepresentation and fraud. Second, it should give us a means by which we can recognize just what size, weight, quality, etc., we are buying; and it should provide the sizes, weights, qualities, etc., that the consumer actually wants. Third, it should tell us not only what quality is good but what is best for our purpose, and what is best not only in itself but best in proportion to price.

It should be pointed out also that the simplification or standardization of production, which frequently must be the normal result of the development of a technology of buying, may improve the quality of the product or decrease its price, or both. With the stabilization of demand that is the logical consequence of the specialization of products it is possible to make goods better and more cheaply than when there are a hundred different varieties and a small demand for each.

OUR NEED OF STANDARDS FOR GOODS AND SERVICES

By far the largest field for technological research to guide the consumer is that which covers the goods and services that he buys to supply his wants.

A dreadful picture is sometimes drawn of the present state of standardization of consumption in the United States. Ten thousand business men, we are told, rise simultaneously from ten thousand hardly distinguishable beds. They proceed to ten thousand 2 x 5 shining white bathtubs (some of them are lavender or green nowadays) and shortly after, clad in ten thousand precisely similar business suits, sit down each to the same breakfast of coffee and grapefruit, toast and eggs. They finish the day at a standardized club or a standardized musical comedy, or in a standardized living room listening to a standardized radio program in the company of a standardized family consisting of a standardized wife and two—partially—standardized children. Such, we are told, is life.

This picture, gloomy or inspiring, as we choose to look at it, does not trouble us here and now. At present we are not trying to entice our business man into the devious and thrilling byways of consumption. We are telling him simply: "If you insist on bathtubs and coffee, you ought to know what you get. If you think you are buying porcelain you ought to get porcelain and not enamelled iron; if you think you are buying coffee you ought to get coffee and not chicory and canary seed." This much is only common sense.

It is amazing how little our business man and his wife know about qualities, about materials, about the relative efficacy of this or that article for a specific purpose; how little they know about measurements and their significance in terms of size, weight, serviceability, and so on. As things are now, they take a chance on whether they are getting the most and the best for their money, and it is a chance on which they usually are the losers. Let us see how this is.

To begin with, even the housewife who is instructed in nutrition knows little about getting the most for her money. She feeds her family as the mores bid her. She does not know whether wheat flour or rye or corn meal gives the greatest food value for its cost. She does not know whether prunes, raisins, or figs are really cheapest, apples or bananas, peanut butter or cheese. She does not know, ordinarily, the quality in the can of vegetables or fruit that she buys, or what, if anything, the brand name means. The price is too often her only guide, frequently an extraordinarily poor one. She does not even know whether first quality refers to food value or to appearance alone.

She does not know how to choose the textiles that will wear best in proportion to their price. In the experiment with sheetings carried on by Professor Rosamund Cook of the University of Cincinnati, Miss Cook found that if a woman picked sheeting blindfold she was just as likely to choose the most economical one as if she chose with her eyes open; and the salesperson's judgment was no better than the housewife's. The housewife does not know what goods will launder best, nor what will keep their color and appearance. It's a mad game of guess.

The consumer does not know what materials are best for his house. What is the most economical type of roofing for his purpose? Guess again. What system of heating will serve him most efficiently? What kind of coal? What make of coal shovel? Three guesses more. Even to know what type or brand or system is best in itself is not to answer our question: we must know what is best in proportion to its price.

How much do we know about the construction of household furniture? Is not superficial appearance and the word of a half-instructed salesman usually our only guide? The writer once sought to find out something about furniture standards from the manager of one of the largest and most reputable furniture stores in the United States. He said that his store kept only first and second grades, but that many high-class stores sold second grade for first. He could not tell, however, what, if any, were the essential differences in serviceability between first and second grade, or second and third grade. For the consumer, he said, the best plan was to buy from a reputable store, such as his, and trust to price. He implied that a consumer who asked for more information would be a crank.

Hundreds of thousands of automobiles, hundreds of thousands of radios, are sold every year. Our technology for buying these consists chiefly of pictorial advertisements, the enthusiastic inducements of prejudiced salesmen, the word of our friends, and our own personal judgment based, perhaps, on unnecessarily unhappy experience.

Before the buyer can know these things, a technology for buying must be developed. Perhaps the greatest difficulty in effecting standardization in products lies in the nature of the competitive system of production as it is practised at present. The goods offered for sale to consumers are the products of hundreds and thousands of competing manufacturers who are much more interested in differentiating, or appearing to differentiate, their own product from others, than in standardizing it to conform to definite grades. Through aggressive methods of sales-making they are striving to create a demand for Cook's canned soup rather than for soup in number 1 cans that is by original weight of contents 15% small carrots, 12% first grade potatoes, 10% each of young corn and green beans, with certain definite proportions of other flavoring, butter, and water added. If approached on the matter of standardization they will be very likely to reply that they are not interested. Why should they be? They see far more chance of increasing their market through their old lines of advertising their product merely as "distinctive" and "different" and "superior."

It is obvious, however, that if one is giving specific advice as to costs there may be considerable difference between recommending prunes and 60–70 prunes, or sheeting and 40–42 unbleached sheeting, twill weave, 60 inches wide, or coal and buckwheat coal. This lack of standardization also makes it very difficult to make comparisons between commercial brands: a grade that falls down in one respect may be superior in another, but there is no way of knowing the relative standings of different grades without experience with each. For the individual consumer such experience is very costly, usually too costly.

RESEARCH, REFORM, AND EDUCATION IN STANDARDIZATION

There are four main agencies whereby research, reform, and education in standardization can be carried on. The first is the producers themselves; the second, professional associations and educational institutions: schools and colleges, particularly schools of engineering and home economics; the third, government; the fourth, organizations of consumers as such.

We have just said that under the present system of production relatively little progress in standardization of competitive prod-

ucts can be expected on the initiative of competing manufacturers. There are, however, certain fields of standardization in
which the producers can and have helped the consumer. One
of these is the field of standardization in sizes of packages or
containers. For many years we have had the standardized
measures of quarts, pounds, and yards. Now we have also No.
1, No. 2, and No. 2½ cans and certain recognized standard
widths of yard goods and recognized standard yarn counts—
though the consumer has usually to do his own counting to
recognize the latter.

In the relatively few cases where producers are producing
exactly the same thing, as fruits and vegetables, they may come
to a common agreement as to grading. The California Fruit
Growers Exchange, for instance, has set up definite grades of
oranges and grapefruit according to their size. Market gar-
deners or the middlemen handling their products recognize
definite grades for vegetables, with which the consumer would
do well to become acquainted.

There is also the standardization that an individual producing or selling company may initiate for the different grades of
its own product. The Great Atlantic and Pacific Tea Company
has several of its own peculiar brand names and there is a distinction as well as a difference in name between "Iona" and
"Grandmother's." Many large manufacturers or selling agents,
the big mail-order houses, for instance, make similar distinctions, although they are not ordinarily interpreted to the consumer except in terms of price. They are, however, a step in the
right direction.

As an indication of the possibilities of the work of the second
group of agencies, professional and educational institutions,
we should note the fact that the American Medical Association
has investigated the claims of many proprietary preparations
and will furnish its findings to the inquirer. There is special
need for some such service as this in a field where the consumer's
health may be at stake. In fact, welfare science as well as
technology is involved here.

Educational institutions, such as schools of engineering and home economics, can and do very well carry on research into grades and qualities of goods not trade-marked and give publicity to their findings. Along such lines are researches into the qualities of different materials for building construction, as copper and slate roofs, the washing, wearing, and fading qualities of different general types of textiles, as cotton and linen, the relative food content of different sizes of fruits, as apples or prunes. We need far more of such information. Educational institutions have done very little in a practical way in a study of patented or trade-marked products. Hitherto they have hesitated to make public, or even to tell their students, what they know about the relative advantages of the Klean-O and the O-Klean electric washers or the differences between Linolome and Corkolome rugs. Doubtless they could do much more to bring about reforms and improvements in standardization than they have done as yet.

Of the general function of government in relation to consumption we shall speak in a later chapter. In theory, one of the most important means of standardization would be law; but the field for laws affecting consumption under our present theory of government is of necessity very limited, and for the most part is confined to matters affecting public health and protection against fraud. In the field of law we have the Federal Pure Food and Drugs Act of 1906, and various somewhat similar state laws. We also have state and municipal laws specifying the butter fat content and the purity of different grades of milk. The recent federal Misbranding Act is an attempt to protect the consumer against misstatements on goods generally. It does not, however, apply to advertisements for the goods.

In connection with government we should mention the general efforts toward standardization in grades and sizes undertaken by the Division of Simplified Practice of the Bureau of Standards in the Department of Commerce. This Division "serves as a centralizing agency in bringing together producers, distributors, and consumers, whenever requested by any of these groups, for the purpose of assisting these interests in their mutual efforts to eliminate waste in production and distribution."[1] This is in accord with the policy of the Department of Commerce to put the government not in business but behind business.

Since the organization of the Division of Simplified Practice in 1921 it has succeeded in reducing the number of sizes and grades of many sorts of producers' goods, and in the realm of consumers' goods has brought about simplification in sizes of bed blankets and in types or sizes of beds, springs and mattresses, and milk bottles and caps.

An indication of what might be done for consumers in the way of standardization is afforded by the Federal Specifications Board, likewise in the Bureau of Standards. This Board was instituted to provide specifications to be applied in the purchase of supplies by the federal, by state, and by municipal governments. In its insistence that all government purchases meet certain definite standards it has set up over eleven thousand specifications and has supplied its needs at much less than the prevailing market price. We are told that for an operating cost of two million dollars it is estimated that the Bureau of Standards saves the government better than one hundred million dollars every year. In the single item of typewriter ribbons the government pays $1.75 a dozen for ribbons which bring $8 to $10 a dozen on the open market.[2] Indirectly the specifications of this Board are influencing processes of production very broadly. The Bureau of Standards will supply to anyone its "master specifications" for different goods, some of which are consumers' goods. It will furnish also a list of hundreds of manufacturers willing to certify their products to purchasers in accordance with these government specifications. Such a service carries great possibilities for aiding the consumer through the retailer. The Board is now going further and supplementing the certification plan by fostering a labeling system. The label

[1] United States Department of Commerce, Annual Report of the Secretary, 1924, p. 18.
[2] An extensive discussion of this matter is contained in Chase, S. and Schlink, F. J., *Your Money's Worth*, New York, 1927.

accompanies the goods as sold. A mimeographed enclosure in
a letter from the Federal Specifications Board reads as follows:

> "Several manufacturers are already applying the labeling system.
> One of these manufacturers makes three grades of liquid soap. One
> grade is said to exceed the requirements of the Government specifica-
> tion by a certain percentage, and is priced accordingly; another grade,
> which is said to 'answer every average requirement,' is sold at a price
> somewhat less than that asked for the Government specification soap.
> The Government specification soap carries the following label:

> ### 'GUARANTEE
>
>> This Liquid Soap is guaranteed to comply with the
>> United States Government Specification No. 27 Liquid
>> Soap as adopted by the Federal Specifications Board, on
>> June 20, 1922, when tested by method shown in circular
>> of the Bureau of Standards No. 124. Copies of specifica-
>> tion and method of testing will be sent gratis upon appli-
>> cation.'"

The possibilities involved in this undertaking of the Department of Commerce are immense. Through it the consumer
is now able to recognize at once the status of a few products,
and the plan might well be applied to everything that we buy.

Another government bureau, Home Economics, in the Department of Agriculture is dealing directly with matters both
of scientific and of technological interest in consumption and
can properly encourage standardization. Several states, notably
North Dakota, have developed rather extensive work for consumers' guidance in buying food products.

This brings us to the fourth main type of possible agency for
furnishing a technology to consumers, organizations of consumers themselves. What the Federal Specifications Board
is doing for the government as a buyer suggests what might
be done by and for consumers as a whole. There is now in
existence an Educational Buyers' Association for large buyers
such as institutions, but no organization doing research or providing education for the great body of consumers. Mr. Stuart
Chase and Mr. F. J. Schlink suggest that the instruction of the
consumer may properly be made an object for an endowment

by some philanthropic millionaire. Or consumers themselves might organize and by paying some small sum, such as a dollar a year, provide a fund for research and publicity, which, if discreetly managed, would certainly save itself many times over. It is as important to institute an organization for publicity as an organization for research, since the relative status of commercially named products, even if determined, can hardly be published in magazines and newspapers dependent on advertising. Such organizations as the Good Housekeeping Institute, which test the products of their advertisers and publish the results, must in the long run please some advertisers or others, and so are obviously limited in what they can accomplish. They tell us truthfully that a certain thing is "good," but they do not tell us in what respects it is weakest, nor how good it is in proportion to its cost, nor how good it is compared with its competitors. And these are important points about which we desire information.

A significant and rather a surprising aspect of the situation with regard to consumers' instruction is the fact that consumers as such seem on the whole less concerned about their ignorance than do producers or government officials or professional societies. This lack of concern is of course largely due to the consumers' ignorance. A strenuous effort is being made to awaken them today.[1]

[1] Two recent and significant books on this subject are Harap, Henry, *The Education of the Consumer*, New York, 1924; and Chase, Stuart, and Schlink, F. J., *Your Money's Worth*, op. cit.

CHAPTER XVIII

CONSUMPTION AS AN ART

"Might not the student afford some Hebrew roots, and the business man some of his half crowns, for a share of the idler's knowledge of life at large and the Art of Living? . . . There is no duty which we so much underrate as the duty of being happy."
—R. L. STEVENSON, *An Apology for Idlers.*

After scientific knowledge has done for us the utmost that it is now capable of doing and indeed the utmost that we can forecast for it at present, it will have answered less than half the questions we should like to have answered for directing our consumption on a scientific basis. It will have told us a good deal about the physical welfare of the body, our food, fresh air, and so on; but there still remain many important questions which do not submit themselves to scientific or statistical analysis at present and perhaps never will do so. Let us illustrate this.

In the preceding chapters we have made repeated reference to the usual more or less unthinking acceptance of a certain standard of living as good or desirable. Granting for the moment that this standard of living is good, how am I to decide, on a scientific basis, certain questions that arise within it? How much formal education shall I seek? What types of recreation are best for me? How am I to know whether it is really better for me to choose a fur coat or a radio set, since I can have but one; a bottle of perfume or the latest best seller; a box of chocolates or a seat at the Orpheum? Are there any scientific principles applicable here?

What is an even more serious question for me, however,—though I admit I think about it less—is the question of the validity of my accepted standard of living itself. How do I know, how can I know after all, whether any of these specific things I have mentioned are good for me? It may be best for me to turn them all down—fur coats and radio sets, perfumes and best sellers, candy and theatre tickets; and, having done so, it may be best for me to put the money they would have cost into a conservatory where I may enjoy flowers all winter. I know a few people with conservatories, but a winter garden could not be called a part of the standard of living of any, even the richest group, of American people. Fur coats and radio sets and the other things, on the other hand, very decidedly enter into the standards of most American groups. How am I to know if the commonly accepted standards present to me the best choices for my own purposes? Should I choose the conservatory, or should I, perhaps, choose something else I do not know about at all? Is there any way by which a person can be truly enlightened without specific experience and without scientific aid?

Science Itself Was Once Unproved Ideas

We must admit, as we survey the historical development of interests, that not all good interests can be accounted for by the hit or miss method of experience, on the one hand, or by the application of scientific principles on the other. Some good interests, and this is most obvious in the case of those related to the arts, seem to have entered or to have been preserved as the result of an apparently more or less spontaneous appreciation of the right, the fitting, or the beautiful under certain conditions. Indeed there are certain interests which all of us would probably call good and yet which we cannot prove good by any processes known to science. Delight in flowers, refreshment in music, pleasure in the company of animals or birds, satisfaction in the study and contemplation of certain books, all of these are aspects of our consumption which it would be hard to demonstrate as desirable in the laboratory, yet we all believe they are desirable.

Tentatively to accept certain things as good, fitting, or significant in advance of being able to prove them so by scientific demonstration, is not necessarily, however, a non-scientific attitude. The scientific attitude is only in part to accept and apply the demonstrable; its other part is the critical building up of new hypotheses on the basis of the best available organized knowledge. We even say that the scientist "feels" his way into the unknown. The scientist, in other words, in so far as he contributes anything at all new to his science, is in some degree a creator and an artist. The difference between the creative scientist and the creative artist is fundamentally a difference in degree rather than a difference in kind. The scientist has more objective and organized knowledge at his command for suggesting and checking his hypotheses. The artist has little objective and organized knowledge for checking his progress as he goes on. He is more dependent on his "feeling" as to whether or not he is on the right track. For this reason he is more liable to failure than the scientist, but none the less he can venture beyond where the usual scientist dares tread. His "feeling" may play him false and his work may have to be discarded; on the other hand it may lead him forward, and aid in laying the foundations of what may ultimately become a science. In fact, by an analysis of the work of a sufficient number of artists one can discover the principles and laws which have been perhaps unconsciously common to all. As science springs from creative perception, so arts are partial or nascent sciences. In our chapter on science it was pointed out that a mathematical basis has now been shown for certain relationships in the field of art which were formerly regarded as being attainable only by a high type of "intuition." Arts always precede sciences, and of course they are far older.

Applied to the art of consumption, this means that one's "feeling" for the fitting, the good, and the beautiful has been, and must continue to be, a guide in the introduction of new wants into life and in the new or better organization of wants already there. Leaders in the art of consumption must do on a broad scale for the race what every individual is called on to practice on a small scale in his own experience.

The more important thing in the development of either science or art is not to demonstrate some idea, but to get an idea to be demonstrated. As we have seen in Chapter XV, the greatest man is the creator. He stands aside from the crowd and listens for the music of the spheres. Then suddenly, perhaps when he least expects it, a new suggestion comes to him, a new idea the source of which he may not be able to explain or understand. This creation to some extent takes place in every life. It may be expressed only as a fresh choice of conventional things, as when the tired business man, let us say, has a hunch he would do better to take up golf than to go motoring every Saturday afternoon; or when a woman surprises her friends by saying, "I had an inspiration the other day. I'm going to give up one of my bridge clubs and join a class in these new rhythmics." It may be a fresh choice of an unconventional thing, as when a college student decides to get up early in the morning and study birds; or it may be the introduction of a new interest altogether, as when one day in the dim past somebody brought music into his own life and the life of mankind.

For most of us most of the time, of course, the art of consumption must be simply the best arrangement of certain conventional interests. Yet that is a tremendous task. It cannot be accomplished by people who are continually rushing from one thing to another. One must take time, first, really to desire it; and second, in the modern United States at least, one must take time to rest, to listen, and to dream. The artist in living may not be able to explain the "feeling" by which he proceeds, but great artists, both in the arts and in living, have frequently declared that they knew well enough when they were working in accordance with a true idea and when they were not.

Of course it is obvious that as soon as we speak about going forward on the basis of "feeling" or a much abused intuition, we are laying ourselves open to all sorts of criticism. In ninety-nine cases out of a hundred, if not in nine hundred ninety-nine out of a thousand, probably, feeling and intuition are used as an excuse for avoiding the discipline of intellectual processes rather than as intellectual processes plus. For this reason, most talk about feeling one's way forward has fallen into disrepute. Nevertheless it is obvious that there is no other way forward except this. Aristotle undoubtedly had the right idea in giving one name to reason as organized knowledge and another name to reason as intuitive perception.

Any valid new perception of the significant, we may be sure, comes not from accident or sentimentalizing but rises upon a foundation of the best organized knowledge available. Whatever else it may be, unusual application of powers of observation, analysis, and intelligence along certain lines are at its root, and discipline of the severest order is necessary to its perfection. It is not because of the dreams of the fool but because of the dreams of the wise man that we go forward. The great dreamers of the world had equipped themselves for their dreams.

What is the foundation of the art of consumption, that foundation which can be recognized and analyzed by the intellect? Doubtless it may be stated in many ways. Its usual statement is not in terms of economics but rather in terms, more or less complete, of the moral life or of aesthetics, or of philosophy. The art of consumption is called the good life, the fruitful life, the beautiful life, the happy life, the balanced life: all these expressions are suitable. But as economics is concerned with the maximizing of satisfactions, the art of consumption is certainly as much a matter of economics as it is of philosophy or aesthetics or morals. The economic and moral and aesthetic points of view are different; their ideal results are the same.

THE ART OF CONSUMPTION AS THE FULLEST EXPRESSION AND UTILIZATION OF HUMAN CAPACITIES

We may state for our guidance certain ends that the art of consumption should attain. To know these ends is to have a certain criterion for our choices. To say that the art of consumption should mean the fullest expression and utilization of human capacities is indeed not only to state an end but to indicate the means thereto.

The development of all human capacities to their fullest point, the expression of all potential interests, is the ideal of consumption as an art. This is, of course, impossible in any one life; but such a statement of the ideal makes clear that in every life the way should be left open for the expansion of all types of interest. No one type of interest should be so developed that it suppresses or atrophies or dulls another type, or so that the later development of another type is made more difficult.

We may call the artist in consumption him who has developed the largest number of interests fully. In practice this means there must be more discrimination of choice of interests even at the start, particularly with regard to interests connected with our physical appetites; for these first of all by relative over-development become destructive to others.[1]

A man's capacities for satisfaction may roughly be classified under certain heads, as, for instance, among others, physical, social, mental, aesthetic. Let us suppose a child of remarkable intellect to be born, whose greatest pleasure is abstruse mathematical speculations. It has sometimes happened that such children have been permitted or encouraged by vain parents to develop still further their intellectual satisfactions, to the suppression or exclusion of most other satisfactions; with the result that in young manhood or womanhood they have ceased to experience as much pleasure in social contacts as they felt in their play as little children, and are never able to regain it. Or they may develop their intellectual life at the expense of their health and physique. On the other hand, certain athletes go to the other extreme. In the same way, we all know people whose desire for financial success, or whose strong physical appetites, have blunted their native capacity for intelligent judgment or for aesthetic appreciation. At the present time,

---

[1] A line of thought suggesting that moral good is "most" good is developed in Perry, R. B., *The Moral Economy*, New York, 1909. To define moral good as "most" good, however, is only one way of defining it.

no doubt, financial success is the most over-estimated and over-worked of all sources of potential satisfaction.

In the present age and situation it is practically impossible to develop all sources of satisfaction at the same rate nor is this necessarily best. Occasionally the expansion of one little-developed source of satisfaction, such as the aesthetic, may be desirable even at the expense of the partial atrophy of another and over-developed source, such as business enterprise, but in such a case the person's interests previously have been very badly balanced. Of course the expansion of one source of interest which involves the atrophy of another is wasteful of energy.

The recognition of the desirability of balance is a first step on which the art of consumption rests. The Greeks taught this lesson in their doctrine of the golden mean: nothing is good in excess and all aspects of the human soul must have a chance at the light.

The artist in creating an harmonious life is restrained, on the one hand, by his energy or drive and his intelligence, and on the other hand, he is limited, first, by the standard of living of his group, and second and finally, by the sum total of interests with which he has had opportunity to become familiar. We know from what has been said in previous chapters that no one man can introduce many new interests into society. He may introduce one or two, but for the most part his artistry is expressed by the choices and combinations he makes among current interests.

The limitations of his energy, which affect his courage, will always to some extent compel him to conform to certain socially accepted standards more than he would really desire to do. He may dislike modern modes of dress and regard the toga of the Romans as a more artistic and comfortable garment than coat, vest, and trousers, but he will hardly go so far as to order a toga from his tailor. The cost in courage is greater than the gain in artistic satisfaction. Courage is required, indeed, for such a private and personal matter as being a vegetarian. None the less there is a wide range of choices which are not accompanied by any social cost; and many more of which the social cost may easily be borne. There is a great field for the choices of the artist in living.

Analyses of interests are to a certain degree artificial yet it helps to analyze interests if dollars are to be distributed to develop them. So it is interesting to work out in tabular form a statement of the minimum essential, the desirable, and the excessive and undesirable satisfactions coming under each main type of human interests, and then to use this as a check on one's own interests, or the interests of the group to which one belongs. Let us consider the main types of interest to include those pertaining to physical health and well-being, those directly economic or acquisitive, the intellectual, the social, the aesthetic, and the religious interests. Then let us ask: In what respects is the consumption of the young people of today best developed? least developed? Do the same conclusions hold for the American people as a whole?

THE ART OF CONSUMPTION AS CHOICES YIELDING LONG TIME SATISFACTIONS

The study of the way of attainment of the art of consumption may be carried one step further. The practice of consumption as an art necessitates foresight in recognizing those sources of satisfaction which have the most enduring good effects.

In this case the part played by intelligent thought is very obvious. If, with five dollars, I buy, let us say, a ten-course dinner, it is quite clear I get a certain definite satisfaction, which, however, has largely evaporated when I have finished my coffee; but if, on the other hand, I buy a ticket to a symphony concert it is probable that I take away from the hall a somewhat greater capacity for appreciating music than I had when I entered. I have bought, in other words, something more than two hours' pleasure; I have bought a permanent addition to my capacities for appreciating satisfaction. One can classify one's interests according to whether they yield satisfactions at the moment, as physical pleasures, or whether they continue to result in satisfactions long after the moment is gone. Interests in nature, in mental cultivation, in aesthetic appreciation, should properly fall in the latter class. Some satisfactions, notably the intellectual and the aesthetic, may never be realized at all unless they are planned for in advance.

The bearing of this on the education of the young is evident. Their future satisfactions are best served if they are placed in environments and subjected to disciplines adapted to the development of their latent capacities. It is true that we no longer believe in the omnipotence of education where native gifts are meagre, but even so the possibilities of education for developing appreciations are as yet hardly sensed. Consider, for example, that with all our talk of education in the United States, probably forty-nine out of fifty children are given the ugly comic supplements of our daily and Sunday newspapers. Only one city in the United States, Boston, has an art centre for children founded to develop within a beautiful environment the artistic appreciations of the young.

This principle necesssarily demands common sense in its application. I should not be sensible if I went hungry, or made my children go hungry, and spent all my money on art and symphony concerts. If after working hard a year I give up my vacation to buy the *Encyclopaedia Britannica* I am probably not so wise as I think. But the American people are not notably addicted to such excesses as these.

One adult can hardly attempt to prescribe for another those contacts and disciplines which will be most fruitful in developing latent capacities for enjoyment. One can only insist on the necessity of such contacts and disciplines, which every adult must choose for himself. At this point the demonstrable basis of the art of consumption passes into the realm of the undemonstrable justification of a "feeling" that this or that is best; and here every man, after applying his intelligence as wisely and as far as he may, had best follow the example of Socrates and do his own listening-in to the broadcasting station of the Universe.

The Quality of Pleasure: Joy

The art of consumption should mean not only the development of latent tastes. It should mean also a more difficult thing, the cultivation of satisfactions not only enduring but joyous. We do not wish to indulge in a philosophic or psychological controversy as to what extent pleasures are quantitative and to what extent they are qualitative, nor how far the same measuring stick, price, may be applied to both. The study of the art of consumption from any aspect involves more than price or money, of course. But even the science of consumption involves more than this. If one must have a seeing eye in order to appreciate a picture, so one must have an efficient stomach in order to appreciate cheese.

The ordinary man or woman knows well enough that there is a difference in the quality or intensity of satisfactions. Certain physical pleasures are very intense. We shall not linger on these, however, since the purely physical pleasures are usually the least difficult to achieve.

There is, however, a certain type of less easily definable pleasure to which even economists should not avoid paying their respects, the pleasure which is perhaps the keenest of all pleasures, the sense of great beauty, great reverence, great nobility, or great love. It is usually believed, perhaps, that such things are matters of character and cannot be bought. It would be degrading to think of buying them. So discussion of them is left to professional philosophers or to men clothed in the vestments of organized sanctity. Yet money does have something to do with achieving these things, in an indirect way. And, strange as it may seem, one can even spend his money so that something of these joys may eventually be purchased. It may be that their connection with economics has been neglected too long.

Let us consider the joy of recognizing beauty. In part this is, or is not, a birthright. In part it comes from cultivation and from being able to betake one's self where beautiful things are.

In this respect an hour in the Bargello is worth a lifetime on Gopher Prairie. There is a money cost even to the pure joy of music. Take the flash of keen pleasure one may feel in recognizing a bird. One must, however, be able to buy a trip to the park or the country, and it helps also to be able to afford a pair of binoculars. One sunrise in the Vale of Chamouni is worth many seen through the framework of an elevated railroad. It is not usually among reeking tenements that men exclaim:

> "To mingle with the Universe, and feel
> What I can ne'er express, but cannot all conceal."

Most of us are not so emancipated but that the setting has something to do with our joy.

There is no doubt but that the majesty of nature, which usually cannot be had without travel, and the majesty of cathedrals or churches, which are built at a price, foster the pure joy of religion and the sense of the presence of God. For love of humanity to have significance, one must know concretely what humanity is, which means that one must be able to mingle with it. Many men who thought they loved their fellows have had a rude shock when they joined the crowd pouring from the gates of a cotton mill or when they descended into a forecastle or padded beside the workers in a rice field. To be able to love one's kind under such circumstances and with such knowledge, that is an experience from which joy rises. And to accomplish this means either an expenditure of money or at least the foregoing of making money for a time.

Now it is indisputable that many of the world's most joyous men had little to spend for even the necessities of their physical body; and it is also indisputable that a man could spend a fortune in the pursuit of joy, and would not achieve it. But to make consumption an art does not mean that one spends to get joy. One seeks the most significant experiences, whatever they may be, and finally joy comes of them. It is not to degrade them to say that they can be planned for, that they are in part a result of how one spends one's money. Too long have we regarded money solely as the vile symbol of man's degradation in mines and factories, shops and stock exchanges. Such it is; it is also the symbol of his domination over the world, and a means by which he may enter into the songs of poets and the dreams of philosophers. To recognize that the development of consumption as an art lies within our capacities is to give a new impetus to living.

SPECIFIC GUIDANCE IN THE ART OF CONSUMPTION

Although we have not all become wise in consuming, we at least have the example of those who are wiser than we. The artist in consumption, as we have observed before, is also the wise, the happy, and the moral man—the man, in Stevenson's words, whose entrance to the room is as though another candle had been lighted; and there is probably a greater consensus of opinion as to who are our good examples than there is on any other subject which human beings discuss. Such men or their recorded lives are always before us to follow, if we do not know ourselves what our choices should be.

As a means of attaining an introduction to the art of consumption, the best general means is still undoubtedly through collegiate institutions. Long before there was any attention to the scientific side of consumption there was much interest in the art of living. In ancient society, and particularly in Athens, a young person who was anxious to live well sought out, if he could, the company of those people who had a reputation for serenity of disposition, breadth of interest, wisdom, and generosity of view. Such people did not give any direct instruction in how to live well. They talked with their students about philosophy, literature, art, politics, economics, or specific problems of the day. Their students gained from them a certain amount of information and a considerable ability to think. Above all, however, they acquired from their acquaintance with the wise certain standards that were often unconscious. Such contacts of teacher and pupil, master and disciple, were, as we know, the foundation out of which the liberal college arose.

Due to their emphasis on knowledge rather than on wisdom, today neither the technical nor even the liberal college is a company of choice spirits from whom a student seeks primarily to learn the art of living well; yet none the less such institutions offer the best approach available to most young people. What their faculties fail to give as individuals is given in part by the books of the wise, with certain of which students must necessarily become familiar; and in part by the sciences, by which more or less unconsciously is discovered the relationship of nature to men, and of men to each other.

As we have already seen in another connection, things can be taught by association that are not taught by word of mouth; and from association we learn more than we realize. We may even become transformed before we realize what has happened. Fortunately we all have the example of great men, the presence of nature, great books and great art, and consciously to seek these is to put ourselves in the way of being unconsciously directed by them.

CHAPTER XIX

ORGANIZED MOVEMENTS TO BETTER CONSUMPTION

"An Old Man had many Sons. . . . One day he called them around him, and producing a bundle of sticks, bade them each in turn to break it across. Each put forth all his strength, but the bundle resisted all their efforts. Then, cutting the cord which bound the sticks together, he told his Sons to break them separately. This was done with the greatest ease. 'See, my Sons,' exclaimed he, 'the power of unity!'" . . .—*Aesop's Fables.*

The control of consumption for the benefit of consumers comes in three ways: through the efforts of individuals acting singly or together without formal plans to improve the consumption of themselves or their neighbors; through privately organized efforts of groups to help themselves or society as a whole; and through governments. In this chapter we are concerned with the vast number of privately organized efforts to better consumption.

PROFESSIONAL SOCIETIES

The members of a professional society are usually engaged as individuals in the professional work which the society represents. Through organization such a society attempts to set up better standards in its field, extend publicity to it, encourage research in it, and otherwise to accomplish more than its members could accomplish as single individuals. Examples of such societies affecting consumption are the American Medical Association, the American Public Health Association, the American Dietetic Association, the American Home Economics Association, and the American Institute of Architects.

We spoke in Chapter XVII of the work of the American Medical Association in analyzing quacks and nostrums and warning the public against their use. It furthers the cause of public health also, along with the American Public Health Association.   The American Dietetic Association does specifically for foods what the American Home Economics Association seeks to do for all branches of household consumption: to determine superior standards and to encourage education in their application.   The American Institute of Architects furthers better town-planning as well as better architecture.

All these societies are the organizations of professional workers in the narrow sense of the word professional.   Students of history will remember the function of the craft guilds in the middle ages in setting up and enforcing standards for all kinds of goods made by ordinary manual workers.   In those days nearly all workmen had their guild, and poor workmanship and inferior materials were unprofessional in the broader sense of the word.   Bakers, brewers, drapers, candlemakers, all recognized their responsibility to their labor and hence to the consumer of it.   It may be that the practical success of this aspect of the craft guilds has been overestimated by those who love to hymn the past, but with changed management and changed control in industry, the burden of enforcing good standards of workmanship and materials is no longer the burden of the workman who makes the goods.   Spasmodic efforts to enlist workmen in setting up professional standards do, indeed, take place, but the modern wage system is not calculated to encourage them. The impetus must come from elsewhere.

GENERAL SOCIETIES

In addition to the professional societies there is a large number of organizations the membership of which is nonprofessional and may be open to anyone.   Some of these organizations exist for the express purpose of improving one special phase of consumption.   Others, founded perhaps primarily for social or other purposes, pay attention to one or more phases of consumption as an incidental part of their work.

In the first place, let us dispose of a number of societies organized to effect reforms in consumption, particularly reforms in the self-indulgence and assumed immoralities of other members of the body social. The efforts of the Anti-Saloon League and the Women's Christian Temperance Union are largely directed against the temptations of drinkers who are presumably not members of these organizations. New England has some rather curious survivals of this Puritanic attitude. They invoke the old Blue Laws through the Lord's Day League, which aims to preserve Sunday from the contamination of labor and wordly recreations, such as baseball; and through the Watch and Ward Society, which, along with some really protective functions, tries to exercise a vigilant oversight over the amusements and even the reading of New Englanders in general and Bostonians in particular.

Most general societies affecting consumption are of a different type. They do not stress reform so much as they stress constructive and progressive welfare. Of such are a number of the societies affiliated with the National Health Council, which serves as a clearing house and coördinating center for agencies interested in general health, physical and mental, and child hygiene. There are many of these.

The American Civic Association and the National Municipal League seek to make living conditions clean and attractive, to promote proper housing, to encourage the beautifying of streets and parks. The National Housing Association exists to improve urban, suburban, and rural housing conditions. The American Country Life Association works for better living conditions in the country.

The National Consumers' League is interested chiefly in labor conditions for women and minors, not primarily in consumption as such, although it has done some work in food problems.

General societies which exist for the purposes of improving consumption along aesthetic lines include many organizations affiliated with the American Federation of Arts. The National Motion Picture League encourages better motion pictures. Many little-theatre and repertory-theatre organizations are working for a better drama.

The Playground and Recreation Association of America is one example of organizations interested in promoting wholesome exercise, sports, and games. The Boy Scouts, which is an international association with troops in almost every civilized country, the Girl Scouts and Campfire Girls, and similar groups should be mentioned for their success in stimulating healthful recreation among young people.

In addition there are a large number of general organizations that pay some attention to certain phases of consumption along with their other activities. Perhaps the most conspicuous examples of these are the general women's clubs, which exist in practically every town and city of the country. They are very likely to have departments of home economics, music, drama, or gardening. In out-of-the-way places they are likely to be the only organization doing anything at all to improve standards of living. The National League of Women Voters studies living costs. Organizations of business men, such as Chambers of Commerce, Rotarians, Kiwanis, and Lions occasionally supply motion picture shows and band concerts at their own expense as a means for advertising their city: a certain interest in better recreation for the people may be present. One of the chief purposes of community centers is to encourage better recreation, and they may hold classes in housekeeping and home making.

The National Education Association and Mothers' and Parent-Teachers' Associations throughout the country further certain educational and recreative aspects of consumption as an incidental part of their work.

The welfare of negroes is served by the National Urban League, which has as one of its objects the improvement of housing conditions for colored people. It encourages also the provision of community activities for them.

PHILANTHROPIES

Philanthropies in the United States are many and varied. We shall speak only of those with a wide constructive influence in consumption. The Rockefeller Foundation organized "to promote the well-being of mankind throughout the world " has devoted itself chiefly to programs of public health and medical education. The work of its International Health Board and of its China Medical Board is well-known and significant.

The Russell Sage Foundation does most of its work in the field of social case work and charities, but has a department of recreation which is of interest to us here. The Russell Sage Foundation is responsible for one of the most interesting experiments in the United States to make homes and their surroundings beautiful. Forest Hills Gardens in the borough of Queens, New York City, sets the whole country an example of what intelligence in landscape- and house-planning can accomplish for a community of relatively well-to-do householders.

The efforts of some employers of labor to improve the living conditions of their workers are in part philanthropic. Provisions for the encouragement of saving, medical care, and recreation rooms and facilities, all should contribute to better consumption. Some firms provide homes for their workers at a standard rather higher than prevails in the community at large. A few firms have built attractive villages for their workers. The beautiful villages created by employers for English workers, as at Bourneville and at Port Sunlight, are known rather more widely than similar efforts of employers in the United States. One interesting American experiment by employers is the Indian Hill Garden Village in the surburbs of Worcester, Massachusetts. Because of lack of understanding between employers and employees, and for other reasons, such philanthropic work in general and such villages in particular have not always served the purposes for which they were intended, but the effort to set up better standards in itself is praiseworthy. The influence of these standards reaches farther than the employees of the company and the people of the immediate community.

Practically every town or city of size has its charitable organizations, some of which, as visiting housekeepers' associations and settlement houses, endeavor to instil better standards of consumption among the people they serve.

SOME IMPORTANT MOVEMENTS ABROAD

The United States seems to visitors to be crowded with organizations. "You have societies for everything!" exclaim our
foreign guests. In fact, by joining and by founding societies
we are able to use up some of our increasing income. At the
same time, having increasing income in the United States, we
need organizations or something else to help us dispose of it
intelligently.

In other countries, where there is a narrower margin between
income and subsistence, we should not expect there would be so
many and so varied organizations to help people spend the
surplus. There is often very little surplus to spend. At the
same time there is more need that people should be instructed
in basic economies and aided in getting and using necessities.
Unfortunately, too, foreign governments do not as a rule offer
free education and libraries so liberally as they are offered in the
United States. Home economics education for rural women,
which in the United States is handled through the extension
service of the state colleges, is in foreign countries largely in
the hands of private organizations, though they may be sub-
sidized by the government. And in many places abroad it is
private organizations that provide such reading rooms and libraries as are available.

Probably the majority of rural women in England, Scotland,
and Wales today have access to a Woman's Institute. There
are about four thousand of these institutes in England and
Wales. The movement began in Canada, where, however, it is
relatively less important than in England. Similar organizations exist in Ireland, Norway, Sweden, Denmark, and Finland,
in France and Belgium, where they are called Circles of Farmers'
Wives (Cercles des Fermières) and in most if not all other
countries of Europe. In Belgium the movement is wide-spread
and important.[1]

[1] See de Vuyst, P., *Women's Place in Rural Economy* (Hunter, Nora, trans.),
London, 1913.

What is done by these women's organizations? In the continental countries, where women are to a large extent agricultural producers, instruction in production and consumption goes hand in hand. So far as consumption is concerned, these organizations often furnish the only opportunity the women have or ever have had to obtain encouragement and education in foods, nutrition, and cooking, in health, housing, laundry work, and cleaning, in sewing and dressmaking, and in applied arts for the home. In addition, the institutes in Britain, at least, have lectures and classes in art, literature, music, and similar subjects. The so-called cultural aspects of life are considered as "practical" as instruction in home tinkering and cobbling.[1] The writer has visited these institutes in out-of-the-way places, where women came on foot over the hills five and six miles to attend the meetings. At one such institute on the borders of Dartmoor, the group, made up of shy dairy-maids, buxom farmers' wives, and gracious titled ladies, discussed with interest the author's talk on American standards of living, and made plans for contests and classes in public health work, cooking, and floriculture. "This is the only place we have," said one, "to learn how to do things better and to hear about the rest of the world."

Coöperative societies abroad contribute effectively to the education and recreation of the people, supplying facilities which among us are provided by the government. The need of libraries for working people was recognized by the Rochdale coöperative pioneers in 1843 and in all societies organized according to the original Rochdale plan a part of the profits is set aside for education. The writer has visited many English villages where the only library was that of the nearest coöperative society—sometimes several miles away—a library open, perhaps, only one evening every other week, but doubtless the more appreciated because it was directly provided by the people who used it.

[1] See Robertson Scott, J. W., *The Story of the Women's Institute Movement,* Idbury, Kingham, Oxon, 1925.

On the continent, community enterprises receive a larger share of consumers' coöperative profits than they do in England. The coöperative societies' headquarters, the *maisons du peuple*, are frequently community centers for reading and recreation.

The Youth Movement of Europe, particularly of Germany, is a spirit rather than an organization which has deeply affected the character of the recreation of youth and has stirred it to protest against meaningless conventions in many lines. "Away with artificiality in dress and in amusement! Let us cultivate physical good spirits and the enjoyment of nature!" is the cry of these enthusiastic *Wandervögel* (birds of passage). They would knock from their pedestals the smug gods of the middle-aged.

These illustrations of foreign movements are given because they are different from our enterprises in the United States. There are, of course, various organizations abroad which perform functions similar to those of our professional, general, and philanthropic associations.[1]

[1] An interesting series of articles which discuss organizations for the improvement of leisure abroad is to be found in the *International Labour Review*, IX (February, April, and June, 1924).

CHAPTER XX

GOVERNMENT AID AND INTERVENTION IN CONSUMPTION

"The sacred truth that the greatest happiness of the greatest number is the foundation of morals and of legislation."—JEREMY BENTHAM, *Works*.

Organized government is a potential source of great influence in consumption. Government may act indirectly, by providing the means of educating consumers to live in the most effective way, or by making possible experiment and research by which the best science and technology of consumption may be determined. It may act directly by offering consumers goods and services cheaply or free of cost; or by prohibiting or regulating consumption believed to be harmful. Its theoretical possibilities for intelligent guidance in consumption are almost unlimited. Reformers have dreamed of utopias where all consumption would be perfectly regulated by government. We here, however, are chiefly concerned with what organized government actually has done, and is now doing, for consumers.

EDUCATION

The part that government plays in education is so well known to every one of us that it is hardly necessary to do more than to mention it. It is often said that a belief in education is the real religion of the people of the United States. It is the one characteristic of their culture which has remained in emphasis and importance practically unchanged since early colonial days.

In the United States almost every child who wants it can secure practically free education through school, college, and university. But free or low-cost educational opportunities are

not limited to the formal routine of schools. Individual municipalities, counties, and the state and federal governments provide
or assist in providing part-time special education for pre-school
children, for immigrants, for housewives, and for other groups;
and part-time general education is offered freely to almost anyone who wants it by extension work, correspondence courses,
and even by radio.

Some of this education deals directly with problems of material consumption, as through courses of home economics, which
are of immediate practical use. All general education, however,
is of significance in connection with consumption, since its
aim is to develop capacities for the good life, which ultimately
means a wiser use of the opportunities offered in the material
world.

EXPERIMENT AND RESEARCH IN CONSUMPTION

Experimental and research work done by governments in the
past has more generally had the producer rather than the consumer in view; but of late, with the increasing complexity of
consumption and the advancement of those sciences from which
consumption may directly profit, there has been a new emphasis
on research and experiments to aid the consumer. The most
outstanding example of this new emphasis was the organization
of the Bureau of Home Economics of the Department of Agriculture. The chief purpose of this Bureau is to improve the
science and technology of domestic consumption.

Certain governmental activities intended primarily as aids
to production may at times touch the consumer as directly as
they touch the producer. The Bureau of Fisheries of the Department of Commerce has done something to determine the
nutritive values of fish and to educate the taste of the consumer
for new sea-foods. In Chapter XVII we mentioned the Bureau
of Standards of the same department, which is aiding the
technology of consumption by leading a movement for standardization and simplified practice in the production of goods.

The Children's Bureau and the Women's Bureau in the

Department of Labor touch the problems of consumption for children and for women, both by way of research and experiment and by education and information service. In Chapter XXIV we shall have occasion to speak of the work of the Bureau of Labor Statistics in the same department, which makes studies of cost of living throughout the country.

GOODS AND SERVICES SUPPLIED BY GOVERNMENTS

It would be possible, of course, for a government to collect all the goods resulting from the productive activity of its people and dispense these goods to them again for use, as some central authority judged best. Such was the case under the Inca government in Peru, to which we have already made reference, but this is altogether exceptional. In Rome it was customary for the emperors to provide free grain and games for the populace out of the rich revenues of the provinces. This was not, however, for the sake of rendering a real service to the people but was primarily a political device to win support and, as we know, it resulted in degrading the population. In both ancient and modern times monarchs or governments have occasionally provided music or entertainment for the people. When the expenditure involved is not great such offerings may be good politics, but the idea has been more generally to put the people in a good mood rather than to further their welfare.

Under all modern governments, of course, some means are furnished for taking care of paupers and others who because of some special misfortune are handicapped in providing for themselves. We are not concerned, however, with such cases as these, which apply to only one group or class in the community. So the provision of mothers' and old age pensions is one made to overcome certain particular social or economic handicaps. These cases should be discussed under the head of poor relief and social legislation rather than under the head of government as an agency of influence in consumption.

At the present time the free or low-cost goods and services provided by modern governments, and particularly by the government of the United States, federal, state, and local, fall into two main groups. The first consists of those goods and services which very obviously serve certain pressing physical needs, and in particular it consists of free medical advice and treatment in communicable diseases. The object here is not only to aid the sufferer but to keep him from spreading his complaint. This group of services is not so large as one logically might expect: frequently, of course, the responsibility for contraction of a communicable disease rests not on the individual but on conditions in his community; and frequently the menace of a case of communicable disease is as great or greater to the community than it is to the sufferer, hence we should logically expect the community to bear the main burden of cost and care.

The second and much larger group which governments furnish free or at low cost is made up of desirable or necessary goods and services which individuals can with most difficulty provide for themselves or which business enterprise is not likely to provide. Some of these are directly educational, as the schools, which have already been mentioned. In this second group fall the postal system and the road system and, in some countries, the telephone, telegraph, and radio service. The postoffice and the roads we consider to be so obviously the function of our government that we hardly need to mention them.

The parks of the country, local, state, and national, do, however, deserve particular attention. With the increase of prosperity in the country which affords means to travel, and with the wide ownership of automobiles, our parks, and particularly our national parks, have come to be used more than even those who struggled to establish them would have dreamed possible.

We have in the United States 51 national parks and monuments, of which the largest is Yellowstone. In the season of 1926 the total number of visitors, most of whom came by automobile, amounted to nearly three million: 2,797,840 people [1] or an average of one visit for every 44 people in the country.

[1] United States Department of the Interior, Annual Report of the Secretary of the Interior for year ended June 30, 1927, p. 131.

At this rate, the average would amount to more than one visit for every citizen during his lifetime. The annual number nearly doubled in the five years previous to 1926. The huge number visiting the parks is the more surprising since there is only one national park in the East, on Mt. Desert island in Maine. All the other parks and monuments are located where the population is thinnest, west of the Mississippi.

While the idea of the desirability of great public parks can hardly be accredited to any one person, one of the earliest and most significant expressions of this idea came in connection with the exploration of the Yellowstone region in 1870. General Chittenden, the historian of the park, describes [1] the members of the Washburn expedition sitting around their camp fire at the junction of the Firehole and Gibbon Rivers, near the present West Yellowstone entrance. They had just visited the geyser regions.

"It was suggested that it would be a 'profitable speculation' to take up land around the various objects of interest. The conversation had not proceeded far on these lines when one of the party, Cornelius Hedges, interposed and said that private ownership of that region, or any part of it, ought never to be countenanced; but that it ought to be set apart by the government and forever held to the unrestricted use of the people."

This view found immediate acceptance with the others, and they vigorously set about to bring it to pass. The act establishing the park was passed in 1872. Before this date in other parts of the world large areas had been set aside for privileged classes, nobles and monarchs. Students of English history remember the enormous expanses of forest which William the Norman, following practice on the continent, had set aside for his personal pleasure in hunting. The New Forest alone contained 17,000 acres for the exclusive enjoyment of the King. The act establishing Yellowstone Park marked an innovation in the policies of governments. It was the first time a vast tract of territory had been dedicated to the use and enjoyment of all the people.

[1] *The Yellowstone National Park*, Cincinnati, 1914, p. 90.

The state park idea as a movement was inaugurated in 1921. The third annual conference on state parks in 1923 expressed as its purpose in part

> "To urge upon our governments, local, county, state, and national, the acquisition of land and water areas suitable for recreation and preservation of wild life . . . until eventually there shall be public parks, forests, and preserves within easy access of all the people of our Nation." [1]

Progress in the state park idea has been very rapid. Metropolitan and municipal parks and parkways are old institutions and every progressive city has a department devoted to parks and playgrounds.

It is obvious that with the increase of population and the settlement of isolated areas in the country, it is of the greatest advantage to set off park areas as early as possible, since the difficulties and expense grow greater from year to year. The potentialities of our parks for giving health and recreation and for spreading appreciation of nature and of natural beauty among our people are tremendous; the actual use of the parks is most encouraging.

The national park movement in other countries has received added impetus since the war, and there are now ten parks in Sweden, several in France, one in Switzerland, one in Italy, one in Argentina, and plans are in progress in Japan and Poland. Canada and Australia stand in the forefront of the movement outside the United States.

Almost every community in the United States has either a public library of its own, or has access to a public library of some sort. Travelling libraries serve rural districts. The museums of art and natural history in our larger cities are usually supported at least in part from public funds. Many municipalities furnish free entertainment, particularly during the warm weather, in the form of band concerts, motion pictures, and fireworks.

It is clear that all the services which have been mentioned

---

[1] United States Department of the Interior, Report of the Director of the National Park Service for the year ended June 30, 1923, p. 17.

are the sort of services through which a government may well serve its people. They are services in which almost everyone is interested, and which are generally educational; services, too, which can be produced most economically if provided on a large scale, and which, for the most part, are nowhere adequately covered by private enterprise.

Other nations provide about the same things for their people except as they are handicapped by lack of funds. Public libraries, for instance, are usually regarded as luxuries in most countries outside of the United States. On the other hand, some nations go further than the United States in providing free or low-cost services along certain lines. In Germany, for instance, public authorities take much more of a hand in providing music and other entertainment free or at low cost. In England, the national government controls all radio programs, and radio owners pay a small fee for the service.

English government authorities are conspicuous for the assistance they give the people in housing, both by way of setting up standards and by providing houses at low rents. Land and housing conditions in England are quite different from those prevailing in the United States.

The most conspicuous modern case of government aid in consumption is afforded by Russia. In favoring the provision of free or low-cost goods and services by the government, the socialist, communist, or syndicalist point of view is looking primarily toward a more equal distribution of income; but the idea of a more intelligent consumption is sometimes present as well. Under the Soviet system, for instance, the motion picture industry is in government hands and the producer is permitted to produce as his artistic sense guides him, without having to consider the "market."

Cost of Services Rendered by Government in the United States

Per capita expenditures of our government are larger than per capita taxes and tariffs, for the government has income from

other sources than these. The National Industrial Conference
Board estimates that in 1923 the average per capita expenditures of governments federal, state, and local in the United
States were $91. Of this the federal government dispensed
about one-third, state governments about one-sixth, local government about one-half.[1]

TABLE VII

PERCENTAGE EXPENDITURES OF THE UNITED STATES GOVERNMENT FOR
VARIOUS PURPOSES FOR THE FISCAL YEAR ENDED JUNE 30, 1927

(United States Department of the Treasury)

Ordinary civil functions		
General government	2.7	
Internal security	2.0	
Development and regulation	3.3	
Public domain, works and industries	7.3	
Local governments and Indians	1.4	
Foreign relations	.4	
Total		17.1
Military functions		31.8
Public debt		51.1
Total		100.0

How much of this rather large per capita expenditure goes
for consumers' services? In the case of the federal government
a very small percentage of all expenditures served consumers
directly, as is shown in Table VII.[2] War expenditures, including military functions and payments and interest on the national debt, incurred largely for war purposes, accounted in
1927 for 83% of all federal expenditures. About one-tenth
of this huge expense is offset by payments of foreign governments to us in return for their war debts. Of the remaining 17%, the major part goes for the general functions of
government and services to producers. Roughly speaking,
about 5% of federal government expenditures serves consumers directly.

A much larger proportion of the expenditures of local govern-

---

[1] National Industrial Conference Board, *Tax Burdens and Public Expenditures*, New York, 1925, pp. 32, 33.
[2] Annual Report of the Secretary of the Treasury on the State of the Finances, op. cit., p. 18.

ments serves consumers directly, since the main expenses of education and of highways are borne by local governments. The proportion of total state and local expenditures serving consumers directly is, however, probably not much more than 50%.[1]

If we combine the expenditures of federal, state, and local governments for all purposes, the results are roughly as follows:

Direct services to consumers	35 per cent
Military defence and past wars	25 per cent
General functions and miscellaneous	40 per cent

Of the $91 per capita expenditure in the United States, therefore, about $32 pays for direct services to consumers, about $23 pays for military expense and past wars, and about $36 pays for the administration of government, police protection, services to producers, the care of wards of the state, etc.

The Protection of the Consumer and Sumptuary Laws

The fourth means by which government directly influences consumption is through laws to regulate or prohibit the sale of certain things.

Such laws fall logically into two groups, those to protect the consumer against deception and fraud, and against buying harmful substances without knowledge thereof, and sumptuary laws properly so-called, the aim of which is to prevent the consumer from consuming things believed to be harmful to him, even though they are what he wants.

Everyone agrees that some laws in the first group are as necessary as the police service. The government of the United States protects the consumers' interests through the Federal Pure Food and Drugs Act of 1906, the Misbranding Act and others to which we referred in Chapter XVII. Organizations in the Department of Agriculture are in charge of food law enforcement and meat inspection. The Bureau of Markets in the same Department serves the consumer indirectly through its work on marketing standards.

[1] Cf. National Industrial Conference Board, op. cit., p. 42. Of course only a part of highway expenditures is chargeable as a consumer service.

State, county, and local governments more specifically protect
the interests of the consumer in buying by specifying standards
of dairy and other products, and in requiring certain minimum
provisions for sanitary marketing.

Such protective laws, both federal and other, are usually
merely safeguarding measures and seek to prevent abuse
rather than to build up ideal or superior standards. In the
past, sumptuary laws were made primarily for one or the other
of two purposes: first to maintain standards of decency, particularly in dress; second to keep fast lines of demarcation
between social classes, as by prohibiting the newly rich bourgeoisie from imitating the consumption of the nobility. The
second type of law is particularly characteristic of periods of
rising economic prosperity. Sometimes such laws were passed
to compel people to patronize home production.[1]

In modern industrial society sumptuary laws for the purpose
of enforcing social distinctions are discredited. Sumptuary
laws or regulations to maintain standards of decency are, however, fairly common. We have laws or ordinances as to the
extent to which the body shall be covered in public places,
particularly at beaches. We have laws governing the sale and
transmission through the mails of publications believed to be
indecent or obscene; and laws under which the proper authorities may suppress dramatic or other performances which they
believe are polluting. In the United States standards of so-
called decency vary much in different cities. In Boston, for
instance, municipal regulations prohibit the sale of a number
of popular books, which Bostonians may easily order by mail
from New York.

In present day society, particularly in the United States,
however, a third type of sumptuary law is receiving very considerable attention. This type prohibits or regulates consumption of goods not on grounds of decency—where the foundation

---

[1] See Baldwin, F. E., "Sumptuary Legislation and Personal Regulation in
England," *Johns Hopkins University Studies*, v. 44; and Greenfield, K. R.,
"Sumptuary Law in Nürnberg," *Johns Hopkins University Studies*, v. 36.

of the protest is moral—but on grounds chiefly of health or efficiency. The prohibition of the sale of opium and other harmful drugs is an example of this, but the most outstanding example is of course the Volstead Act, which prohibits the legal sale of intoxicating liquors to the general public. Some of the same people who were interested in pushing the Volstead Act are now turning their attention to the prohibition of the sale of tobacco, and particularly of cigarettes.

The chief good argument for laws to compel people to desist from practices deleterious to their morals or health is that such laws educate and eventually do away with desire for the evil that is legislated against. They work themselves out of business. But if a majority or even a significant minority is opposed to a particular restriction, the restriction may have a contrary effect, and even increase the desire for the thing prohibited. Then the law may be neither obeyed nor enforced.

Sumptuary laws seem at first an easy way of improving consumptive standards; their efficacy, however, is probably usually overrated, and sometimes they cause such resentment as to do actual harm. They can be really successful only when most of the people are so wholeheartedly behind them that they are able to lead any recalcitrant minority chiefly by enthusiasm and good will. In a democratic country their success depends upon education. When most of the people have been educated to the desirability of a sumptuary restriction, the law may aid in the education of the rest, and in preventing the rising generation from acquiring injurious interests.

The League of Nations and International Consumption

There are certain problems in regulating consumption that cannot be effectively handled by legislation within any one country alone. A country, for instance, that desires to prohibit the manufacture and sale of a particular commodity believed to be harmful may find itself greatly handicapped by importations of this commodity from some other country.

In the middle of the last century a Chinese province sought to prevent the use of opium and to prohibit its cultivation. The British government, however, was able to introduce so much opium from India as to render the Chinese effort of no avail. We all know what difficulties we had with Prohibition when some states had it and others did not. Now when we have a nation-wide act liquor is smuggled into our harbors and across our borders. As international trade increases, so such difficulties increase. It is thus desirable that there should be some agency for international regulation of trade in prohibited goods or services.

The League of Nations through various committees has been making a beginning toward a solution of some of the worst difficulties that have so far been faced. The work of the opium committee of the League is one of the best known parts of the League's work. The Committee is investigating the world's need of this drug for medical and scientific use, with the object that self-indulgent private consumption shall in a few years be completely suppressed. The League is also engaged in attempting to prevent international traffic in women and children and in obscene publications.

The League of Nations is likewise making a beginning in the provisions of certain services from which all peoples and nations can benefit. Through its health organization it is working for the standardization of remedies, for the universal provision of sera and vaccines, and for the control of epidemics: matters obviously of international interest, which one nation alone can hardly take care of. Experience in 1920 taught us that customs boundaries present no barriers to influenza.

The League's committee on intellectual coöperation is improving the technology by which new discoveries of scientists and others are made available for the world.

It is significant that the League of Nations has already concerned itself with such matters of human consumption. These far-sighted views give us a glimpse into a future where safety and economy in the consumption of any one nation shall both alike demand international good faith and international coöperation.

PART V

THE CONSUMPTION OF CULTURES, NATIONS AND GROUPS

CHAPTER XXI

WHAT IS A CULTURE TYPE?

"The world which we ordinarily think of as real is an arbitrary selection from experience."—W. R. INGE, *Outspoken Essays, First Series*, XI.

We all know the story of the seven blind men who tried to describe an elephant. The man who got hold of his tail said he was like a rope, the man who put his hand on his side said he was like a wall, the man who grasped his leg said he was like a column; and so on. The story is an illustration of the familiar doctrine of philosophers, expressed in the quotation from Dean Inge at the head of this chapter: our perceptions and conceptions cannot extend beyond our own personal explorations, and even within these we are limited by our pre-perceptions and our preconceptions.

Now what is true for men as individuals, what is true for you and for me as separate human beings, is true also for men as groups. You and I are limited, first in separate ways because we are two individuals, let us say, Pericles and Aspasia; we are limited also, in a common way, because we are members of a group of narrow experience living in Athens in the fifth century B.C. In the same way, today, we have Michael O'Brien, contractor, and Julius Kleinberg, men's ready to wear, both living in Chicago. Mr. O'Brien and Mr. Kleinberg as individuals obviously bring different points of view to life, and might find themselves in hearty disagreement on certain aspects of it. But Mr. O'Brien and Mr. Kleinberg would make common cause against the ideas and customs of Japanese or Filipinos. "Say," we can hear them exclaim in the same breath, "We won't stand for any of this nonsense. We've got to protect our institutions."

Michael O'Brien and Julius Kleinberg would have some

sympathies as citizens of Chicago, and more as citizens of the
United States; but we are interested in them chiefly as common
exponents of one great culture type, attaining its purest form,
no doubt, in the United States, but extending over most of the
Western world—over Canada, and at least partially over Mexico, Central and South America, over most of Europe, over
South Africa, even over Australia.

Now we must confess at once that we are likely to get into
trouble when we attempt to delimit definite cultures. More
than one good ship has gone on the rocks here. So for the time
being we shall not attempt to mark them off, but merely to cast
some light on the general nature of a culture.

A Culture More than a Sum Total of Interests

In our first chapter occurred the following words:

"A 'culture' is not a mere sum of beliefs, practices, and goods and
services consumed. It is beliefs, practices, goods, and services linked
and bound together first by a mutual dependence on some common
point of view, and second by a mutual interdependence on one another. A culture, in other words, is organic."

Now up to the present we have been analyzing culture and
consumption into their elements rather than treating cultures
as a whole, and it is right that we should have done so. It is
well to understand the separate influences—the geographic
environment, heredity, the state of social and economic development, and so on—to begin with. For some purposes we might,
of course, stop here. Surely if there were only one culture in
the world, these separate and discrete elements affecting it
would be all we should ever inquire about.

The man on the street, who is familiar with no peoples but
his own, has no curiosity about cultures. He has nothing to
start him thinking. Carlyle's healthy countryman never knew
he had a digestive system, and the man on the street does not
know that he has a culture. It is only when we come to compare
the modes of life and thought of peoples remote from one another
in time and space that we begin to see something in cultures

which has not been accounted for in our previous analysis, and which piques our curiosity.

Although in mathematics it is axiomatic that the total is merely the sum of its parts, in the sphere of life no one would claim that a human being is the sum total of 208 bones plus nerves plus blood vessels plus muscles, and so on. A culture is not a living creature in the sense that human beings are; there is, nevertheless, a sort of resemblance. The meaning of a culture cannot be understood merely by studying the separate elements that enter into it. The underlying idea or ideas must be grasped first.

OUR DIFFICULTIES IN UNDERSTANDING THE MODES OF LIVING OF OTHER PEOPLES

It would be a very superficial student who could claim to be able to understand Chinese culture and its attendant consumption by studying the geographic environment, the physical heredity, the social contacts, the state of the industrial arts, and so on, in China. Chinese culture is not a sum of tea plus jade plus rice plus paper lanterns, plus Shanghai cotton mills plus a certain type of art; nor is it even the sum of all these plus the recorded teachings of Lao-Tse, Confucius, and the rest. All of these things we can trace to their apparent sources and study them separately; but no such analytic study would tell us what they mean in the life of the Chinese, or what they really "are." In some cases, as particularly with physical necessities, it is obvious why they came in, but in many other cases we have no way of knowing, from our analytical study, why one thing rather than another was taken up, nor why things happen to be used in the particular way the Chinese use them. For instance, we are told that the Chinese invented gunpowder, but did not use it for firearms. They used it for fireworks and firecrackers. Why did they use it chiefly in one way and we use it in another?

One might, in fact, spend his lifetime studying the separate and discrete influences lying back of Chinese consumption and yet never understand it in more than a superficial and mechanistic sense. From such an analytical study as we have outlined in our earlier chapters he would have a good background for approaching the study of Chinese culture, but no more. He could give an explanation of the probable source of the material elements in the culture, but he could not understand the significance of the elements, taken either individually or together. From such a study he could not possibly know what it was all about.

The significance of basic differences in culture types is a matter of relatively recent recognition among students. This is natural, for it requires a detached point of view which we are only now beginning to achieve.

It is universally recognized, however, that in actual life, people of different cultures usually have difficulty in understanding one another in an intellectual way. The more different the cultures, the greater is the difficulty. For instance, Westerners who go to India or China frequently speak of the attitudes and actions of Indians or Chinese as "incomprehensible" and send home such comments as: "They think backwards"; "We are unable to meet on any common intellectual basis"; "They seem wilfully to misunderstand everything I say."

This failure of persons of one culture to understand those of another is not necessarily due to mere superficial differences of appearance or bearing or even to modes of expression. In many cases its source is profound. A significant book [1] not long since sought to prove that, so far as primitive cultures are concerned, the thought processes there are different from ours. It is probable, however, that it is thought forms rather than processes that are different. The following observation recorded by the distinguished ethnologist, W. H. R. Rivers,[2] illustrates the point well.

[1] Lévy-Bruhl, Lucien, *Les fonctions mentales dans les sociétés inférieures,* Paris, 1910.
[2] *Psychology and Ethnology,* New York, 1926, pp. 40–41. His whole discussion, pp. 36–50, of "The Primitive Conception of Death" is worth reading in this connection.

"Death is so striking and unique an event that if one had to choose something which must have been regarded in essentially the same light by mankind at all times and in all places, I think one would be inclined to choose it in preference to any other, and yet I hope to show that the primitive conception of death among such people as the Melanesians is different, one may say radically different, from our own.

". . . On looking up any Melanesian vocabulary you will find that some form of the word *mate* is given as the equivalent of dead, and that dead is given as the meaning of *mate*. As a matter of fact, such statements afford a most inadequate expression of the real conditions. It is true that the word *mate* is used for a dead man, but it is also used for a person who is seriously ill and likely to die, and also often for a person who is healthy but so old that, from the native point of view, if he is not dead, he ought to be.

"I well remember an early experience in the island of Eddystone in the Solomons when a man whom I knew well was seriously ill. I heard that he had been visited by a great native physician, who was shortly expected to return, and presently there came along the narrow bush-path the usual procession in single file, headed by the doctor who, in answer to my inquiries about his patient, mournfully shook his head and uttered the words, '*Mate, mate.*' I naturally supposed that the end had come, only to learn that all he meant was that the man was still very seriously ill. As a matter of fact he recovered. . . .

"It is clear that it is wholly wrong to translate *mate* as dead or to regard its opposite *toa* as the equivalent of living. These people have no categories exactly corresponding to our 'dead' and 'living,' but have two different categories of *mate* and *toa*, one including with the dead the very sick and the very aged, while the other excludes from the living those who are called *mate*."

Oswald Spengler points out a similar significant contrast between classical and modern Western culture. "Infinite space," he says,[1] "is the ideal that the Western soul has always striven to find, and to see immediately actualized, in its world-around;" but "the whole Classical world never expended one word on it, and indeed did not even possess a word by which the problem could be exactly outlined." A footnote adds: "In the true Classical literature, the idea not being there, there was no necessity for a word to describe it." In the same way, he declares that the classical culture had no understanding of the

[1] *The Decline of the West* (Atkinson, C. F., trans.), New York, 1926, p. 175.

notion of our "will." [1] And as they did not have our concepts, so we do not have theirs. The Greek *sophrosyne*, usually translated self-control, carries a far more positive idea than our word self-control, for *sophrosyne* was an expansive word, leading out into culture building. Nothing like a proper idea of the Indian Nirvana can be gained without understanding something of the Indian culture first. Scholars have always declared that translations of the literatures of peoples remote from ourselves could never carry the idea of the original; the reason is, of course, that there are no abstract "things " but only attitudes; and we must get the attitude before we can understand the word.

The art of other cultures often seems incomprehensible to us likewise. What, for instance, is the impression on the mind of the Westerner the first time he sees a Chinese painting of a landscape? It seems at first childish, then over-sophisticated, and finally simply different. We get along better with Greek art, but we produce nothing in the true Greek manner, nor could we enjoy it in the Greek manner if it were produced. The idea of form without content is alien to us, and we must always put something inside. The Lincoln Memorial in Washington is a good example of an attempt to be Greek; but by the visitors who crowd into it to read the Gettysburg address it is made even less Greek than it was left by the architect. To the classic Greek form meant something more than it does to us, that is all. A temple "empty " to us would not be empty to him in the same way.

Our difficulties in understanding the music of other cultures are perhaps even greater than our difficulties in understanding their art. Music is, unfortunately, no universal language; the strains of the bagpipe sound quite differently on the two banks of the Tweed. Spengler remarks [2] of Greek music: "the few fragments that remain suffice to show us that the sensuous charm of this art is something outside our comprehension," and goes on: "Equally incomprehensible to us is Chinese music;

[1] *The Decline of the West*, p. 310.
[2] Op. cit., pp. 227, 228.

in which, according to educated Chinese, we are never able to distinguish grave from gay. Vice versa, to the Chinese all the music of the West without distinction is *march music*. . . . Such is the impression that the rhythmic dynamic of our life makes upon the accentless Tao of the Chinese soul. . . . We ourselves have accent in our blood and therefore do not notice it."

These illustrations have perhaps carried us far afield, but they do make clear the fact that ideas which seem axiomatic and feelings which seem obvious to the people of one culture may be completely unintelligible to the people of others. Cultures, in other words, are distinguished from one another not only by the separate interests within them, but more fundamentally by the different attitudes toward life of the people.

These attitudes toward life may be and in most cases are of profound significance in determining what the consumption of a group shall be. As we have previously said, they influence what interests will be taken up, to what extent they will be taken up, and how, when taken up, they shall be used. The attitude colors the interest and gives to it its life.

Every one of those external influences which we have been discussing in our previous chapters exerts its power within a more or less closed circuit; its power is limited by the attitude of the group toward life. Even the important factor of deliberate intelligence, to which we devoted six chapters, is itself almost altogether a function of the fundamental cultural attitude of the group and dependent upon it. "There cannot occur to anyone a thought which is not implicit in the general possibilities of the spirit of the age." [1] Even in our most abstract thinking we are the children of our *Zeitgeist* and *Kulturgeist*.

It would not be true, of course, to say that every one of the interests of a group is influenced by the cultural attitude of the group, any more than it would be true to say that the interests of animals presuppose a cultural attitude on their part. For

[1] Keyserling, Count Hermann, *The World in the Making*, op. cit., p. 216.

instance, whatever their culture, men have to eat; and it was not cultural attitude that determined the fact that they ate rice in the valley of the Yangste-Kiang and maize in the valley of the Mississippi. This was an accident of geographic environment; and, in general, the closer are interests to the basic necessities of physical sustenance, the less they are determined by cultural attitude, for physical sustenance itself is pre-cultural. Yet even the cases of rice and maize afford us, in another way, an illustration of our point. It is the cultural attitude that has determined to what extent and how rice and its products and maize and its products are being used today. Rice in the valley of the Yangste-Kiang remains rice, but maize in the valley of the Mississippi is not only maize but oil, syrup, sugar, and even paper, as industrial research provides a means of transforming the original product. That is to say, the state of production and the development of markets are not things-in-themselves but are bound up with the prevailing culture attitude.

CULTURE TYPE DEFINED

In Chapter II we suggested that at the dawn of man's life on this planet the first expression of the new humanity may not have been in connection with utilitarian activities but in connection with speculative thought. Man was the first animal to realize that something about this universe of ours is left to the imagination. He was the first animal to ask *Why?* Of course the low-browed hairy creature did not give his speculations the elegant expression of a nineteenth-century German philosopher; he perhaps gave them no expression at all, but he was vaguely troubled. All the earliest cultures show us this. Nature, suffering, dissolution,—he asked himself, in his poor stumbling way, what these were and how their apparent evils could be averted. In his poor stumbling way he tried to avert their apparent evils himself. From the very beginning, so nearly as we can tell, man was concerned with religion, magic, superstition, call it what you will.

At first he made charms, fetishes, and other sacred objects

and invented tabus to invoke good and avert evil. Later, when
he had amassed more experience, he gave his speculations a
maturer form.   A comparative study of cultures shows that
there are certain modes of thinking or feeling characteristic of
each; each culture has its own philosophy, its own way of attempting to deal with the mysteries of life.   Such modes of
thinking or feeling characteristic of a culture appear not only
in one but in every important aspect of it: not only in its formal
philosophy and religion, but in its politics, its art, architecture,
literature, its social relationships, its industry, its ordinary
everyday modes of passing the time.   Their influence, in other
words, is pervasive.   In every case there is a definite relationship between the nature of man's attitude toward the mystery
and the character, significance, or extent of his consumption.

These characteristic modes of thinking and feeling determine
to some degree what of the various interests offered by the
general environment shall be taken up; and in themselves they
in part provide the forces that determine to what degree certain
of the social and economic influences we have already discussed
shall prevail.   That is to say, even a merely analytical study of
consumption would not be complete without reference to these
fundamental modes of thinking and feeling.

To us, however, they have a more important aspect here.
They determine in part what of the eligible interests possible
shall be taken up, but even more important is their function of
determining to what extent these interests shall be taken up,
and how, once taken up, they shall be used.   Through these
fundamental modes of thinking and feeling interests receive
their vitality.   Consumption is the study not of mere goods and
services in themselves, but of the uses to which goods and services are put, of the way goods and services are translated into
life.   The fundamental modes of thinking and feeling are the
synthesizing elements in a culture; they furnish, therefore, the
only bases by which cultures *as a whole* can be compared.

For our purposes, therefore, a culture type may be defined as
a mode of thinking or feeling which interprets the significance

of consumption in terms of man's way of meeting the ultimate problems of life.

THE GROWTH OF BASIC CULTURE TYPES

How culture attitudes get started and differentiated is a question about which we know little and into which we cannot enter here. But however once started and differentiated, we can point out, in the light of our previous chapter on the mechanism of interest, Chapter III, how they grow, expand, and develop their potential ramifications.

There has never yet been, it appears, an all-inclusive attitude toward life. We cannot, in fact, comprehend such. All world-views are partial. Of these various partially comprehending attitudes, any one that was once achieved by a people, any one that had once taken hold, would stand a good chance of continuing until something catastrophic happened to dislodge it. As we saw in Chapter III, the human tendency is to save its energy by clinging to the familiar. It expands what is known, and even its so-called novelties tend to be related to the old ways. Even when the introduction of a new interest involves no direct competition with the old, it is hard for it to get in. Where, as in the case of a world attitude, the introduction of the new involves the replacement of the old or its synthesis into something immensely more comprehensive—as the union of two world views would be—it will be seen that it would have almost no chance at all. Thus the world attitude once established, whatever it is, is related to all aspects of life and continually refined in its applications, just as in Chapter III we saw a material trait expanding into a complex and stimulating continually more and more refined applications of itself. As the human mind economizes its energy, so the social group creates and extends its institutions.

CHAPTER XXII

WHAT IS WORTH WHILE TO CONSUME?
THE DIFFERENT ANSWERS OF SIX CULTURES

"Then go forth, my son
Dare the wide seas and brave the stormy tracks
To Indian islands now beyond thy ken.
The men who greet thee, mark! so shalt thou learn
Strange manners, stranger thoughts: what man has been,
What man perchance may be."—*Old Play*.

For the lack of a better method of interpreting life we must always be jumping from analysis and comparison to synthesis. We must study the parts but not forget the whole; we must study the whole, but to do so we must analyze it. We have said that a culture was more than a sum total of interests, nevertheless we studied interests. We now say that life is more than a sum total of cultures. Nevertheless we study cultures. At the same time we must keep them in their place.

There is a good deal of argument nowadays about the definition of a culture and just how many cultures there are and have been in the world. What a man has to say on the latter point will depend very much on what aspects of cultural life he is most interested in. It seems impossible to separate cultures exactly in a way that will be satisfactory for all purposes. Cultures are not sharply defined; they are always flowing into one another on the borders of time and space, and sometimes one is almost altogether absorbed by another.

Take, for instance, Roman culture. Is that a separate type? Is it the final aspect of Mediterranean culture, superseding the Egyptian, the Minoan, the Babylonian, and the Greek? Or is it to be linked merely with the Greek? Or, by chance, is it the beginning of modern Western culture; or of mediaeval culture? One might conceivably answer the question in each of these ways, depending on what purposes the analysis was wanted for. All analyses have something artificial about them, ours among the rest. As we have said, nothing with a vitality of its own is merely the sum of its parts, however cleverly you classify the parts.

We are studying cultures from the point of view of their influence on consumption and in this chapter we take examples of six cultures or culture types. They are not proposed as an exhaustive list, but they illustrate our point.[1]

PRIMITIVE CULTURES

We are going to treat all primitive cultures together. Now we recognize that in perhaps most material and in many immaterial respects primitive cultures are distinct from one another. Wissler tells us there are about fifty separate types. For our purpose here, however, the essential thing about a culture is its answer to the question: what sort of things are most worth while or most necessary for consumption? Primitive cultures may all be treated together as illustrating a certain immaturity of attitude in the face of the mysterious and unknown. The first expression of this attitude is fear; its second expression, an effort to avert the mysterious and unknown by spells, charms, sacrifices, and magic of all sorts.

In our second chapter, "The Beginnings of Culture," we were impressed by the fact that primitive cultures were so rich in culture traits in comparison to the few useful culture traits they had in common or even exclusively. We saw that all of them had a large body of culture traits not immediately useful at all. Now a considerable portion of this second class of interests came in because of man's recognition of the alarming mystery of the

---

[1] The Hebrews, of whom we do not speak in this chapter, are a most interesting example of a people who have maintained their racial integrity without preserving any very definite culture of their own. The Hebrew's attitude toward life might be described as a confidence in God so great that it did not need the "artificial" elements of a culture to support it. In a sense, perhaps, the destruction of the peculiar elements of Hebrew culture served to strengthen for centuries their racial integrity, so firmly did they feel that the chastening of the Almighty was the proof of his love. Such, at any rate, was the spirit of the greatest among them. "Whom the Lord loveth he chasteneth, and scourgeth every son that he receiveth." "Though he slay me, yet will I trust him."

unknown; he recognized it by making totems, fetishes, charms, and sacred objects in general, of which most primitive cultures knew many.

A considerable part of such early art as there was found its expression in or stimulation from man's awe. For instance, it is now very commonly held that the remarkable Paleolithic rock paintings and other remainders of primitive art found in northern Spain and the valley of the Dordogne were inspired by a belief in sympathetic magic.

Far more has been written about primitive religion than about the material side of primitive life, partly because there was so much more in primitive religion to write about. When primitive man had taken care of the immediate needs of his body, food, shelter, and warmth, he turned his attention not so much to direct methods of increasing his material comfort, as to pleasing, placating, or otherwise dealing with the unknown.

What the effect was on his consumption is obvious enough: his energy was spent not in improving his standard of living in what a modern would call a rational way, but in attempting to deal with the mysterious unknown, by whatever name one calls it. His purpose in approaching the unknown was often, indeed, to improve his material condition: his painting of animals transfixed by spears, for instance, was supposed to make it easier for him to transfix real animals with real spears; his images of symbols of fertility were supposed to be means of increasing material fertility. Nevertheless it is obvious that whatever the purpose—to improve material life, to avert disease and death, or anything else, the result was to use up a tremendous amount of effort and energy in a way which, to a person educated in our own culture, seems wasteful.

Neither were the fetishes, charms, and idols the direct seed of a more mature religious life. In such cultures as we can trace growing upward from a quasi-primitive to a maturer cultural stage, as for instance that of the Egyptians and that of the Hebrews, these fetishes, charms, and idols withered by the way while the seeds of the scanty material life grew and multiplied.

We can, therefore, make the general statement that, greatly as primitive cultures differ, there is in all or most a dread or awe of the unknown and an idea that its favors can be bought in round-about ways. This sense of uneasiness demands of man a considerable part of what energy he has. The earliest culture-building, because of the nature of culture-thought, consists of a great deal of economically fruitless activity.

EGYPTIAN CULTURE

Egyptian culture, even at its height, was not free from all the superstitions or animistic ideas of the primitive culture from which it arose, but its characteristic attitude was the expression of a much more mature point of view. The emphasis is no longer on fear of the unknown; fear of the unknown has now passed into an assurance, however gained, of a future life where good will effectively triumph over evil, and compensate for sufferings here. A righteous future was the single most important concept that transfixed the attention of the Egyptian, and his culture as his thought was engrossed by his idea of a resurrection. The ultimate meaning and reality of being for him lay on the other side of the grave.

What, precisely, was the effect on his consumption? He went about his daily affairs and had his various economic interests, but a very large part of his attention was diverted to interests and practices connected with death, burial, and resurrection. He has gone a step beyond primitive man, yet not such a long step.

Egypt has given us far more remains than any other ancient culture, partly because of its dry climate, but more fundamentally because more attention was paid to burial there than elsewhere. The dead body must be preserved in order that the soul might have a habitation, hence the tremendous amount of effort given to embalming and all the subsidiaries thereof, the unguents, the perfumes, the spices. The dead must be laid away in many wrappings and in coffers which demanded the highest art. It is said that the first piece of masonry known to have been made was constructed not for a dwelling nor even for a temple, but for a tomb. It was necessary that the tombs be built to endure as long as possible.

It will be remembered that the Pyramids are tombs, and thousands of men gave years of their lives to the building of one pyramid. Herodotus says that the construction of the pyramid of Cheops required the services of one hundred thousand men for thirty years.

The tomb temples and, in fact, the temples in general bear testimony to the dominance of a rather limited religious idea. The great temple of Karnac at Thebes, nearly a quarter of a mile long, covers three times the area of any religious building ever erected by any people other than the Egyptians. Luxor, in the same city, was nearly as large. A large part of the city of Thebes seems to have been given over to memorials for the dead and to the industries connected with the keeping up of these memorials. There were inns to entertain visitors to the necropolis and many shops for the sale of funeral offerings. The necropolis furnished means of employment to an army of stone masons, builders, painters, sculptors, and embalmers.

It is said that nine-tenths of all the papyri found in Egyptian remains are copies of the great Book of the Dead, which were buried with the dead bodies, and in which the soul was to read of his appearance before the gods Anubis and Thoth who would weigh in the balance the good and evil of his life.

It is obvious enough that however greatly Egyptian culture was influenced by the material state of production, by the trade internal and external of the Empire, and by all the other influences, including the geographic, which bore heavily upon it, the controlling culture idea of the importance of the future life most differentiates it from other types of consumption and gives it its distinctive character.

EAST INDIAN CULTURE

The Egyptian left the mysteries of life, destiny, and evil, to be redressed in a future state. The East Indian met them in a totally different but equally interesting way. "What men call mysteries," he said, "are simply the mysteries of their own nature. The evil in this world we have brought upon ourselves by our own former deeds of evil. God is not sending this pain to you to test you; you were yourself the author of it in some previous state. Neither can he redress it in a brighter future. You must redress it yourself by your own efforts." Then he adds: "Nothing outside of you is real, anyway. The soul is the only reality. All else is illusion."

If the solution of the problem of evil is within ourselves, if the soul is the only reality and the world is illusion, it is obvious there is not much place, theoretically at any rate, for culture. Culture must be an illusion too. And so, according to the strict interpretation of Indian teaching, it would be. Such doctrine does not simply ignore culture, it strikes at its very root.

East Indian practice has been by no means wholly consistent with the spirit of the teaching of both Brahmanism and Buddhism with regard to the illusion of material things. India had in the past and still has an indigenous material culture; but, in conformity with what we should expect from this teaching, the glory of India has always been in the least materialistic aspects of her culture. Never has East Indian invention been important; East Indian art has a considerable claim to distinction, East Indian poetry even more; but it is in the field of philosophy, the least material of all, that India has made its great contribution to the world.

The lowest depths of material misery have been the lot of the Indian masses for centuries. Today as we know, Gandhi, perhaps the greatest living Indian and one of the greatest men in the world, is obstructing the advent of machine goods and machine production into India, on the ground that the advantages of machine goods and machine production, whatever may be claimed for them, do not compensate for the fact they inhibit the development of the soul.

But if the lowest depths of material misery are reached in India, it is true that here also men have attained the sublimest heights of spiritual power and bliss. To the typical Westerner, meditation under the sacred Bo-tree seems worse than a bore, and he perhaps feels with the American clergyman who said, "Those statues of Buddha look so stupid I want to smash every one I see." But meditation is not necessarily a bore, nor Buddha stupid, nor Nirvana nothingness in a Western sense. The East Indian had hold of a real idea, so important to him that it seemed to him all else was worth sacrificing to it. No human being, certainly no human race, is so stupid as to dedicate itself to a Westerner's concept of a vacuum and call it bliss. But more than this; the example of the lives of many individual Indians proves they have attained a spiritual mastery at which Westerners can only marvel.

It is clear how profoundly the East Indian's attitude has held back his material consumption, while it has enriched other aspects of his culture.

GREEK CULTURE

To the Greek this flesh was solid enough. The material world to him was a real world; destiny was outside of his own control. The problems of the world and of destiny were very serious problems to him, but he devised his own way of meeting them. He defied them.

There is something extraordinarily inspiriting in the spectacle of the Greek, a lone man facing ruthless destiny, unconquerable evil, dreary death, looking them squarely in the eye, accepting them and attempting to match them with the magnificence of his own poor little strength. The spirit finds one of its best expressions in literature in the great tragedy, *Prometheus Bound*. Prometheus, it will be remembered, stole fire from Olympus and gave it to men. For this immeasurably great gift Zeus punished him by having him chained to a rock where vultures continually pecked at his liver. But in his destiny he is superior to all destiny. The glory of his soul requites him for his suffering, and from his desolate rock he hurls words of defiance at the god.

In actual life essentially the same spirit in a gentler form is given us in the death of Socrates, Plato's account of which should be familiar to us all. With the just man, everything is always well. Why trouble about death? Man never came closer to showing that he himself was the equal of the gods.

The Greek made no claim to understand the meaning of life nor to govern its content. He felt himself challenged merely to give it what lay within his power: a perfect form. But note how this idea of perfect form controlled the expression of his whole culture.

The great contribution of the Greeks to the world was their art. Art is itself primarily a form; to the Greeks it was the form of a form. The Greek sought no meanings, but projected himself outward in a sense difficult for us to understand. His temples were not erected for the purpose of containing something within but to be something acting without. Appearance was everything, for, to the Greek, appearance was the only attainable reality.

But Greek culture in all its aspects emphasized form. The human mind must be developed to the fullest degree, not for the sake of controlling anything, but merely to prove its own perfection. Greek mathematics reached a high development but it was regarded chiefly as an exercise showing how great were men's capacities. It was not used for practical problems, such as for sanitation engineering. Practical use was not the point.

With all his potential control, the Greek put no emphasis on the material side of life, because he believed it developed mean qualities in human nature. But the beautiful was not for the service of one man alone. The beautiful is most appreciated when we are not encumbered by sentiments of personal possession. The Greeks did not approve of the spending of much time or money on any article of private ownership. Even the time that could be spent on the decoration of gravestones was limited by law.

Hence the tremendous emphasis on public life in the Greek

state. The temples, the statues, the monuments were for all the people. The private houses of the great leaders were simple affairs on some back street, and a wealthy man considered it a high privilege to use his wealth by making a liturgy or gift to the city. Said Pericles: "National greatness is more for the advantage of private citizens than any individual well-being coupled with public need." [1]

CHINESE CULTURE

If the primitive man feared, the Egyptian hoped in, the Indian denied, and the Greek defied the unknown, the Chinese had still another way of approaching the ultimate mystery. He ignored it.

It has often been said that the Chinese alone of all peoples has a philosophy rather than a religion. His philosophy, moreover, is not made up of those abstruse speculations that characterize the philosophies of other peoples. It is essentially pragmatic; and even when it is mystical, as in Taoism, it is practical. Confucius deplored inquiries into the unknown. They were fruitless. This life is enough. Leave the unknown alone and it will leave you alone; what we don't know can't hurt us—such is the spirit of the Chinese attitude toward life.

This attitude, though it seems at first thought childish, also partakes of an extreme degree of sophistication. After all, why not? Take the things of the world as they come, do with them what you will, don't worry about anything. Human energy is too precious to spend worrying. If you are sufficiently patient, Destiny itself will come and eat out of your hand. As a matter of fact, in the case of the Chinese, this philosophy worked. They are the only ancient people who succeeded in keeping their culture to the twentieth century. Several times they have been conquered in arms but their conquerors have always turned around and themselves adopted the Chinese culture.

When Tennyson penned the line, "Better fifty years of Europe

---

[1] An excellent account of Greek culture is to be found in Zimmern, A. E., *The Greek Commonwealth*, op. cit.

than a cycle of Cathay," he was looking at the unprogressive aspects of this attitude. It is indeed anything but progressive, but the Chinese is not worried about that. What is this Western progress but a flash in the pan? After things have quieted down a bit, if there is anything in it at all, we shall quietly absorb it, but no need to worry now. In the meantime let us take life in a dignified manner. The world is given us for our philosophic enjoyment.

If there is something sophisticated, there is also something playful in the attitude of the Chinese; it is, however, a profound playfulness. The learned philosopher who refuses to concern himself with wars and rumors of wars, but sits for an hour looking at the arrangement of leaves on a vine; or listening to the song of a frog; or watching the graceful play of a cat, and smiling the while; what does he get out of life? Whatever it is, it is evidently something that we do not get. Students of Chinese life agree that one remarkable characteristic of this people is their ability to get enjoyment under conditions of the hardest labor and with only the most meagre physical necessities. But a man who can get an evening's pleasure from hearing crickets chirp does not need a Packard six.

The Chinese differs from the East Indian attitude in just this, that whereas the Indian flees the material world, the Chinese welcomes the material world just as it is and proceeds to use it for his soul's pleasure. Plenty of inventions were first made by the Chinese—they were ingenious enough: block printing, the compass, gunpowder, formed a part of their culture centuries ago. All of these, however, were used for enjoyment rather than for what we would call profit. To what end should all be taught to read if they cannot profit by reading, the Chinese asks. If the development of printing should mean that the majority of people would read material on no higher level than street-corner or chimney-corner gossip, better let printing alone. And as for the compass, to what end should we sail the seas? For trade? What satisfactions can that bring? For conquest? It is more trouble than it is worth. Gunpowder in skyrockets and firecrackers has given the Chinese a great deal of amusement. Is not this better than, for whatever purpose, to use it in killing other men? This point of view shows us why Chinese culture is to so large a degree a culture of ornament, games, ceremonies, courtesies, and art in everyday life.

THE CULTURE OF THE WEST

We come now face to face with our own culture, the culture that finds its most highly developed expression in the United States today. What is our attitude in the face of the ultimate mystery of existence, the mystery before which our primitive ancestors trembled? We are out to make it a mystery no longer. We are out to conquer it, to hold it in our hands and stand on it with our feet and tear its meaning to pieces in our textbooks. The goose that lays the golden egg!—if we could only once catch it, it would never be permitted to cackle again!

There is, however, something rather inspiring about this, too, is there not? Surely man should do what he can with his powers and the powers of nature, at least as a beginning. In a way this attitude, the attitude of conquering nature, would seem logically to precede some of the other attitudes. It would seem more logical for men to do what they could to conquer nature first, and afterwards determine what aspects were better ignored, what aspects better denied, and what aspects had better be met by defiance. But it did not come about so. And if our cultural neighbors tell us that this mad scramble of ours makes us look ridiculous, we can turn the tables by observing that their sublime aloofness is equally narrow-minded.

How is our attitude expressed? Oswald Spengler believes that one of the early ways it found expression was in the building of the great mediaeval cathedrals, the high towers of which are an expression of the aspirations of men toward the beyond. Modern skyscrapers would be a similar illustration.

In science we are analyzing the elements of things to electrons and further, and carrying our sight to that far point where the telescope reveals no more stars. By television and radio we are making ourselves masters of distance. By experiments in biological chemistry we work on the problem of creating life.

By invention we have set ourselves to control the powers of the earth, the sea, and the sky, the rivers, the winds, and the tides, the rays of the sun and the lightning. We use these for transforming the materials of the earth. What is the result? The mountain is in labor, and from our factories proceed a succession of watches and fountain pens, rubber boots and velvet damask, waffle irons and vacuum cleaners, and heaven knows what other symbols of our mastery over Nature. The consumption of the West is distinguished from the consumption of other parts of the world by its vast numbers of factory-made goods.

This is the way the Western attitude toward life reacts on consumption.

CHAPTER XXIII

WHAT IS A STANDARD OF LIVING?

"Lord, Thou hast given me a cell
Wherein to dwell. . . .
A little buttery, and therein
A little bin. . . .

"Some little sticks of thorn or briar
Make me a fire
Beside whose living coal I sit
And glow like it."
—ROBERT HERRICK, *A Thanksgiving to God for his House.*

We have heard the words "standard of living" a good many times in the years since the beginning of the War. This is a topic on which there has been a great increase of knowledge and of interest in the last fifteen years. Everyone nowadays wants to know whether college professors have to do the washing and whether street-car conductors can have grapefruit for breakfast. How many pairs of silk stockings can a coal-miner's wife afford in a year? Does the ordinary plumber go to work in a Rolls-Royce or in only a Packard?

A large part of all that has ever been done in the field of consumption has been done in terms of standards of living. But what precisely is a standard of living? What is its relation to a culture?

RELATION OF STANDARD OF LIVING TO CULTURE

Let us answer the second question first. The territory of most great cultures has several or many standards of living within it. These standards within a great culture may be quite different from one another, but in their important respects they will presumably be more like one another than any one of them is like a standard of living in some "foreign" culture. The standard of living of a wealthy man in ancient Egypt was

241

more like the standard of living of a poor farmer by the Nile than it is like the standard of anybody in China, then or now, or is now like that of anybody in the United States.

There are really as many standards of living in the world as there are people; nevertheless, standards of living within cultures tend to group themselves, as groups of people have common characteristics. In this way we speak of the standards of living of different occupational groups, as those of farmers or those of coal miners, those of government clerks or those of college professors; or in some countries, we may divide them by social groups, let us say the landed gentry and the yeomen. Or we may speak of the standards of living of different nationalities or racial groups within a culture: the standards of the French as compared with the Germans, the standards of Negroes and of Indians within the United States. We may speak of the standards of living of different geographic sections of a country, comparing Northumberland with Cornwall, or New England with California. Finally we may divide standards of living by the income groups they represent: those people receiving over ten thousand a year with those receiving less than two thousand,—and so on. One may use almost any basis he likes for distinguishing groups, though some bases obviously mean much more than others. Groupings merely on the basis of money incomes, though convenient, are perhaps the most arbitrary of any that are likely to be used.

STANDARD OF LIVING DEFINED

Let us distinguish two phrases, scale of living and standard of living. The first refers merely to the things consumed that can be definitely measured in some way, as by pounds or yards, calories or dollar's worths. The measures of pounds, yards, calories, and dollars are a good starting point for approaching standard of living, but standard of living is more than the material things consumed. It is a sum total, not of things, but of satisfactions. A standard of living consists of the satisfactions considered essential by an individual or group.

The scale of living of a poor country doctor is very much lower than the scale of living of a millionaire wastrel. The doctor's standard, however, is higher. If we were describing it we would probably start by enumerating the items in his scale of living: he lives in a four thousand dollar house and pays ten dollars a week for such and such food for his family; and so on. Then, however, we should have to add: he takes great pleasure and interest in his home; his children are receiving the best possible education; the conversation of the family is always delightful; the man loves his work. Few men have a higher standard of living than he.

Scales of living can be precisely compared, one with another, but when we have compared them we have, after all, done relatively little. Standards of living cannot be precisely compared, but such comparisons as can be made are worth very much more than comparisons of scales merely.

Most studies of "standards of living" that have been made have been really studies of scales: studies merely of goods and services consumed, which have not taken account of appreciations of goods and services; nor have they taken account of interchangeable satisfaction between goods and services consumed and work performed. The reason for this narrowing of definition is to be found, of course, in convenience, and a study merely of goods and services consumed casts sufficient light on the problem for many purposes. It is assumed that in the same class of society appreciations of the same material goods are approximately similar.

It must be emphasized, however, that just as we cannot tell how well a man lives by knowing how much money he spends, we cannot know what satisfaction he gets by knowing what he spends his money for. The same radio set, for instance, may mean two quite different things to two different families, both in the amount and the kind of pleasure received from it. A fur coat may be used to keep one warm or to triumph over one's neighbors; a bathtub may serve for daily baths or for show to guests or for a coal bin. A house and a garden mean one thing

to one man, another to another. Hence a thorough study of
standards of living must take account of how goods and services are appreciated and used. It must also consider little
things, such for instance as flowers, pictures, trips to parks,
which may yield to certain individuals a satisfaction out of all
proportion to their money cost. In the quotations at the head
of the chapter, the standard of living is the man's pleasure before
his fire rather more than it is the little house, the flour bin, and
the fire itself.

We must note, also, how the same standard of living may
express itself in part either through purchasable satisfactions or
through work. This point, again, has received almost no attention in studies of standards of living although the principle
involved therein—psychic income as distinct from an income
in money or goods—is well known. Most standard of living
studies have been made of one group or class of people, usually
people at more or less monotonous labor, and it has been assumed, for the most part rightly, that their satisfactions from
work, if any, were about the same. With the development of
comparative standard of living studies, however, the question
of satisfaction assumes a new importance. How shall we know,
for instance, which is better off—a farmer or a sailor, a teacher
or a mechanic, with the same purchasing power?

After a certain minimum consumption standard is assumed
we find many evidences of men's willingness to substitute satisfactions from labor for satisfactions from consumption. Anyone who hesitates between accepting a job he likes at low pay
and a better paid job that he does not like so well is illustrating
the point, and in fact the principle is an important one, from
the point of view of distribution, in explaining the differences
in wages in different employments.

The fact that study of standards of living must take account
not only of what people actually have, but what they believe is,
in the words of our definition, "essential," is closely tied up
with the matter of appreciations. Since, however, a person's
standard of living is a product of his experience, that which

people believe is really essential is not usually much beyond what they have. A person who has fallen from prosperity to penury, however, keeps, at least for a time, the standard of living of his prosperous days. A student working his way through college considers certain things to be in general essential for him, but nevertheless he may not yet be able to afford them. They are properly to be considered, however, a part of his standard of living.

In our earlier discussion of cultures we said that the various interests within a culture were interdependent and bore an organic relationship to one another. We did not, however, explain this in detail. In connection with a standard of living this relationship is very clear. Not only are interests within a standard of living related by similarity and contiguity through the medium of culture complexes; they are related also by contrast.

We have already seen that the human mind is expansive as well as conservative and is hence attracted not only by what is similar but by what is complementary. It is led by similarity but it adventures into contrast. The total standard of living, then, is in part made up of similar interests or complexes, and in part of contrasting and complementary interests and complexes.

Let us give an illustration which will at the same time show how misleading it is to pass judgment on one item of consumption apart from the total standard of living situation. In the lower ranks of industrial society many men spend most of their working hours in extremely mechanical and monotonous tasks. Due to various causes, most of the interests available to them outside of working hours are likewise more or less mechanized. The available interests and the men themselves are both, so to speak, products of the same industrial system. Their standard of living is thus very largely mechanized. Most of their interests are built into one great industrial and mechanical complex. The human mind, however, has characteristics and attributes which the mechanical complex fails to satisfy, and the industrial worker, though he may not realize it, seeks to gratify himself by what is contrasting and complementary. Out of the few contrasting interests available to him the most intense and concentrated contrast is, or was, offered by drink and the saloon. Its pleasures were illusory so far as permanent satisfaction was concerned, but, in the common phrase, they went straight to the right spot and did the job while they lasted. They were a poor antidote, but they were at least an antidote, for a mechanical way of living.

Now if drink is considered simply and solely as one separate element of consumption, without reference to the standard of living of which it is a part, it must be condemned at once. In and by itself it is almost entirely injurious. If, however, it is considered as a part of an entire standard of living situation it will be condemned with a difference. The intelligent solution would be to lay emphasis on other interests that would take the place of drink in giving play to one important side of man's nature. It is, as a matter of fact, very fortunate that the law prohibiting the consumption of intoxicating liquors in the United States came at a time of increasing prosperity. The lower-paid workers today are able to buy substitutes for the satisfactions of liquor. Fast driving of old Ford cars is nowadays furnishing its own share of thrills.

An example of the same principle, given by John A. Hobson in *Work and Wealth*, is the very large expenditure and display frequently made on funerals by lower-paid industrial employees. To some social workers it has seemed most unfitting that a bereaved widow should cast away the entire small savings and insurance of the family in one big display. But who knows? Man does not live by bread alone. Music, flowers, a long procession, a big gathering of friends—this may be the most fitting disposition of money conceivable, at the end of a drab and monotonous existence.

The truth is we should be careful how we judge separate elements in the scales or standards of living of others. The benefit or harm caused by any good or service consumed must always take account of the relation this good or service bears to all the other interests in the standard of living.

Scales and Standards of Living Continually Changing Today

Although standards of living are products of experience they have changed much in the past and they are continually changing today in countries that have come under the influence of the Industrial Revolution. It is a commonplace that most people are continually after more. The question arises, how is it, granting the strength of the natural impulse to propagate, which we shall discuss in Chapter XXV, that a standard of living can ever get itself established in the first place.

In general, the scale or standard of living is influenced by the same causes that determine the appearance and development of individual interests, but it is influenced by other causes as well. Scales and standards of living react as a whole to certain historical conditions, and the psychology of individual interests alone is not sufficient to show how great social changes are effected. Changes in scales and standards take place only when people have had the opportunity for some time to see others enjoy comforts and luxuries, or to enjoy comforts and luxuries themselves. Under such conditions they may be led to think seriously about the matter of restraining their numbers, in order to insure the establishment, or the continuance, of these comforts and luxuries.

There have been some periods in history more favorable than others for the establishment of new scales and standards of living. Probably the Black Death in England, which carried off such a large number of the people in 1348 and 1349, was indirectly responsible for raising the scales and standards of English workers. Wages were so high, due to the scarcity of labor, for a long time after the Black Death, that a superior standard of living had time to establish itself.

The same result in outstanding degree has of course followed the Industrial Revolution. One result of the vastly increased production of the period has been to make possible a taste for the new economic goods and to establish this taste so firmly that reproductive impulses could not break it down.

There are two major influences through which pressure is continually bearing upon people to increase their incomes and to raise their standards of living here in the United States today. Young married people in setting their scale or standard are influenced by what they formerly enjoyed in the homes of their parents, where the economic income was the fruition of years of experience; or they are influenced by what they were able to afford as single individuals.

In the second place, in a democratic society, people in the lower-paid ranks are influenced vicariously to some extent by the higher scales and standards they see all about them. They are able to know precisely what they want before they get it. When they claim that this or that new thing is essential to their welfare it is to some extent quite true, although there are always, to be sure, complaints without real substance. The pressure for higher incomes on the part of lower economic groups is one of the great stimuli to increased production in economically progressive countries.

Today the greatest pressure for improvement in scales and standards is at the lower end of the income scale. Emulation plays a great part in this. As we saw in Chapter IV, emulation is of more service in bringing up the rear than it is in advancing the van. In the economic vanguard today money incomes and expenditures are increasing very rapidly, but satisfactions probably not so rapidly in proportion to their increase at the lower end of the income scale. The fact is that as consumers we are still overwhelmed by the Industrial Revolution and do not know quite what to make of it.

CHAPTER XXIV

THE STUDY OF SCALES AND STANDARDS OF LIVING

"To-day's problem is less a problem of increasing riches than of assuring stability and social peace; of assuring, in a word, that consummation of welfare to which man may legitimately look forward. Therein lies the aim of social science founded on observation."—*Opening words of program of Frédéric Le Play's Réforme sociale, Vol. I, no. 1.*

The collection of data on scales and standards of living has been pursued by many methods and for many motives. Up to the present time the study of consumption as such has been, avowedly at least, one of the less important motives. Yet all scales and standards of living studies, whatever their motive, furnish material to the student of consumption.

STUDIES MOTIVATED BY INTEREST IN DISTRIBUTION OF INCOME

"We haven't enough to live on!" Such is the burden of complaint which has led to many a study of scales of living. Through investigations of how people live and of how much they have to live on, it is possible to prove that they cannot reach a certain desired or desirable standard. Most of our important studies have been motivated to some extent, many of them chiefly, by concern about the distribution of wealth and income.

Such concern springs from two sources. First, it may be that wage-earners and other workers, their sympathizers or their representatives, are demanding for labor a greater share of the national dividend, and are supporting their contention by statistics relative to their modes of life. Second, it may be that dire conditions of poverty are clamoring for attention, and there is need of collections of facts to demonstrate the necessity of philanthropic aid or poor law reform.

The presentation of budgets is a means by which wage-workers, clerical workers, and professional workers may set forth their claims for need of greater incomes. Their employers sometimes counter by gathering their own statistics as to the cost of a "reasonable" scale of living. Many such studies have been made in the United States, but most are local and few are individually important.[1] The use of cost of living studies as a basis for the determination of wages is common in some foreign countries, particularly in Australia and New Zealand, but was practically unknown in the United States until the increased cost of living brought about by the war called the whole subject of scale of living to the attention of employees and employers. The Ship-building Labor Adjustment Board, the National War Labor Board, and other government organizations used such studies in conciliation, mediation, and arbitration during the war, and they were also taken into account in bargains made between employers and employees directly. On the whole, however, since the war, this method for determining a wage bargain has rather fallen into disuse in the United States. It was useful when prices were rapidly rising, for it was an excellent means of showing that wages were not keeping pace with prices. It was a good way to seek to maintain the status quo. But the American workmen are now seeking, not to maintain a status quo by appealing to old scales, but to bring about the improvement of wages as speedily as possible. The theory of the ordinary American workman today is not that he should be paid according to a certain scale of living but that he should be paid all he earns: it is his own business how he spends it.

Practically all studies motivated by a desire to increase returns from labor have been studies for the benefit of wage-earners, but we have two interesting examples of the application of this motive for the advantage of other groups. One is a study of the standard of living of government employees,

[1] See National Industrial Conference Board, *Family Budgets of American Wage-Earners*, New York, 1921, Ch. VII.

clerical workers in Washington, on the basis of goods and services customarily consumed by clerical workers.[1] The other study is based on the expenditures of ninety-six members of the faculty of the University of California.[2]

Many of these studies serve a necessary purpose in their own field, but in the field of consumption their value is limited. They deal almost exclusively with scales rather than with standards. The student of consumption is interested in such data as are presented in all these studies, but his ultimate interest is, as we have seen, not in money nor in goods, but in the use of goods and the satisfactions received from them: a much more difficult thing to report on. Except for families on the margin of subsistence, the student of consumption would emphasize not the need of more money, but the need of more intelligence in using it.

Some of the most important studies ever made have been motivated by a sympathy for poverty. While these studies have been undertaken primarily with a belief that distribution of income was defective, they mark a transition to the consumption point of view.

As we know, the combined effects of the new Industrial Revolution and a bad poor law made living conditions very wretched for English villagers in the last years of the eighteenth century. In the year 1787 the Rev. David Davies made a study of family expenditures in his parish to determine why so many of his parishioners were in receipt of poor relief, and later collected similar data from several other rural parishes. His study was published in 1795 under the title *The Case of the Labourers in Husbandry*. Better known than this is Sir Frederick Morton Eden's *The State of the Poor* or "an History of the laboring classes in England from the Conquest to the Present Period in which are particularly considered, Their

[1] United States Department of Labor, Bureau of Labor Statistics, "Tentative Quantity and Cost Budget," *Monthly Labor Review*, December, 1919, pp. 22–29.

[2] Peixotto, Jessica B., *Getting and Spending at the Professional Standard of Living*, New York, 1927.

Domestic Economy with respect to Diet, Dress, Fuel, and Habitation;" etc. This study, published in 1797, is a mine of interesting information on the everyday life of the common people.

Perhaps the most distinguished of all studies of poverty was the great work of Charles Booth, *Life and Labor of the People in London*, published in 1891–1903, a profound and illuminating inquiry into the facts and the significance of the life of the poor. In 1901, B. Seebohm Rowntree published his *Poverty*, which was a study of conditions in York.

In the United States, social settlements and other charitable organizations have shown considerable interest in the standards of living of the economically handicapped. We have, for instance, Mrs. More's *Wage-Earners' Budgets*, made in the lower west side of New York City, published in 1907, Chapin's *The Standard of Living Among Workingmen's Families in New York City*, published in 1909, and Miss Byington's 1907–1908 study of the standards of steel workers in Homestead, Pennsylvania. Though these were studies of wage-earners' families, the families were hovering on the verge of dependence. In 1927 appeared a study of the *Income and Standard of Living of Unskilled Laborers in Chicago* by Dr. Leila Houghteling. This is written from the point of view of a social service worker interested in relief giving. The United States Bureau of Labor has made several studies of the condition of women and child wage-earners, which deal with budgets at the poverty level.[1]

INTEREST IN CONSUMPTION AS A MOTIVE

As we have said, many studies of poverty deal with consumption as well as distribution, and it is often difficult to tell on which is the primary emphasis in any particular study. Indeed, the student of poverty does well to follow a pragmatic policy, emphasizing whatever purpose or method of improvement promises the best means of relief. The first important

[1] Vol. XVI of Report on Condition of Women and Child Wage-Earners of the United States, Senate Document No. 645, Washington, 1911.

study in which an interest in consumption seems to be dominant is the great work of Frédéric Le Play.

In the year 1829, when Le Play was an ardent youth of twenty-three, he and a friend set out on a tour of 200 days, in which they walked 4,000 miles. They dwelt among the families of miners, founders, wood-cutters, and wagoners of the Hartz mountains, they lived with agricultural families on the Saxon plain, with fisher families in Hanover, Oldenberg, and the Netherlands, and with industrial families in Westphalia, Belgium, and the Rhine basin. This was the introduction to a lifetime work accomplished in Le Play's vacations over many years. His method was to live eight days to a month with a family which he regarded as a fair type of its class. In 1855 he first published *Les ouvriers européens*, which contained thirty-six of the most representative out of 300 family monographs compiled by him in several countries during this long period. He "struck an unworked mine of research in the matter of the consumption of wealth." [1]

Shortly after the appearance of Le Play's book, Ernst Engel published the *Cost of Living of Belgian Workingmen's Families*, in which for the first time a statistical analysis of family expenditures was presented on a large scale. He used Le Play's studies and others of his own. Engel's name is known to all students of consumption because of the so-called laws of consumption which he formulated. We shall refer to him again.

In our own country, in 1900–1902, the United States Bureau of Labor made a study to give information as to living conditions among American wage-earners. Field agents of the Bureau collected data on incomes and expenditures of 25,440 families in 33 states. The Federal Bureau of Labor Statistics in 1918 and 1919 made a somewhat similar study of 12,837 wage-earners' families in 42 states. Of these families, 12,096 were white and 741 were colored. This study was made for the immediate purpose of providing information on cost of living,

[1] Higgs, H., "Frédéric Le Play," *Quarterly Journal of Economics*, IV, p. 422.

but information regarding living conditions in various parts of the country was given as the real purpose.

In the meantime, in 1909, the British Board of Trade had made a study of 7,616 families in 29 American industrial towns east of the Mississippi River. Its purpose was to provide information for making international comparisons of conditions affecting wage-earners.[1]

The most definite emphasis on consumption in the United States has come in connection with the study of standards of living of rural families. The United States Department of Agriculture, working in collaboration with departments of sociology in some of the land-grant colleges, has made a number of studies of rural standards of living. In 1925 under the Purnell Act a federal fund for financing home economics research in the land-grant colleges became available: one object of the research is to make consumption studies with a view to finding out how families are living and to suggesting improvements in consumption.

Local or national government authorities in many foreign countries have collected family budgets and studied them for various purposes. Such government investigations have been made in Canada, in Argentina, in most countries of Europe, in the Union of South Africa, in India (Bombay), in Japan (Osaka), and in Australia and New Zealand.[2].

The student is at first likely to be somewhat confused by the varying methods and motives of all these studies and the difficulties of classifying them. The confusion indicates not that there has been great accomplishment but that we are still in the preliminary stages of studying standards of living. We are

[1] The 1900–1902 study was published in the Eighteenth Annual Report of the Commissioner of Labor, Washington, 1903; the 1918–1919 study in the *Monthly Labor Review*, May-September, November, December, 1919; January, July, September, 1920. The British Board of Trade study was reprinted as Senate Document No. 22, 62nd Congress, 1st Session, Washington, 1911. For a short summary of these three American studies, see National Industrial Conference Board, op. cit., Ch. I.

[2] International Labour Office, *Methods of Conducting Family Budget Enquiries*, Geneva, 1926, pp. 55–78.

still evolving modes of procedure and still discovering purposes
to which these studies can be applied.[1]

In What Ways Are Standards of Living to Be Ascertained?

Most of the "standard of living" studies of which we have
spoken have been studies of expenditures only. We have made
some reference to the methods of conducting them, but the most
important of these methods may well be reviewed here.

Obviously the ideal method of studying standards of living
would be for the proper investigator to live with selected families
after the manner of Le Play. A period of residence plus the
family accounts for a year would furnish the best possible
basis for a study. This method is not only very costly, but it
requires the services of a most exceptional investigator, a man
or woman not only both keen and sympathetic, but one prepared
to undergo hardships of living. Owing to the cost and the difficulties of this method the number of families studied would
necessarily be few. Nevertheless such a study in the right
hands would yield results of inestimable value. Such experiences in actually living with people are suggestive and enlighten-
ing as no other method of study can be.

A method of study approaching this in thoroughness is illustrated by an investigation now in progress at Iowa State College
under the Purnell Act already referred to. One hundred and
fifty farm families, fifty in each of three sections of the state,
are enlisted as coöperators and furnished with simple account
books. These families are visited monthly by a sympathetic
investigator who is herself personally interested in the problems
of farm housewives. She collects the accounts and all com-
putations are made at the office. Through the monthly visits
she and the women become friends, and her insight into their

[1] A study unlike any other that has come to the author's attention is *The
Equipment of the Workers* by the Members of St. Philip's Settlement Education
and Economic Research Society of Sheffield, England, published in London in
1919. It approaches consumption from the point of view not of goods but of
the satisfactions derived from them.

true standards, their equipment, their ambitions for their families, grows as their acquaintance increases. It is obvious that such a method also is costly and requires an investigator of a high type.

The method most usually followed in studies casting light on standards of living is the so-called schedule method. An investigator visits a family once or twice with a printed list of questions calling for data on their expenditures and perhaps on other aspects of their life. The questions on expenditures are usually answered by guess, but the theory is that under-estimates and over-estimates will balance one another if the body of material is large enough. It will be remembered that the Bureau of Labor collected records from 25,440 families in 1900–1902. This method is of course not exact nor thorough, but it has the considerable merit of being relatively inexpensive.

A trained investigator may use still a fourth method which is less expensive yet and which is of some value in local studies. A person familiar with the general standard of living of a large group of people in a certain area can get a good deal of light on the particular standard of a sub-group in that area by a brief campaign in the place where the sub-group resides. Let us say, for example, that the investigator knows a good deal about the standard of living of industrial workers in New England. He is given two weeks to report on the standard of cotton-mill workers in New Bedford, Massachusetts. He goes to New Bedford, finds out average wages, range of wages, size of families, age of children at leaving school. He visits real-estate men and tenement districts to get rents. Coal dealers tell him the average yearly coal bills. The central organization of the gas and electric companies, the theatres, the doctors and dentists, give him other data relative to particular expenditures of the industrial population. Social service agencies and perhaps the Chamber of Commerce furnish more general information on standards. Stores in industrial districts furnish prices of grades of goods most commonly consumed. If, in addition, he makes a few calls on the workers themselves, he will have

at the end of two weeks an estimate of standards of living in
New Bedford which will have some value for a limited range of
purposes.[1]

COMMON DENOMINATORS OF ALL SCALES; ENGEL'S "LAWS"

The various expenditures making up a total scale of living
are classified into groups in various ways. The simplest method
is to make five groups, one for food, one for shelter, one for
clothing, one for fuel and light, and one for sundries. Sundries
may, in turn, be divided into its various parts. The term
sundries is a colorless one, but no other sort of term can characterize such a heterogeneous group of expenditures as medical
care, carfare, reading material and entertainments, society
memberships, church contributions, candy and tobacco, and
household furnishings and cleaning supplies. The terms "Advancement" or "Development" which are sometimes used as
a way of grouping expenditures for reading and education,
social and religious activities, and recreation of all types are
hardly satisfactory. Some of these things are often not "advancement" or "development"; on the other hand, proper
expenditures for shelter, food, clothing, and operating expenses
mean "advancement" and "development" themselves.

We are interested to know if the various studies of expenditures that have been made in different countries and different
social groups point to any generalizations about scales of living.
A few can be made.

In general the largest proportion of small total expenditures
goes for food. Engel's estimate for Belgium in 1852–1854 was
that from 50 to 62% of total income was spent for food alone.
He estimated that 12% went for shelter, 16 to 18% for clothing,
5% for fuel and light, and from 5 to 15% for sundries. It is
interesting to compare these percentages with those brought

---

[1] This method was followed in a number of studies made by the National
Industrial Conference Board for the purpose of ascertaining the so-called minimum standard of health and decency in various cities. See Research Reports
22, 24, Special Reports 7, 8, 13, 16, 19, 21, published from 1919 to 1922.

out by the two large studies of the United States Bureau of
Labor and Bureau of Labor Statistics already referred to.
The first gives the percentages of expenditure of 11,156 families
of wage-earners in 1900–1902, and the second of 12,096 families
of wage-earners in 1918–1919. These percentages are presented
for comparison with Engel's in Table VIII. From this table
it is seen that the American wage-earners spend proportionally
much less for food than did the Belgian families in 1852–1854,
and that Americans spent less in 1918–1919 than they did in
1900–1902. At the same time Americans spent appreciably
more than the Belgians for sundries. With a rising standard
of living, the proportion spent for sundries by American wage-
earners' families increased between 1900–1902 and 1918–1919.

In poor countries and among poorer people in our own
country today, the percentages of income spent for food are
still as high or higher than the percentages Engel found in
Belgium. In Bombay a study of expenditures of 2,473 working
men's families showed that they spent 57% for food. The
percentage spent for food in China, Egypt, and the East Indies
is even higher than this.[1] We shall refer on page 297 to a
study of American negro families who spent 54% of their
incomes for food.

What do these facts indicate? On the basis of his study,
Engel believed that certain broad characterizations held good,
which have since been known as Engel's "laws." He declared
that as income increased:

The proportion of income going for food decreases;

The proportion of income going for rent, clothing, fuel, and
light remains for the most part unchanged;

The proportion of income going for sundries increases.

Common sense would suggest that the proportion of income
spent for food would decrease, and that for sundries would
increase, with increasing income, and Table VIII shows this
was the case so far as comparisons between Belgian and Ameri-

[1] " Working-Class Expenditure in Bombay," *International Labour Review*,
VIII, pp. 235–238.

can families are concerned. This "law" is generally though
not universally true.[1]

Engel's generalizations with regard to fuel and light are
correct for relatively low expenditure groups, but expenditures
for shelter and clothing do not conform to any particular law.
The trend of shelter and clothing expenditures is particularly
subject to influences that vary between nations and groups
within nations. We shall refer to this matter of proportions
for shelter and clothing again when we come to the study of
scales and standards of living in the United States.

TABLE VIII

PERCENTAGE OF TOTAL YEARLY EXPENDITURES FOR EACH OF THE MAJOR
ITEMS IN THE COST OF LIVING FOR BELGIAN FAMILIES IN 1852–1854
AND FOR AMERICAN WAGE-EARNERS' FAMILIES IN 1900–1902 AND IN
1918–1919

(Engel, United States Department of Commerce and Labor, and United
States Department of Labor)

| | Percentage of Total Expenditure | | |
Expenditure Group	Belgian Families	11,156 American Families 1900–1902	12,096 American Families 1918–1919
Food.........	50–62	43	38
Shelter.......	12	18	13
Clothing......	16–18	13	17
Fuel and light	5	6	5
Sundries.......	5–15	20	27

[1] The "law" as to food did not hold among families included in Chapin's
study of the standard of living in New York City previously referred to. It
was only approximately true in the Bombay study.

CHAPTER XXV

POPULATION, CULTURES, AND STANDARDS OF LIVING

> "'Why,' said I, 'how many children do you reckon to have had at last?'
> 'I do not care how many,' said the man, 'God never sends mouths without sending meat.'
> 'Did you never hear,' said I, 'of one Parson Malthus?'"—WM. COBBETT, quoted by Leslie Stephen, *English Utilitarians*.

While the total amount of consumption by human beings is obviously dependent on production, by which alone are furnished the goods to be consumed, the amount available for individuals is also obviously dependent on the number who must share the total. If population increases as fast as goods increase, other things being equal, we are no better off than before. If population increases faster than goods, we are worse off. The relationship of population and the growth of population to the supply of available goods is therefore of great significance.

In the plant and sub-human animal world the numbers of any species are limited by the depredations of their enemies and by the available food supply. There is no consideration, conscious or unconscious, as to whether the offspring can be kept alive after birth. An increase in the food supply means, other things being equal, that some which would otherwise have died will now live, and the numbers of the species will increase proportionately to the food supply. We can see that if the human population increased in proportion to the food supply, actual or potential, improvements in the arts of production in so far as they could be applied to foods would in no way increase the satisfactions available for individual persons.

THE RESTRICTION OF POPULATION BY CULTURES AND STANDARDS OF LIVING

Fortunately for us, the laws governing growth of population are not necessarily the same in the human as they are in the sub-human world. As we glance up the course of history we see there is no general rule that population keeps pace with increased means of livelihood. Material standards of living have been rising, though not continuously, ever since man made his appearance on the planet.

The single most striking case in history of greatly increased means of production is the Industrial Revolution. Population began to increase rapidly in England, and indeed in Europe, about 1750, and continued to increase rapidly down to the present century. The increase was caused in part by a rising birth rate; in part, especially in the latter years of the period, by a falling death rate due to advances in medicine and sanitary science. Yet the increase in population, great as it is, has not been at all commensurate with increases in total consumption. In the United States the correlation between growth of population and increased total consumption has been even slighter than in Europe. Individuals and families have demanded for themselves an increasingly greater share of the return from industrial improvements and from the exploitation of natural resources. The birth rate reacts to this demand, and it must react the more because the death rate has fallen.

If the knowledge possessed by the Western world were applied merely to increasing food supply, its surface would support many more people than are actually on it. All around us in the West, moreover, we see evidences that the birth rate is being half-consciously or consciously and deliberately restricted. The East presents a different situation, as we shall soon see. But students of the population problem tell us that restriction of numbers has been practiced in some degree in many periods and among many people.

In the year 1798 the economist Thomas Malthus sought to

tie the human to the sub-human laws of increase, by declaring
that human beings tended to increase in a geometric ratio,
whereas the food supply increased in arithmetic ratio only.
The increase of human beings, like the increase of animals, was
subject to certain positive checks: famines and plagues, and
wars to which men would be driven in order to take food from
their neighbors. Many would die and be killed, but the rest
would multiply again, and the unhappy process would be repeated. He pointed in particular to India and China, whose
famines, plagues, and wars afforded many instances of this
very thing.

This gloomy interpretation was made just at the time when
the growth of the factory system of the Industrial Revolution
and the new applications of science to agricultural purposes
were promising to increase on a large scale the world's supply of
goods. Thus it appeared that human beings could not hope to
be much better off as a result of the Industrial Revolution. Its
improved processes would be called upon primarily to furnish
means to provide, not more enjoyments for the numbers then
existing, but more bare subsistence for an increasing population.
Hence the newly expanding science of economics was dubbed
by Carlyle the dismal science.

Malthus' argument seemed to do very well for India and
China, but it was another matter to apply it to Europe and
England. Malthus soon realized this and in subsequent edi-
tions of his book came to modify his original propositions, in
the light of the obvious facts, so far as to say that education
and voluntary control of population, moral restraint, as he
called it, might save the situation.

Today there is considerable superficial disagreement as to
whether or not Malthus was right, but the real point of the disagreement is as to just what Malthus meant. The facts of the
situation are generally accepted by all parties, though some
lay more emphasis on one limiting influence and some on another.
If Malthus is interpreted narrowly, he was certainly wrong.
If he is interpreted very liberally and very generously, his

limiting factors may be stretched into an admission that growth of population is limited, not by food supply, but by people's ideas and standards.

An examination of the facts as to what actually takes place among peoples makes clear, first, that the ideas governing every culture have a general relation to the growth of population within that culture. Second, in most cases, also, different nations within a culture or different groups within a nation have standards of living which specifically affect their own growth. Population, in other words, tends to conform to the "idea" of a culture, a nation, or a group, as to what constitutes a suitable or sufficient population.

In Chapter XXII we discussed the fundamental attitudes toward life of six different types of culture, and saw how these attitudes affected consumption by determining what was worth while to consume. Such culture attitudes affect consumption indirectly as well, by their influence on the growth of population.

Neither the primitive man nor the Egyptian had much idea of how to improve the world as it was. Neither was satisfied with it, but both were sidetracked from attempting to deal with it. The primitive was deflected by his fears, the Egyptian by his too-ready assumption that the future life was the real object of this one. While they were engaged in these preoccupations, the growth of population was left to run its course, save as it interfered with the needs of physical subsistence.

The attitudes toward life of the East Indian and the Chinese were attitudes which would on the whole deprecate interference with the unrestricted growth of population. The East Indian, as we saw, denied the reality of this world anyway, and the Chinese sought to accept fate with the pragmatic attitude of enjoying it if he could. In neither case could we logically expect to find much effort to control the growth of population beyond the needs of subsistence, if indeed to control it at all. The status of population in India and China, it will be remembered, afforded the main support to Malthus' first doctrine that the growth of population was held in check by plagues, famines, and wars. It is of considerable significance that the reforms of the British Government in India, which are said to have increased means of consumption 50%, have resulted not in higher standards of living but in 50% more population. That result surprised the Britishers, who thought that other men must act and react as they. In their ignorance they had believed India's troubles were due to material deficiencies. The real point, of course, was her cultural attitude, so different from their own.

When we come to the cultural attitudes of the Greeks and the modern West, the situation changes. In the one case we have a people seeking to show themselves superior to fate and nature, in the other case a people seeking to get fate and nature within their own control. In both cases the deliberate control of population would be means of achieving these ends, and in both cases we find a control of population for purposes beyond those of maintaining physical subsistence. In a stimulating essay on the Birth Rate, Dean Inge observes that even in the days before the Trojan War, the Hellenes had believed "the world was too full of people." Hesiod, writing in the eighth century B.C., advises a father not to bring up more than one son, and daughters were sacrificed even more frequently. Inge quotes Wilamowitz-Moellendorff to show that in one graveyard 233 out of 570 burials were those of infants who had been left to die. Abortion also was freely practiced.[1] We recollect Plato's advice in the *Republic* that undesirable children should be "concealed, as is fitting, in some mysterious and unknown hiding place." [2]

On our own culture attitude as it affects the growth of population we do not need to comment more than we have already done.

We said that the culture attitude bore a general relation to the growth of population, and that the standard of living bore a specific relation. Even in the primitive, the Egyptian, the East Indian, and the Chinese cultures a standard of living at a sub-

[1] Inge, W. R., *Outspoken Essays*, First Series, London, 1923, pp. 60–63.
[2] Translation of Davies and Vaughan, V, 460.

sistence or slightly higher level has been enforced to some extent
by foresight as well as by plagues, famines, and wars. In primitive societies, as Carr-Saunders has shown,[1] definite efforts
were made to limit the number of children. Infanticide was
practiced, and means even more preventive were found in abortion, in tabus enforcing long periods of abstinence from sexual
intercourse, and in prolonged lactation, which was believed to
lessen the liability of conception. Incidentally, it is worthy of
note, also, that in parts of India and China today the spreading
of knowledge of infant welfare is sometimes definitely deprecated
on the ground that the extremely high infant death rate is one of
the chief safeguards the people have for their meagre scale or
standard of living. A high infant death rate, native social
workers have said, is an evil, but its present alternative is worse.

Among the nations of the modern West there are considerable
differences in the rates of population growth as related to available consumption goods. There may be said, therefore, to be in
a sense a national idea of a suitable standard of living, even
though this idea is expressed no more explicitly than the birth
rate expresses it. France, as everyone knows, has kept down
her population by reducing the birth rate. Her neighbor, Italy,
with a lower scale of living is more prolific.

Quite as striking are the differences in birth rates among different social, economic, or occupational groups within a nation.
As the standard of living varies, so the birth rate of the poor
and unskilled groups in civilized countries is much higher than
the birth rate of the well-to-do and the professional groups. In
England and some other countries, however, where aristocratic
ideals are stressed and "family" is important, the families of
the wealthy classes are likely to be large. In England, for which
the best statistics are available, the correlation between standard
of living and birth rate is, with the foregoing exception, remarkably close.[2] It is not exact, as doctors' families, for instance,

[1] Carr-Saunders, A. M., *The Population Problem*, Oxford, 1922.
[2] Florence, P. S., *Overpopulation*, London, 1926, pp. 34–37. The statistical
data are taken from the British Census (1911) Report on the Fertility of Marriage.

have a lower birth rate than that of the Church of England clergy, but here it is obvious that the one class, the doctors, have the greatest possible knowledge; the other class, the clergy, may in some cases be restrained on religious grounds from utilizing what knowledge they have.

This actual minimum standard which determines the birth rate has been established by custom or convention and seems to the people as real as subsistence itself. In fact in studies of minimum cost of living the actual minimum standard is frequently called "mere subsistence" although an analysis of the items included under it would indicate that more was included than was physiologically necessary for the human body. The "minimum standard" is not a physiological subsistence minimum in most civilized countries, but a psychological subsistence minimum on the basis of the most firmly fixed of prevailing customs and conventions. It is sometimes argued that such "minimum subsistence" standards in any given place are true minima under economic conditions as they exist there. In certain places one cannot, for instance, rent a house for less than thirty dollars or buy a pair of shoes for less than seven. In part this is true. But the very fact that there are no houses built at less than a certain physical standard and none of the roughest and cheapest clothing offered for sale, is the strongest proof that a standard of living above the physical subsistence minimum is firmly established in the community.

It is, then, a psychological minimum which determines the absolute limits of population within a country, or within a group. It may be so little above physical subsistence as to amount to practically the same thing, as among uncivilized peoples; but whenever there is any psychological standard at all, that, and not the food supply, is the real issue in setting the bounds on the natural growth of population. The standard of living acts within a culture, and the cultural attitude determines the general disposition of the people toward limitation of population, as the standard of living determines the lengths to which they will go.

Population and Decadent Standards

It is sometimes hastily assumed that a declining national birth rate is a sign of men's increasing intelligence and foresight and therefore a thing to be viewed with rejoicing. This is true only up to a certain point. If a high standard of living limits the growth of population, a decadent standard does the same thing. In the essay previously referred to, Dean Inge speaks of the decline of population in Greece, in Italy, and in Spain after the high points of their culture had been reached. These periods were characterized by luxurious living among the upper classes, desire for luxuries among the lower, and by cynicism and despair among all classes alike.

We have already mentioned the fact that within our own culture it is the people on the upper social and economic levels who are propagating themselves least rapidly. Is this, or is this not, an indication of superiority? The question is difficult. On the one hand, it is desirable not only that superior people should survive but that high standards of living survive too; and at a given time the only way to save the one may be partially to sacrifice the other. If superior mentality leads to superior standards of living, it is also only superior standards of living that can make superior mentality effective; and while in our so-called high standards of living we can see much that is undesirable from the point of view of an artificial or an ideal standard, it may nevertheless be that in the long run we should lose more from insisting on more children from the superior economic stocks than we should gain thereby.

On the other hand, as we observed in our chapter on race, the importance of the problem of increasing our superior stocks can hardly be over-estimated. If acquired characteristics cannot be transmitted, our biological inheritance must be fundamentally the most important thing of all. The standard of living of a business man who, because he has a two thousand dollar car and a yearly trip to Miami, can afford only one child, would seem to be decadent.

We must admit, however, that the question is relative and today largely academic. At present, at any rate, we can do very little by way of insisting on more children from superior economic stocks. We can probably accomplish more by attempting to bring about a lower birth rate among the inferior economic stocks.[1]

When we ask, however, what the birth rate should be, or what in fact is an optimum population from the point of view of numbers, we are faced again with a question no one can answer yet. The answer involves our knowing what is the best standard of living and how it can be best attained. It is clear that the solution is dependent on many circumstances and conditions beyond those which seem to be most immediately concerned.

MEANS OF RESTRICTING NUMBERS

When once a standard of living is established or strongly desired it is maintained or secured by keeping down the number of children in various ways. The death rate has always tended to fall as standards of living rise, due to the improved living conditions and greater knowledge of disease; so more than proportional emphasis must be placed on lessening the number of children.

There is some disagreement among students as to the relative importance of various influences affecting the birth rate in modern society. How important is and can be the direct moral restraint advocated by Malthus no one assumes to know. All students agree, however, that there is a considerable indirect restraint, partially moral, in the social attitude that frowns on very early marriages or on marriages consummated before a certain standard of economic support is assured. The community in these cases emphasizes the standard at the point

[1] Ellsworth Huntington has collected some data indicating that while it is in general true that the less intelligent people have the largest families, the most superior married people of all have more than an average number of children. There are some places already where the spread of birth-control knowledge has resulted in cutting materially the birth rate of the poor and ignorant.

when the individual is most tempted to minimize its importance. As we have noted, primitive communities accomplished the same end by the institution of various tabus. Of all the influences affecting the birth rate this social attitude is perhaps the most important. Indirectly, of course, it reacts also on the practice of artificial birth control.

The chief disagreement among students is as to the relative importance of two[1] further means by which the birth rate is affected, and no one can finally settle that question without further research.

The first of these means is an assumed natural decline in fertility with advancing civilization. It is pointed out that the lowest forms of life as a rule are the most fertile; and that apparently women might have thirty or forty children, but since they do not there must be some unknown physiological hindrance affecting fertility. It is pointed out further that with advancing civilization more and more husbands and wives who desire children are unable to have them; although we have no statistical evidence on this point. It is suggested that the development of great nervous energy, accompanying a complicated culture, tends to bring about a bodily condition in which conception is difficult; a certain degree of alkalinity in the immediate environmental situation has been demonstrated as highly favorable for conception in a number of recent experiments, and it may be, for instance, that high nervous tension tends to increase the acidity of certain body secretions.[2]

The second influence is the practice of abortion and the use of artificial contraceptives and other deliberate methods of interfering with conception. It is people of the most advanced civilizations, and, in the United States, of the most advanced

[1] Another influence suggested, but probably of minor importance, is that there is less sexual intercourse as civilization, wealth, or social position improves, due to the fact that with such improvement people find a wide and diversified field of pleasures. A small number of statistical data have been collected which tend to confirm this point within a very limited field of study. Pearl, Raymond S., *The Biology of Population Growth*, New York, 1925, Chapter VIII.

[2] Pell, C. E., *The Law of Births and Deaths*, London, 1921.

economic classes, who have knowledge of contraception, and so this may very plausibly be the reason for the decline in the birth rate with increasing civilization or improving economic or social status. It is said that in the various countries of Europe a decline in the birth rate was noted just as soon as birth-control methods began to be generally known.[1]

We shall not attempt to evaluate the relative importance of these two influences on which disagreement is so great. At present the largest number of students put the greatest emphasis on the second.

OVER-POPULATION

But if, as we have said, the population problem is taken care of by the culture and the standard of living, what is the meaning and significance of the term over-population, of which we hear so much?

In the first place, the word over-population is often used quite loosely. We say, for instance, that China is over-populated because there are too many people there to maintain a standard of living such as ours by means of the resources available there at present. Or a person of one social class says his own country is over-populated, meaning there are too many people to maintain a standard like his own. From the point of view of the people themselves who know no better standard, however, the word over-population in either case is, strictly speaking, incorrect. What one should say, rather, is that the standard of living is low.

There is another connection in which we speak of over-population more correctly. Since the war we have heard that certain countries are over-populated because of the devastation of armies, or because of the partial paralysis of industry and agriculture due to the extraordinary depression. Here, due to war conditions, the usual supply of goods is cut off, which in effect is the same thing as increasing the population. From the point of view of consumption such a situation is menacing,

[1] Florence, op. cit., pp. 31–32.

for it may result in a permanent lowering of the standard of living. In times of general mental depression it is extremely important that no economic standards be permitted to decline. The danger is, that if they once decline, the people who are suffering from an abnormal state of affairs will not have the courage to pull them up again.

There is still another and broader sense in which the term over-population is a just one. Although population follows standard of living it may follow several steps behind, and if standards of living are changing very rapidly there may be a considerable discrepancy at any given moment. In this sense it was said that England and Germany were over-populated even before the war. Had the war not intervened the situation would have taken care of itself, but, as it was, the unrest due to the temporary discrepancy probably did something to stimulate the war. The saying that over-population leads to war means just this; but war between modern nations not only fails to cure; it postpones the day when relief could have been expected.

CAN STANDARDS OF LIVING BE RAISED BY TEACHING BIRTH CONTROL?

Can consumption standards be raised by such comparatively simple instruction as that of birth control? The advocates of birth control have the most sanguine hopes as to what it can do. Many of them claim it is the solution of the problem of low standards and "unprogressive" cultures. It is a claim which we must challenge. Our knowledge of the ways in which interests arise must already have made it clear to us that one can never raise the standards of living merely by making it possible for people to have more income, more wealth, or more resources. The improvement of standards of living is not a negative process. Specific interests have to be stimulated, wants have to be aroused, before standards of living will change at all. Just as standards of living will not be improved by giving people more resources, so they will not be improved merely by providing information as to how to keep down the population. In a country where standards are rapidly rising and population has not had time to adjust itself to them, a knowledge of birth control may help to bridge the gap and, whatever its permanent results, it may be a temporary advantage. In other situations, to teach birth control would have probably no effect at best.

It is a matter of some significance that the time when knowledge of birth-control methods began to be widespread coincided with a time of very great expansion of desires in the last century. The fact that the spread of birth-control knowledge is prohibited by law in the United States probably bears a close relation to the fact that the country is a new one and in some parts of it there is still a demand for more men.

CHAPTER XXVI

AMERICAN CONSUMPTION

"He has income who knows how to use it."—Roman Proverb.

How significant are statistics of national consumption as a means of casting light on consumption translated into life? Obviously they are but a starting point, yet an essential starting point. With them as a basis we shall be prevented from aërial flights of fancy. Our statistics will keep us in touch with earth.

Per Capita Consumption in the United States, Compared with That in Other Countries

The American people have more purchasing power per capita than the people of any other nation. We do not have the exact figures for average per capita consumption in the United States compared with that in other countries, but we do have average per capita incomes, which, for relative purposes, will serve us fairly well. These figures are for 1914 and conditions have changed since then, but the essential significance of the comparison still holds good. According to the National Bureau of Economic Research,[1] if we take the average per capita income in the United States as 100%, that in

Australia	would	be	78%
Great Britain	"	"	73%
Canada	"	"	58%
France	"	"	55%
Italy	"	"	33%
Spain	"	"	16%
Japan	"	"	9%

Further light is cast on the situation by the National Industrial Conference Board's figures of the purchasing power of

[1] *Income in the United States*, Vol. I, op. cit., p. 85. These estimates were made subject to correction.

273

hourly wages in terms of food prices and rent. If the purchasing power of Philadelphia is taken as 100, the status in Ottawa and abroad on January 1, 1927, was as follows: [1]

Ottawa (Canada)	86%
Sydney (Australia)	78%
Copenhagen (Denmark)	69%
Dublin (Irish Free State)	63%
London (England)	57%
Stockholm (Sweden)	51%
Amsterdam (Netherlands)	50%
Berlin (Germany)	35%
Riga (Latvia)	30%
Prague (Czechoslovakia)	30%
Vienna (Austria)	29%
Rome (Italy)	29%
Brussels (Belgium)	26%
Warsaw (Poland)	24%

How Is American Money Spent?

Percentages of the national income estimated as spent for the various goods and services entering into consumption are given in Table IX. [2]

First let us compare these figures with Table VIII on page 259 and with the generalizations of Chapter XXIV which were based on Engel's laws. According to this table, the proportion of income spent for food declined from a maximum of 62% in Belgium in 1852–1854 to 38% for wage-earners' families in the United States in 1918–1919. At the same time the proportion of income spent for sundries rose from a minimum of 5% in Belgium to 27% for American wage-earners' families in 1918–1919. It was said that the major part of small incomes was required

[1] Information supplied directly by National Industrial Conference Board.

[2] This table must be regarded as only a tentative estimate. It has been made up from many sources. In part it is the work of graduate students in economics at Iowa State College, Miss Grace L. Pennock, Miss Jessie L. Welch, and, particularly, Mrs. E. C. Morgan. Cf. table in Edie, Lionel D., *Economics: Principles and Problems*, New York, 1925, p. 81. At this date there has never been a comprehensive and exact compilation of statistics of consumption in the United States. The National Industrial Conference Board has a study in contemplation.

for food, the basic necessity of life; but that as incomes rose, relatively less was spent for food and relatively more for sundries. In these estimates for the United States as a whole it will be seen that the proportion spent for food is only 27% and the proportion spent for sundries (including savings) 44%. This indicates, as would be expected, not only that the scale of living in the United States is immensely higher than that of Belgium in the middle of the last century, but also that the general scale in the United States is much higher than the wage-earners' scale.

Changes in American per capita expenditures for certain budget items between 1919 and 1926 have already been given in Table I on pages 6 and 7.[1]

TABLE IX

PERCENTAGE OF TOTAL NATIONAL CONSUMPTION ATTRIBUTED TO EACH MAIN CLASS OF GOODS AND SERVICES IN THE UNITED STATES

(Author's Estimates on Data from Various Sources)

Articles		Percentage
Food		27
Clothing		13
Shelter		12
Fuel and light		4
Sundries		
Furniture and furnishings	2	
Tobacco, candy, soft drinks and gum	5	
Education and reading	1	
Health	2	
Automobile	5	
Other recreations (Theatres, ball games, club dues, etc.)	3	
Miscellaneous (Cosmetics, writing materials, street-car fares, contributions, etc.)	4	
Savings and insurance	12	
Taxes	10	
Total sundries		44
Total of all		100

[1] For a discussion of different per capita expenditures at different times and for different groups, the student is referred to Winslow, Emma A., "Contributions from Budget Studies," in Berridge, W. A., Winslow, E. A., and Flynn, R. A., *Purchasing Power of the Consumer*, op. cit.

CONSUMPTION OF FOOD

On the basis of the 1926 income figures of the National
Bureau of Economic Research,[1] our estimate of 27% of national
income spent for food is $207.90 per person per year, $4.00 per
person per week, fifty-seven cents per person per day. This
would amount to about seventy cents per day per adult.

Food is the one field of consumption wherein we can discuss
not only costs but adequacy with some degree of assurance. We
shall take these up first on an average and second on an actual
per capita basis.

Professor Sherman, arguing from various small investigations, has given us estimates of the distribution in expense of
the main items entering into the American food budget. He
believes these estimates are representative not only of total
American expenditures but of typical families' expenditures
as well.[2] At the same time, Professor Pearl gives us a careful
study of the distribution of American food consumption in terms
of calories.[3] Their classifications are not precisely uniform, but
it is interesting to put them together as closely as we can.

TABLE X

AMERICAN CONSUMPTION OF MAIN ARTICLES OF FOOD IN TERMS OF
PERCENTAGE DISTRIBUTION OF EXPENSE AND OF CALORIES
(Sherman and Pearl)

Items	Percentages of Expense (Sherman)	Calories (Pearl)
Meats, poultry, fish, eggs.........	35–45	23
Dairy and fats (Butter, oleo, vegetable oils, nuts, etc.)......................	20	22
Grains......................	15–20	33
Sugars......................	5	13
Vegetables and fruits.............	15	9
Unclassified....................	5	
	95–110	100

[1] See p. 137.
[2] Sherman, Henry, *Food Products*, New York, 1924, p. 553.
[3] Pearl, Raymond, *The Nation's Food*, Philadelphia, 1920, p. 229. Figures
are for 1917–1918. Averages for the six years previous are closely similar, which
argues that there has not been a great change since.

The most interesting thing about Table X is the fact it so well brings out, that we are by no means getting our calories from the cheapest sources. The caloric value of the diet is only one test of its nutritional adequacy, of course, but these estimates are significant so far as they go. According to this table, our cereal products are yielding us in energy value twice as much as they cost, and meats, poultry, fish, and eggs are yielding us a little over half as much as they cost.

It is well known, of course, that people who have to economize on foods do so by choosing a cereal diet. Of all the grains it is said that rye yields the greatest caloric value for cost of production, yet rye flour is practically never used by American housewives, and most Americans know it only through reading about the black bread eaten by European peasants. The poor people of other countries eat very little meat indeed. Meat is a Sunday luxury in many parts of Europe. Of 2,473 working-men's families studied in Bombay, about 750 of them never tasted meat from one year's end to the other.[1]

From the point of view of national production, it is obviously more economical for people to get their nutriment from primary sources, from vegetable products, rather than from secondary sources, animal products. Pearl's estimates of the percentage of our calories and our proteins, fats, and carbohydrates drawn from primary sources is as follows:[2]

Calories	61%
Proteins	48%
Fats	20%
Carbohydrates	95%

For very poor people in other countries, of course, the percentage following every one of these headings would be 100. Hence we see that, however we may complain about our food, other peoples would consider we were rolling in luxury.

Most estimates of the calories necessary for an adult man

[1] See p. 258.
[2] Op. cit., p. 219.

run from 3,000 to 4,000 per day, depending on the labor at which he is engaged. Pearl estimates that our consumption plus edible waste is 4,273 calories a day per adult man, or 3,424 calories actually ingested.[1]

It is generally agreed also that the sum total of American food consumption if equally divided according to food requirements would give the people plenty of protein, if not too much. When proteins are adequate, fats and carbohydrates are likely to be adequate also. The greatest problem as to the general adequacy of the American diet comes in the question of our consumption of certain minerals, notably calcium, and of the vitamins. We do not know whether our total or average per capita consumption of these is adequate, but students of nutrition incline to believe that it is not.

To know the significance of food consumption, we must of course consider it not only by averages but by the amounts consumed by actual individuals. The average caloric consumption, as estimated by Pearl, does not give a great deal of leeway to those who consume less than the average. Professor William F. Ogburn calculates that from 15 to 20% of the nearly 13,000 wage-earners' families studied in 1918 were receiving insufficient quantities of food to take care of the energy requirement.[2]

Our greatest nutritional problem in the food consumption of actual people is, as we indicated in our discussion of averages, the problem of getting sufficient minerals and vitamins. At present it is believed there is a very considerable deficiency in consumption of calcium and vitamins on the part of large groups of people, including many city wage-earners and most of the poorer agricultural population of the South. Growing children are probably on the whole less well-fed than their elders. Percentages of under-nourishment indicated from medical examination of school children run from 10 to 50%, with an average of perhaps 20.

---

[1] Ibid., pp. 246–248.
[2] This is the investigation referred to on p. 253. Professor Ogburn's article is " A Study of Food Costs in Various Cities," *Monthly Labor Review*, IX, p. 322.

As we have said already, and as Table XI to follow shows in detail, the percentage of money expenditure for food definitely falls with increase in income, bringing actual per capita expenditures up or down toward the average. A man cannot go on eating more calories indefinitely, and it is hardly good form in the United States to proclaim one's increasing income by one's increasing avoirdupois. One can, of course, choose more expensive foods, turning from oatmeal and molasses to mushrooms and *paté de foie gras*, though there is a limit even here. Wealthy Romans used to dine on peacocks' tongues, but we prefer to take our greatest refinements along other lines than food. The 12,096 wage-earners' families whose expenditures are given were spending in 1918 about thirty cents per person per day, which was about thirty-eight cents per adult. Owing to the rise in the scale of living of American people between 1918 and 1926, it is presumable that a study of wage-earners' families made in 1926 would have shown considerably greater expenditures for food.[1] The average value of the food of 2,886 farm families in the same table was thirty-seven cents per person per day in 1924, or about forty-seven cents per adult.

In schools of home economics fifty cents well spent per day is regarded as sufficient not only to cover the cost of nutrition of an adult but to cover it with considerable attention to convention. Carefully invested, it may even bring something in the way of tomato salads, asparagus, and beefsteaks. In practice, of course, not all housewives buy intelligently: some buy very foolishly indeed. Yet the American people have considerable money leeway even if they do spend unintelligently for foods. The estimate of American average per capita expenditures per adult in 1926, seventy cents, and the per capita adult expenditures of wage-earners in 1918 and farmers in 1924 derived from Table XI, thirty-eight cents and forty-seven cents, should be compared not only with the conventional figure of fifty cents, but with a figure set to cover minimum necessities of nutrition, based

[1] According to the National Bureau of Economic Research, purchasing power per capita rose 25% from 1918 to 1926. See p. 137.

on the best standards so far available. This standard costs
not more than thirty cents per adult according to present
prices.[1]

Our net conclusion, then, is that while American nutrition is
not always adequate, our expenditures for food are much more
than adequate to cover desirable standards of nutrition. Custom and convention in food expenditures have actually interfered with nutrition. No one expects housewives to be mathe-
maticians dealing in grams and milligrams, and no one expects
customs and conventions to disappear. Yet in foods we have a
field where fairly definite and scientific standards obtain, and
where it should be a relatively simple matter to put them in
practice.

CONSUMPTION OF SHELTER

Twelve per cent of the national income spent for housing
amounts to $92.40 per capita or about $425 per household. If
the home is rented, this equals an average monthly rental of
$35, which obviously will provide only very simple quarters.

In order that $35 should be the average, many families, of
course, must pay less than this. The wage-earners and the
farmers whose expenditures are given in Table XI spent only
about $16 a month for rent in 1918 and in 1924. One recent
investigator declares that housing conditions in the tenement
districts of our large cities, notably Boston and New York, are
worse than any in London, Paris, Brussels, or Amsterdam.[2]
In the foreign sections of large cities households of eight or ten

[1] This figure is based on a study made at Iowa State College in June, 1926.
A food budget was worked out on the basis of supplying 3,300 calories per day
per adult, at least 70 grams of protein, .68 grams of calcium, 1.32 grams of
phosphorus, 15 milligrams of iron, and a certain content of vitamins A, B, and
C. An allowance of 10% was made for waste. At prices prevailing in Ames,
Iowa, in that month the daily cost of the budget amounted to twenty-eight cents
per adult. The budget included twenty standard but inexpensive foods. In
making it no attention was paid to conventional menus. The purpose was to
find basic costs with food conventions eliminated. See Gillette, Lucy A., "A
Minimum Food Allowance and a Basic Food Order," *Journal of Home Economics*, XII, pp. 319-324.
[2] Wood, Edith E., *Housing Progress in Western Europe*, New York, 1923,
pp. 2-3.

people are not infrequently crowded into four or five rooms. Conditions in the negro cabins of the South are also far below the American average.

The expenditures of families for shelter show a very considerable variation not only according to the families' incomes but according to the town or city in which they live. Expenditures for food and clothing are fairly well equalized by transportation, but there is no way of transporting ground rents. Other things equal, the cost of shelter roughly increases with the size of the city.

In the year 1920, 45.6% of families in the United States owned their own homes, a decrease of half of 1% since 1900. The percentage of home ownership was largest in the West North Central and the Mountain states, 56% and 55%. In the Middle Atlantic states the percentage of home ownership was smallest, 37%; in New England it was 40%. Des Moines had the greatest percentage of home ownership, 51%, of any city of over 100,000 inhabitants. New York City, as would be expected, had the smallest percentage, 13%; in the borough of Manhattan, it was only 2%.[1] Home ownership is not always feasible, but a large percentage of home ownership argues better housing conditions than a small percentage does. The home-owner has many incentives to improve his home and its surroundings; his ownership tends to stimulate his enjoyment.

According to Engel, the proportion of income spent for housing remained the same, whatever the income. This so-called law is no law in the United States. Among the wage-earners' families whose expenditures are presented in Table XI the proportion of income spent for housing declined as income rose.

CONSUMPTION OF CLOTHING

That 13% of the national income should be spent for clothing means an average expenditure of $460 per family, or $100

---

[1] *Better Homes in America. How to Own your Home*, Washington, 1924, pp. 3, 4. Data are compiled from U. S. Census.

per person. When these figures are contrasted with the average expenditures for housing, it will be seen that American people are relatively better clothed than they are housed. An average expenditure of $100 per person is not a munificent sum. It will not permit a person to appear in many of the latest creations of the Rue de la Paix, but it is enough to allow the expression of good taste and of variety, and much more than enough to provide for warmth and hygiene. It will more than take care of everything essential to well-being, apart from convention and emulation.

As a matter of fact, of course, as we have seen before, convention and emulation have a tremendous amount to do with our clothing expenditures. A family does not ordinarily choose five rooms and bath chiefly because of convention and emulation but because it needs that much room to be able to live with some degree of peaceful privacy. But a family's choice of clothing stands much more on a conventional basis.

Engel found that with increases in income, the proportion spent for clothing tended to remain the same. That does not hold true among the lower income groups in the present day United States. Among the lower income groups, the proportion spent for clothing increases with increasing income, indicating the importance placed on clothing in the workingman's budget. The proportion of income spent for clothing declines only in the higher income groups. This will be shown later in Table XI.

But how much do actual people spend for clothing? In the farm study it was found that the cost of the husbands' and wives' clothing was practically the same, $58 per year, but their sons and daughters between 19 and 24 spent $90.40 and $99.00.[1] The expenditures for adults in a selected group of wage-earners' families in the 1918 study of the United States Bureau of Labor Statistics were as follows: [2]

---

[1] United States Department of Agriculture, Bureau of Agricultural Economics, *The Farmer's Standard of Living* (Kirkpatrick, E. L.), Washington, 1926, p. 19.

[2] "Cost of Living in the United States—Clothing and Miscellaneous Expenditures," *Monthly Labor Review*, IX, pp. 1303–1316.

	Husbands	*Wives*
Northern cities	$68	$56
Southern cities	$76	$62

To see the social significance of these amounts they should be related to the previously given expenditures of the same families for food and for shelter. Compare Table XI.

We have said that by averages Americans are better clothed than they are housed. The same observation applies in the case of most actual families, and the reason for it is not far to seek. It requires a longer training of appreciation to develop a taste for good housing than it does to develop a taste for good clothes or at least for more clothes and more expensive clothes. Dressing-up appeals to the child and to the savage. Clothing shows. It tells the world, because its benefits are obvious and available at once. It is conspicuous consumption. Hence when incomes are increasing rather rapidly the increases are more likely to go for clothing than for other things which require considerable training of tastes to be enjoyed. If we could have a study of the expenditures of "old" families, those which have held an approved social position for several generations, we should doubtless find that for them expenditures for housing took long precedence over expenditures for dress.

CONSUMPTION OF FUEL AND OF SUNDRIES

The expenditure for fuel and light needs no special comment, save the often-repeated criticism that American people waste much fuel by keeping their homes too warm.

The expenditures in the sundries group present a good opportunity for the observations of the moralizer and the moralist. We shall not attempt to justify nor to condemn any of these percentages, but to add a side light or two.

Two per cent for furniture and furnishings is in line with a conventional dictum that the cost of furniture and furnishings should approximate one-fifth of the cost of housing.

Expenditures for sweets have increased since the sale of liquor was forbidden by law. This expenditure, if compared with expenditures in other countries, should be interpreted as in part compensation for the loss of liquor. There is probably no great difference in the amount of tobacco and sweets consumed by average families in different income classes, but a very considerable difference in their expensiveness.

The direct expenditure for education and reading material should be considered in relation to the fact that public agencies provide most of the people's education out of public funds and public libraries provide books.

The 2% spent on health is one of the national expenditures most unevenly divided on a per capita basis. For one thing, health service is given to people in part according to ability to pay. The health service of the poor is paid for to some extent by contributions from the wealthy, which are included in the miscellaneous group.

The satisfactions received from cars are very widely distributed. Most American families who wish to have a car either have a model of some kind or at least are looking forward to owning one. There is one car in the United States to every five people,[1] but a part of the total expense of car ownership and operation is chargeable to production, and so is not included in our estimate of 5%. In the world as a whole there is but one car to every 66 people. Canada has one to every 11 people, New Zealand one to every 12, Australia one to every 17, and the United Kingdom comes next, with one to every 43 people. In China there is one car to every 23,040 people.[2]

Not only amounts but proportions of income invested in savings and insurance are unequally divided among income groups[3] and among members of the same income group as well, since men differ very greatly in their degree of foresight. Savings and insurance are usually the most private items of

[1] United States Department of Commerce, Bureau of Foreign and Domestic Commerce, *Statistical Abstract of the United States, 1926*, Washington, 1927, p. 373.

[2] Ibid.

[3] See King, W. I., "The Net Volume of Saving in the United States," *Journal of the American Statistical Association*, XVIII, pp. 305-323; 455-470.

all budget items, and hence not subject to the levelling tendencies of convention and emulation. High-pressure salesmen of insurance, however, are now doing something to cause men to feel conventions in buying insurance, and their efforts seem to be making toward more of a "standard" than has existed in the past. One possible standardizing factor, in view of the large proportion of automobiles, is suggested by a leaning toward compulsory liability insurance for personal injury. This car insurance is the law in Massachusetts, New Hampshire comes close to it, and other states have it under consideration.

The cost of taxation is, as we have said in Chapter XIV, unequally divided, and we gave there the reasons why this unequal division was desirable from the point of view of consumption.

CHANGES IN PROPORTIONS SPENT FOR THE MAIN BUDGET ITEMS WITH INCREASING INCOME

We have referred throughout the preceding section to changes in proportions of income spent for the main budget items as income increases. At this point we shall summarize those conclusions.

In Table XI are presented the changes in the proportions of expenditures of various types of families as income increases. The 12,096 wage-earners' families were studied by the United States Bureau of Labor Statistics in 1918–1919.[1] The 2,886 farm families were studied by the United States Bureau of Agricultural Economics in 1924.[2] The figures given for the higher income groups are estimates only.[3]

---

[1] United States Department of Labor, Bureau of Labor Statistics, "Cost of Living in the United States," *Monthly Labor Review*, IX, p. 420.

[2] United States Department of Agriculture, op. cit., p. 34.

[3] These tentative estimates are based in part on a small study made by W. I. King, reported in National Bureau of Economic Research, *Income in the United States*, op. cit., Vol. II, p. 26; on a small study made by M. B. and R. W. Bruère, reported in *Increasing Home Efficiency*, New York, 1916, p. 316; and on Miss Peixotto's study, *Getting and Spending at the Professional Standard of Living*, op. cit., pp. 124, 134.

TABLE XI

PER CENT OF EXPENDITURES FOR THE PRINCIPAL GROUPS OF ITEMS OF
COST OF LIVING OF AMERICAN FAMILIES DIVIDED INTO INCOME GROUPS

(United States Department of Labor, United States Department of
Agriculture, and Author's Estimates on Data from Various Sources)

12,096 White Wage-Earners' Families, 1918–1919

Income Group	Number of Families	Size of Household	Average Value	Proportion of Total for			
				Food	Clothing	Shelter	All Other
		Persons	Dollars	%	%	%	%
Below $900....	332	4.3	843	44.1	13.2	14.5	28.2
$900–$1,199....	2,423	4.5	1,076	42.4	14.5	13.9	29.1
$1,200–$1,499..	3,959	4.7	1,301	39.6	15.9	13.8	30.6
$1,500–$1,799..	2,730	5.0	1,537	37.2	16.7	13.5	32.5
$1,800–$2,099..	1,594	5.2	1,756	35.7	17.5	13.2	33.5
$2,100–$2,499..	705	5.7	2,055	34.6	18.7	12.1	34.5
$2,500 and over	353	6.4	2,467	34.9	20.4	10.6	34.2
Total.....	12,096	4.9	1,434	38.2	16.6	13.4	31.7

2,886 White Farm Families, 1924

Value of Living Group	Number of Families	Size of Household	Average Value	Proportion of Total for			
				Food	Clothing	Shelter	All Other
		Persons	Dollars	%	%	%	%
Below $600....	58	3.3	486	54.4	11.6	12.5	21.5
$600–$899.....	280	3.6	779	52.1	11.9	11.6	24.4
$900–$1,199....	579	4.0	1,055	47.6	12.6	13.0	26.8
$1,200–$1,499..	614	4.5	1,339	45.3	13.8	12.7	28.2
$1,500–$1,799..	492	5.1	1,639	43.0	15.1	12.2	29.7
$1,800–$2,099..	332	5.3	1,932	39.8	15.4	13.5	31.3
$2,100–$2,399..	196	5.9	2,240	37.2	15.8	12.6	34.4
$2,400–$2,699..	116	6.0	2,529	36.2	15.5	12.3	36.0
$2,700–$2,999..	83	6.5	2,854	33.6	16.0	13.1	37.3
$3,000 and over	136	7.0	3,779	30.7	16.4	10.9	42.0
Total.....	2,886	4.8	1,598	41.2	14.7	12.5	31.6

Families in Higher Income Groups (Estimates)

Income Group	Proportion of Total for			
	Food (Including Food for Servants)	Clothing	Shelter	All Other
$ 5,000..........	17	12	15	56
15,000..........	12	10	15	63
25,000..........	10	8	15	67
35,000..........	8	7	15	70
50,000..........	6	6	15	73

In Chapter XXII we saw that Engel's so-called laws held generally in so far as they applied to food and to sundries. Table XI bears this out in more detail. With increases in total expenditure, the proportion spent for food decreases and for sundries increases; this seems practically invariable. The proportion of expenditure for fuel and light, not specifically included in this table, decreases slightly with increases in income.

The percentage of expenditure for clothing is seen by the table to increase with increasing income among these wage-earners' and farmers' families, but to fall in the higher income groups.

Proportions of income spent for shelter conform to no general law. They dropped as income rose among the wage-earners' families, they were erratic among the farm families, and among the higher income groups they were assumed not to change. As a matter of fact, one study of higher income groups indicated that they rose and two studies indicated that they fell. We should be obliged to have a much larger body of data than is available to draw general conclusions. In any given case it all depends, of course, on whether families of large income choose to spend for more and for more costly houses and grounds, and this is chiefly a matter of personal taste.

CHAPTER XXVII

AMERICAN SCALES AND STANDARDS OF LIVING

"In America, the passion for physical well-being is general.
. . . Never in America did I meet any citizen so poor . . .
that his imagination did not possess itself by anticipation of those
good things which fate still obstinately withheld from him."—
ALEXIS DE TOCQUEVILLE, *Democracy in America*.

American scales of living and standards of living may be
approached from at least four different points of view. First
are differences according to the amount of income, to which
our last chapter was an introduction. Second are differences
according to occupation or profession; third, differences according to country of origin or race. Fourth and finally, some
differences are to be distinguished on the basis of life in different
geographic sections of the country.

DIFFERENCES BY AMOUNT OF INCOME

So far we have discussed differences in consumption in the
United States solely with reference to different proportions
of expenditure for the main items as expenditure increases.
It is clear also that there is some difference in the kind and type
of goods that can be bought by families of high income. In
countries where economic stratification tends to conform to
stratification in customs and tastes these differences in kind
and type of goods may be very considerable indeed. In England, for example, differences in taste between rich and poor
would be much more striking than they are in the United
States.

In the United States, although there are great differences in
scales of living, amount of income is rather a poor index to
tastes. We have considerable great wealth, and we have still

288

some distressing cases of poverty, but here neither wealth nor poverty is in itself an indication of social status nor economic appreciations; and differences in expenditure between income groups are differences in degree to a greater extent than they are differences in kind. People of low income are able to copy those of higher income in almost every detail of living. Their dwellings are less costly, but they are the same kind of dwellings and furnished in a cheaper version of the same style. Their clothes are so nearly the same that only a practiced observer can detect the difference in quality. Their amusements are the same: like the rich they have their cars, with a difference only of make and model. Rich and poor thrill and laugh together over the same motion pictures. Coney Island caters to the same tastes as Miami and Palm Beach. And, most important of all, education is essentially the same, for if, by any chance, the rich should discover something superior, the public education system would furnish it to everyone as soon as it could get it. The great differences in education in the United States are not the differences in standards among income groups but the differences in standards among sections of the country.

Though statistics of consumption vary among income groups, these statistics mean little unless translated into satisfactions. The rich man, as we have seen, has much more to spend on sundries, but what does this signify if the results obtained from these sundries are no better? Those mink-coated travellers who indulge in the luxuries of first-class ocean travel are no superior company to Carolina mill hands or Kansas farmers or Maine fishermen. Said Viscount Bryce: "To the pleasantness of American life there is one, and perhaps only one serious drawback—its uniformity."[1]

To say, however, that the larger incomes in the United States are in themselves no indication of superior ability to spend them is not, of course, to say that they carry no potential advantage.

[1] *The American Commonwealth*, New York, 1910, Vol. II, p. 878.

DIFFERENCES BY OCCUPATION

Our standards are not altogether uniform, however. We should expect there would be some real if slight distinctions among the standards of people engaged in different types of occupations. In particular, we should expect professional workers to have some more or less unique standards of their own.

So far as the statistical evidence of scales is concerned, our fullest information lies in contrasts between wage-earners and farmers. We have already referred to the statistical studies of their scales of living and now let us turn again to Table XI in our preceding chapter. First we must note that the study of wage-earners' families was more extensive, and too close comparisons should not be made between it and the study of less than 3,000 farmers' families. The percentages are more valuable for our purposes than the actual amounts spent. The wage-earners' study was made in 1918, the farmers' study in 1924, and as we see by the chart on page 286, the cost of living was slightly higher in 1924. Moreover, the families in the two groups were selected by the investigators according to standards which differed in the two cases, and this would differently affect the money values of their living. The size of the farmers' households, including hired men, was 4.8, and the size of their families, 4.4. The size of the wage-earners' families was 4.9. The figures are, however, roughly comparable for the purpose for which we desire to use them.

From Table XI the following significant comparisons as to distribution of expenditures can conveniently be repeated here:

	Average Value	Food	Per Cent of Total for Shelter	Clothing	All Other
Wage-earners.....	$1,434	38.2	13.4	16.6	31.7
Farmers.........	1,598	41.2	12.5	14.7	31.6

It will be seen that the proportion of expenditure for sundries, including fuel and light, was almost exactly the same for farmers' and wage-earners' families, but the farmers had relatively more

food and the wage-earners relatively more clothing. The
wage-earners' cost of shelter was a little higher, but ground
rents in town are much more expensive than in the country.

These figures suggest that the conspicuous consumption of
clothing is more important in the town than in the country, as
Veblen declares in his *Theory of the Leisure Class;* yet the difference is not so great as in theory might be supposed. It is not
so great even as it appears, since the 16.6% of the wage-earners'
total expenditure went to clothe 4.9 persons and the 14.7% of
the farmers' expenditure clothed only 4.4 persons.

The farmers' households were smaller than the wage-earners'
households and the average total expenditure was more, but
the economic value of the farmers' food, nevertheless, was the
higher. In terms of calories the farmers' food value was probably higher yet, since the economic value of products raised on
the farm was taken not at the retail price, such as the wage-
earner would have to pay, but at an average of the retail price
and the farmers' selling price. Farm work requires a greater
caloric expenditure than many types of wage-earning, but other
factors also must combine to raise the proportion of expenditure
for the farmers' food. The fact that the farmer raises a part
of his food, and it is therefore on the spot, means that his
family consumes more than would otherwise be the case.

The most striking thing about this comparison is not the
differences but the similarities. There are, however, more
differences between the standard of living of farmers and the
standard of living of wage-earners than can appear in any table
of statistics. Chief among these is the outstanding difference
in the nature, and perhaps also in the degree, of psychic income
received from work. To a large extent the farmer is his own
master, and this to many men is of great importance. The
farmer, who watches his own crops grow and who cares for and
develops his stock, receives a type of pleasure which the industrial worker but seldom enjoys.

Nevertheless the steady movement from the farm to the city
indicates that the city is offering attractions with which, for

some men, the farm cannot compete. Of great importance is the fact that the industrial worker is tied to his task for a shorter time per day—averaging perhaps two hours per day less than the farmer.[1] The social contacts of industry and the excitements of the town are in themselves inducements and it is certain the city offers a far greater variety of interests.

The advantages of farm life and industrial life must in the long run be compensating for the country as a whole, but they are not usually compensating for individual workers. On the contrary, one type of work selects one type of man, and the other type, another.

We have few statistical studies of the scales of living of professional people. In 1912 Mr. and Mrs. Bruère made a study of the budgets of a small number of educators, physicians, clergymen, and of people in "miscellaneous professions,"[2] and we have the study of the 96 faculty families at the University of California, referred to in the footnote on page 251. The number of families in each group studied by the Bruères was too small, and their data too restricted, to be of much value to us here.

The median[3] income of the California faculty families[4] was $4,893.22, and so we should expect the percentage of their income spent for food to be much smaller than that of industrial workers or that of farmers. It was 16.8% as against 38% for wage-earners and 41% for farmers, but as the median expenditure of the faculty people was $807.50 for food, and since the faculty families averaged only 3.5 people, they had considerably more food or more expensive food than the wage-earners and the farmers. Relatively speaking, this does not point to much difference in standard.

[1] In the farm study referred to, the average length of the farmer's work day for the 1,875 families reporting on this point was 11.3 hours. Op. cit., p. 48.

[2] Bruère, Martha B. and Robert W., *Increasing Home Efficiency*, op. cit., pp. 296–318.

[3] The median is used as more significant than the average, since the average was weighted rather heavily by income received from investments and other sources not professional income.

[4] The following data are from Miss Peixotto's table, p. 124. The number of children is given on p. 63.

A difference in standard is indicated, however, by the fact that the faculty families' median percentage of expenditure for shelter was $684.50 while it was only $440.33 for clothing. They obviously ascribed less importance to the pleasures of dress than to the pleasures of home surroundings. This would be an expected result of education.

When, however, we look into the expenditures in the sundries group, we find that the largest single item is the cost of the automobile, $364.00, and that recreation claims $197.85 more. Education took $69.30, professional expenses $60, church and charity together $57. In other words, the combined median expenditures for automobile and recreation were over three times as much as the combined median expenditures for education, professional expenses, and church and charity.

It is unfortunate that we do not have more studies of professional scales and standards.[1] In so far as this California study is typical, it would show that the standards of college faculty as indicated by broad scales of expenditures are not very different from the standards of other Americans; though we may perhaps suppose that the satisfaction these faculty families received from their professional work was more distinctive in amount and character.

We have here a second indication of that uniformity which Viscount Bryce considered the most unfortunate aspect of American life. It is comparatively easy to reach the standards of the great mass of the people, comparatively hard to achieve what might be better.

DIFFERENCES BY COUNTRY OF ORIGIN AND RACE

The standards of living of recent immigrants to the United States naturally differ considerably from the standards of living of natives, and vary among immigrants according to their

[1] It was Miss Peixotto's impression that this study is generally typical of university life in the United States (p. 58). The present author feels sure, however, that relatively smaller expenditures for automobiles and recreation and greater expenditures for education and professional life would be found among the faculties of the three New England collegiate institutions with which she is most familiar.

country of origin. The distinctive character of such foreign standards of living is not, however, maintained long in the United States. It is usually considerably modified even in the first generation of immigrants, and in the second or third generation is likely to have passed away altogether. The newly arrived immigrants who set up housekeeping in one room on the lower East Side of New York come to see their children established in an apartment in the Bronx and their grandchildren enjoying a house of their own on Long Island. Furthermore, such different standards of immigrants' living as these are have decreased in importance, owing to our greatly restricted immigration.

While they last, however, these foreign standards within the United States are of much interest to the student of culture. Sometimes a considerable section of a large city or the greater part of a small city is almost entirely dominated by a foreign standard of living, and in country districts small towns have occasionally been so completely foreign that even the public-school teaching was conducted in a foreign tongue. The largest study that has ever been made of the standards of living of foreigners in the United States is contained in the Pittsburgh Survey of conditions in steel mills and among steel workers.[1]

The fact that foreign workers have a less expensive scale of living and hence are willing to work for lower wages than native-born Americans has lately been stressed by the American Federation of Labor and other labor interests in seeking for further restriction of immigration by law. It is argued that the presence of large numbers of foreigners willing to work for low wages is tending to bring down American scales and standards of living and is injuring American workmen. This was also the argument that led to the Chinese exclusion act of 1882.[2]

European immigrants are usually assimilated to American

[1] Russell Sage Foundation. Six volumes under the editorship of Paul U. Kellogg, of which the most important for our purposes here is *Homestead* by Margaret F. Byington, New York, 1910.

[2] Cf. "The Battle of the Standards" in Carver, T. N., *Principles of National Economy*, Boston, 1921, pp. 608–615.

standards within two or three generations, but there are at least four fairly sizable groups in the United States among whom racial or national differences have been fairly persistent for some time. These are groups the members of which have not had the opportunity to mingle to any great degree with white native-born Americans. The oldest of these groups comprises the descendants of the American Indians, many of whom are living in an unhappy cultural condition which retains the defects but not the integrity of the standards of their ancestors. A second group is the so-called Cajans, the descendants of the Acadians who were expelled from French Canada in 1755, and who live in the Redbone district of Louisiana. A third group is the Mexicans, in settlements of their own throughout the Southwest. By far the largest of the groups is the agricultural negroes, living almost entirely by themselves in the South.

About one tenth of the population of the United States is negro. We hear relatively little about the scales and standards of living of the negroes, though one of our greatest social problems is here. The scales of living of the negroes are almost universally lower than those of the whites of the same localities. In 1917 the United States Bureau of Labor Statistics made a study of scales of living in the District of Columbia,[1] covering expenditures of 1,481 white and 629 colored low-income families. The average expenditure of the negro families (average 3.5 persons in the net family) was $769.12, as contrasted with $1,216.03 spent by the whites (average 3.8 persons in the net family). In the 1918 investigation of wage-earners' families made by the Bureau of Labor Statistics, 741 of the 12,837 families studied were those of negroes. Their average expenditure was $1,115, while that of the whites was $1,434.[2]

The Southern negro engaged in agriculture is, however, much more badly off in a material way than his urban brothers. Conditions in the agricultural South as a whole are the worst conditions in the country, but for the negro they are the worst

[1] *Monthly Labor Review*, V, pp. 639–655.
[2] Ibid., IX, pp. 420–421.

not only absolutely but worse in comparison with the whites in the same regions. As characteristic of Southern conditions, we have a small study of 154 colored families in selected localities of Kentucky, Tennessee, and Texas, which was made in 1919 by the United States Department of Agriculture in coöperation with the State College of Agriculture in the states named. The more important findings for our purposes are presented in Table XII. For purposes of comparison the same data for 861 white farm families believed to be comparable in the same regions are given also.[1]

TABLE XII

AVERAGE EXPENDITURES, AND PROPORTIONS OF EXPENDITURES, FOR THE MAIN BUDGET ITEMS, SHOWN BY A STUDY OF 154 COLORED FARM FAMILIES IN SELECTED AREAS OF THE SOUTH, 1919; TOGETHER WITH THE CORRESPONDING DATA FOR 861 WHITE FARM FAMILIES IN THE SAME REGIONS

(United States Department of Agriculture)

	Amounts		Percentage of Total Expenditure	
	Colored Families 4.8 Persons	White Families 4.6 Persons	Colored Families 4.8 Persons	White Families 4.6 Persons
Food............	$326.7	$ 631.8	53.5	44.0
Shelter..........	41.0	139.9	6.7	9.7
Clothing........	107.1	254.7	17.5	17.7
Furnishings......	4.5	28.5	.7	2.0
Operating.......	55.8	172.9	9.1	12.0
Health..........	24.8	67.0	4.1	4.7
Advancement....	28.3	84.3	4.6	5.9
Personal........	8.9	16.9	1.5	1.2
Insurance........	14.0	36.9	2.3	2.6
Unclassified......		3.1		.2
Total.......	$611.1	$1,436.0	100.0	100.0

The number of negro families studied, 154, was too small to provide a basis for very definite conclusions as to the negroes' scale of living in detail. Nevertheless the facts brought out by the table are fairly representative for our purpose. Anyone who travels through the South with his eyes open must be impressed

[1] United States Department of Agriculture, Bureau of Agricultural Economics, *The Cost of Living among Colored Farm Families of Selected Localities of Kentucky, Tennessee and Texas*, a preliminary report, Washington, 1925.

by the wretched living conditions of the colored people: the ramshackle cabins standing in puddles of water and looking as if the next wind would blow them down; the ragged pickaninnies and the lean dogs hanging around the doors. Could he enter those miserable cabins he would be still more impressed by the old barrels and boxes taking the place of furniture. He would not care to taste the family's dinner of corn meal mush, fat pork, and molasses.

The most striking thing about Table XII is that the negroes' total expenditure was less than half that of the white families. The second most striking thing is the differences in distribution of income between the two groups. The negroes, as would be expected, had to give a larger proportion of their total expenditure to food, for which they spent 53.5% of their total. They spent, however, relatively as much for clothing as did the whites, and they spent relatively more than the whites for the small item of "personal" (barbers' fees, tobacco, confectionery, etc.). This indicates they were looking upward in superficial or conspicuous consumption. For shelter and house furnishings they spent not only absolutely but relatively considerably less than did the whites: an average of forty-one dollars a year went for the shelter of average families of 4.8 persons.

Differences in the intangible aspects of the standards of living of negroes and whites in the same district are also as striking, although not so easily reducible to statistics. In particular the low status of education among negro families is a menace to standards of living of negroes and whites alike.

DIFFERENCES BY SECTION OF THE COUNTRY

There are appreciable differences in average per capita ability to spend between different states and different sections of the country. From Table XIII, compiled by the National Bureau of Economic Research,[1] it is seen that in 1919, which is taken as the most nearly normal of the three years studied,[2]

[1] Leven, Maurice, *Income in the Various States*, New York, 1925, pp. 260–261.
[2] Ibid., p. 259.

the Pacific states and the Middle Atlantic states enjoyed the highest average per capita incomes, $793 and $781, respectively, while the average per capita income in the East South Central states was only $345.   Among individual states, the highest per capita incomes were received in New York, Massachusetts, Rhode Island, and Connecticut, and the lowest in South Carolina.   These figures do not tell us a great deal about the welfare of the people, since incomes are particularly unequally distributed in the Middle Atlantic states and in Massachusetts, Rhode Island, and Connecticut.   In the South the very low incomes of negroes bring down the average greatly.

TABLE XIII

DISTRIBUTION OF TOTAL INCOME PER CAPITA IN DIFFERENT SECTIONS OF THE UNITED STATES, 1919

(National Bureau of Economic Research)

Continental United States..................$614

New England............................. 715
Middle Atlantic.......................... 781
East North Central....................... 669
West North Central....................... 582
South Atlantic........................... 445
East South Central....................... 345
West South Central....................... 469
Mountain................................. 634
Pacific.................................. 793

Certain material differences in living in different sections of the country, particularly those due to public expenditure, are, nevertheless, quite in harmony with what we should expect from these figures.   The East, particularly the Northeast section of the country, and the Pacific states are regarded as materially progressive.   On the whole they have good schools, good public buildings and libraries and good roads.   In the South, on the other hand, much progress for better schools, better public buildings and libraries and better roads must still be made.

With regard to the more intangible and less material aspects of the standard of living, certain sectional differences in the country are obvious to the attentive traveller. We hear a great deal of the New England emphasis on culture and on economy, the "plain living and high thinking" of the Puritan. "Culture" is institutionalized in New England. All good New Englanders take many of their cues from old England and from Europe; they have nothing to learn from the American West, and all good New England children go to Athens when they die.

New York, as everyone knows, is the place for variety and excitement. The true New Yorker is never at home. Why should he be? He has the theatres of the country at his service, and he can dine out with sumptuous satisfaction every day in the week. Luxury, however, is secondary to variety for the New Yorker. He dashes about, professes to be a cosmopolitan, and in fact has probably a greater number of superficial interests than any other American.

The true Southerner seeks neither the aspiring interests of intense New England nor the varied interests of energetic New York. Life to him is not worth such a struggle. He is sometimes shiftless and often unambitious. Yet he is the only one who knows the spirit of social amenities and the secret of social charm.

The Far Westerner is the most materially minded of all Americans. Big cars are the very breath of life to him. The love of luxury and the conviction that luxury has a divine mission spur him on to greater and greater income heights.

In the Middle West, the most homogeneous and by consequence the most democratic part of the United States, the standard of living has a certain tentative character. The Middle Westerner also emphasizes the material side of life, but more because of lack of experience than because of conviction. He has the least institutionalized of all American standards of living. The Middle Westerner is generally ready to be set right, if anybody knows how to do it.

Too much general emphasis, of course, should not be put on sectional differences in the United States, interesting as they are to the student of culture. To the foreigner these differences may be swallowed up in the peculiar similarities that are common to all Americans. John Drinkwater was once asked whether he was conscious of sectional differences as he travelled about the United States, and he replied, with some embarrassment, that Americans seemed to him more alike than they seemed different.

Is There a Minimum American Scale of Living?

Is there any sense in which we can rightly speak of a "minimum American scale of living"? In wage adjustments in the United States considerable attention has been focused on the nature and cost of what has been called a "fair minimum" or a "minimum of health and decency."

Any such scale arbitrarily set up must take account of the facts of consumption, yet it obviously depends very largely also on the investigator's personal opinion as to what is a fair or decent amount or quality of food, clothing, shelter, fuel and light, sundries. None the less, there is a reasonable degree of conformity among the scales proposed on different occasions by different people. Each student compares his own estimate with those of others.

It is of interest to us to know that these expressions of opinion as to a "fair minimum" American scale of living for wage-earners show a range, ordinarily, from about $1,500 to $2,000 or more at present prices.

From 35 to 40% of the expenditure is usually allotted to food, 15 to 20% to shelter, 15 to 20% for clothing, about 5% to fuel and light, and 20 to 30% for sundries. An American scale is generally assumed to include an adequate diet, including plenty of milk and meat, vegetables and fruit daily; at least four rooms (and in cities usually a bathroom) for a family of four or five; clothing sufficient in quantity and chosen with some regard to style; and, among the sundries items, carfare, a daily and Sunday newspaper and a magazine, movies for the family now and then, and a modest sum for club memberships, for church and charity, and for insurance or savings. The expenses of operating the house, including renewal of furniture and furnishings, are also of course provided for. So many of these estimates are easily available for study that we shall not give more space to them here.[1]

It is worth noting that every minimum proposed as the least consistent with health and decency turns out to be higher than what a large number of the workers concerned are receiving. Since, however, as we have seen, the scale of living of the lower income groups in the United States is looking upward, it comes about as a matter of course that any artificial minimum scale proposed is a little in advance of what is actually attained. If all the workers in a group should reach the minimum scale once proposed for them, it would be found that already another minimum scale a little beyond that attained would automatically have arisen in their own ambitions.

[1] A discussion of minimum and of comfortable American scales and standards is given in Andrews, Benjamin A., *Economics of the Household*, New York, 1924, pp. 105–110. See also National Industrial Conference Board, *Family Budgets of American Wage Earners*, op. cit., Ch. III, and the Board's reports of estimates of minimum standards referred to in the note on p. 257. See also Meeker, Royal, "Relation of Cost of Living to the Public Health—A Standard Minimum of Health Budget," *Monthly Labor Review*, VIII, pp. 1–10; and ibid., "What is the American Standard of Living?" *Monthly Labor Review*, IX, pp. 1–13.

CHAPTER XXVIII

THE INDIVIDUAL AND THE STANDARD OF HIS GROUP—THE MATERIALS FOR BUDGET BUILDING

"Come over into Macedonia and help us."—The Book of Acts.

The ordinary man or woman who thinks about consumption seriously is likely to ask for specific advice with regard to his spending. "How much ought a person of my income to spend for rent?" "How much ought our family to save?" "What make of car is suitable for me?" Even "What allowance shall I make to my ten-year-old daughter?" These and similar questions bombard the economist who presumes to speak of consumption. Precise advice is what the world demands, but what the economist must be slow to give.

One great danger of giving precise advice as to the spending of money is that it may encourage undesirable standardization. There is no fixed amount or percentage which can be named as "best," and the consumption economist is more interested in recommending intelligent divergence from custom on the basis of the needs of particular individuals and families than he is in bringing about a standardized world. Advice is not his province. His eye is fixed on that "tomorrow and tomorrow" when men's standards will be better than any he can possibly advise today. The great advances in civilization come chiefly by men's thinking for themselves.

Nevertheless there is some point in the question so frequently raised, "What do you advise for me?" There is unintelligent as well as intelligent divergence from standardization, and one who is diverging in the wrong direction may well ask what he "ought" to do. He may be answered, first, by being given typical practice, by being told what the majority of other people like him are doing; second, by being informed of principles

302

which should lead to improvement over those typical standards. Materials for both of these possible ways of answering him have been implicit in our preceding discussion, but it is well to make them explicit here.

TYPICAL PRACTICE

In the first place, the individual starts out in life as a member of a group with its own standard of living, and his individual standard has its basis in the standard of the group of which he is a member. This applies to his expenditure for food, housing, clothing, and all his incidental expenditures, and it also applies even more fundamentally, as we have seen, to his views of what is worth consuming. All intelligent individuals to some extent set up their own standards and conclusions as to what is best for them and of course it is through its individuals that the group from time to time changes its institutions. Nevertheless, members of the group they still are, and members of the group they remain. Though they may come to raise themselves in some degree into the free air of individual responsibility, their roots are planted in the group. Obviously, therefore, we can well begin by checking an individual's consumption by the typical practice of the large group of which he is a member. We should ask him to show that any divergence on his part from typical standards is due to superior rather than to inferior intelligence on his part.

The materials for determining typical American practice have already been given. We have already discussed American consumption and American standards of living. We have given in Chapter XIII some available facts of American incomes and in Chapter XXVI have estimated the percentages of total American expenditures for the main budget items. It will be a matter involving some considerable judgment to deduce from these facts and estimates the average expenditures of a "typical" family of two adults and two minor children of average income. On the basis of evidence for earlier years presented in Chapters XIII, XXV, and XXVI and the sources from which the statistics in these chapters are drawn,[1] we suggest in Table XIV the average income and expenditures today of a "typical" American family taken as two adults and two minor children. The typical American family has more than two children born to it, but on an average not more than two are dependent on their parents at any one time. It must be clearly understood that we are attempting to present conditions as typical as possible, so we may have the best point of departure for considering actual ones. There would be a time in its history when the typical American family would be having more of an economic struggle than is indicated in Table XIV, as well as a time when its economic struggle would be less.

TABLE XIV

ESTIMATED INCOME AND EXPENDITURES FOR THE MAIN BUDGET ITEMS OF A "TYPICAL" AMERICAN FAMILY OF TWO ADULTS AND TWO MINOR CHILDREN

(Author's Estimates on Data from Various Sources)

	Amount	Per Cent
Income	$2,000	100
Expenditures for		
Food	660	33
Clothing	345	17
Shelter	300	15
Fuel and light	100	5
Sundries	595	30

Table XIV now becomes our point of departure. We can

[1] Income figure based on National Bureau of Economic Research, *Income in the United States*, Vol. I., op. cit., p. 134. In 1918, 39% of personal incomes in the United States were under $1,000; 47% were under $1,100; 55% were under $1,200; 61% were under $1,300; 67% under $1,400; 72% under $1,500. We assume that the lower personal incomes were more commonly those of boys and girls, women and unmarried or recently married men, and place our typical income figure arbitrarily at $1,430. To this is added arbitrarily 35%, which represented the increase in income per capita of the gainfully employed from 1918 to 1926, according to the *News Bulletin* of the National Bureau of Economic Research for February 21, 1927, p. 3. To this figure of $1,930 we have added arbitrarily $70, to take care of the cases in which mothers with minor children contribute financially to the family income. It will be seen that the percentages of expenditures do not conform to those of any of the classifications in Table XI. This is in part due to the fact that the groups comparable in income to our typical family were not comparable to it in size. Much more research on the subject of income and expenditures would have to be done before we could put our arbitrary assumptions to a conclusive test.

supplement it at the outset by laying down the following propositions, based also on typical practice:

Families of four with incomes larger than $2,000 will ordinarily spend less than $660, or 33%, for food and more than $595, or 30%, for sundries; the converse also holds.

Families larger than four with incomes of $2,000 will ordinarily spend more than $660, or 33%, for food; more than $345, or 17%, for clothing; approximately the same as or even less than $300, or 15% (unless the family is very large), for shelter and fuel and light; less than $595, or 30%, for sundries. The converse also holds.

Families larger than four with incomes of less than $2,000 tend to spend a smaller percentage of their incomes for shelter. Not only the lowest amounts but the lowest percentages for shelter are likely to be found among the poorest families.

Families living in the city will spend slightly more than $300, or 15%, for shelter and families living in the country will spend slightly less. They will ordinarily pay more for shelter the larger the city, though this depends somewhat on the kind of accommodations the city offers.

There will be only slight differences in expenditures between industrial workers and farmers. Professional and clerical workers will ordinarily spend less than $660, or 33%, for food, more than $300, or 15%, for shelter; more than $595, or 30%, for sundries. Business people will tend to do the same, though at these low incomes their standards are more like those of industrial workers than like those of professional people. Professional workers with incomes above $2,500 or $3,000 will spend a smaller percentage for clothing. The third section of Table XI previously given casts light on typical practices of professional and business people of higher income groups.

IMPROVEMENTS ON TYPICAL PRACTICE

All the foregoing, as we have said, is based merely on current practice. The matter cannot be left here. We have indicated in our preceding chapters that with intelligence the typical

American family might be better fed than it is on a percentage for food expenditure smaller than the one we have given; that a percentage for clothing somewhat smaller and a percentage for shelter somewhat larger than those we have given would be more in accord with a matured attitude towards life in society. These adjustments would, in most cases, leave a larger percentage for sundries.

All this has related to the division of the family's money among the main items of the budget. Within the separate budget items certain further recommendations may be made. The best of these recommendations available are those for food, since it is in this field that exact science has expressed itself most clearly. Psychological factors are not and need not be so important in the case of foods as are the measurable physiological factors. In eating, the main point is to be adequately fed, and a healthy appetite does not require the stimulation of costly foods, like sweetbreads, nor of foods elaborately prepared, as potatoes à la Canary. As Horace—though an Epicurean—once observed:

> "'Tis not in costly flavors pleasure lies
> But in thyself. Go, seek thy appetite
> In stress of labor."

There is, indeed, something to be said on psychological grounds for ceremonious arrangement of service, for delicate nuances of flavors and for diversification of foods stimulating to the imagination, in which the French are masters, but the excessive expenditures which socially-minded dietitians in the United States condemn are due to unwholesome eating habits rather than to the cultivation of aesthetic tastes in eating.

Professor Sherman gives two simple rules for good food consumption under all conditions and at all income levels.[1]

"(1) At least as much should be spent for milk (including cream and cheese if used) as for meats, poultry, and fish, and

"(2) At least as much should be spent for fruits and vegetables as for meats, poultry, and fish."

[1] *Food Products*, op. cit., p. 573.

The assumption, based on American practice, is that meats will be consumed and that expenditure for meats will itself be adequate. During the war, the United States Food Administration advocated that, for economy, not more than 20% of the food money should be spent for meat, fish, or eggs, and 20% or more should be spent for bread and cereals. Milk and cheese; fruits and vegetables; and fats, sugars, etc., would each require a fifth more. One would not recommend that a diet consist solely of cereals, but of all foods cereals give the greatest value for the money.

Such recommendations as these furnish a means by which a family can check its own food consumption, but they should not be taken as absolute in any sense. They are time-savers in checking, and that is what most people want. Any individual family might develop superior standards if it would apply nutrition principles carefully to its own preferences and conditions.

In the field of shelter, a common piece of advice is that families should not ordinarily spend more than 20% of their income for housing, although in large cities an expenditure of 25% may occasionally be necessary. This recommendation is useful, though individual circumstances may counsel divergence even here. When a family knows that it will probably remain some time in a place, and feels justified from the point of view of permanency in buying or building its own home, it may properly spend rather more than on a rented one. By and large, and in the long run, all economic costs and risks considered, the economic status of buying and of renting are the same, but more pleasure is ordinarily derived from the house if the family owns it, and more of the family's time is likely to be spent in it and about its grounds. For this reason a family owning its home can afford to spend less for something else, commercial recreation, for instance, and more for the house.

A friend remarked to the author recently: "You know, since we've got our house and garden we've scarcely gone into the city for dinner at all. We're going to build a sleeping porch with the money we're saving." As a family's conditions change, its allocation of expenditures normally changes with them.

Clothing expenditures are based so largely on fashion and convention that specific recommendations here are almost necessarily rather of the nature of moral advice than of economic principle. From our discussion of the mores the reader should be able to draw his own conclusions. The requirements of warmth and cleanliness could be met for expenditures much smaller than those prevailing among nine-tenths of our people. The cost of beauty, if it were really demanded, would be less than the cost of fashion.

The operating expenses of the household include fuel and light, and furniture and furnishings, including cleaning supplies. The cost of fuel and light runs from 4 to 6% in almost all cases of moderate incomes, and there is no reason to suppose an increase is needed nor that very much of a reduction can satisfactorily be made, with present methods of heating. When a family is furnishing a house anew, an arbitrary principle is sometimes set up that the furniture and furnishings should be about one fifth of the cost of the house. A long-run average of one fifth of the annual cost of housing applied to the upkeep and renewal of furniture and furnishings would amount to the same thing. This fraction, however, would be less than one fifth when the furniture was new, and later, when larger replacements were made, would be more than one fifth in some years. But the writer recalls one home she has visited where the furnishings cost more than the house, and were so choice that provision had been made for their eventual custody in a museum. On the other hand, there is no reason why an American family might not, if they wished, emulate the Japanese and live happily in a home atmosphere largely free of the encumbrances of furniture. The ultimate test is not in the percentage but in the reason.

In even more striking degree there is a difficulty in setting up desirable amounts or percentages to be spent for the various other items described as sundries. Typical practice here, if there is such a thing as typical practice, is hardly worth noting even as a point of departure. A family's expenses for carfare to or from work or school are not adjustable to an arbitrary budget. Their expenses for the maintenance of health cannot be forecast, except for periodic examinations by physician and dentist. Their expenditures for recreation, education, societies, church and charity are and ought to be dependent on a wide variety of circumstances of which there would be no typical combination. The best thing a family can do in making a sundries budget is to take care of necessary and predictable expenditures for carfare and health, and exercise its own judgment as to whether a contribution to the Fourth of July fund of the Rotary Club is or is not worth more to it than a subscription to the *American Mercury*. Even such advice as "Take more magazines," "Buy more pictures," "Travel!", good as these things are, is not necessarily good advice. In this field where quality, not numerical measurement, is above all the test of value, it is far more important to get the family to think for itself, even though it sometimes goes wrong, than to induce it to conform to somebody's idea of "culture." The arbiter of culture would be our most dangerous citizen if he succeeded in wielding any real influence.

There is, however, one field in which guidance is more frequently asked than in any other, and where some economic principles can be applied, though it is not a simple matter to apply them—the field of savings and insurance. "How much should I save?" What answer can justly be given?

John Stuart Mill long ago observed: [1]

"With the same pecuniary inducement, the inclination [to save] is very different, in different persons, and in different communities. The effective desire of accumulation is of unequal strength, not only according to the varieties of individual character, but to the general state of society and civilization. Like all other moral attributes, it is one in which the human race exhibits great differences, conformably to the diversity of its circumstances and the stage of its progress."

[1] *Principles of Political Economy*, Book I, Chap. XI, 2.

The virtue in saving, of course, resides not in the saving itself but in the object for which the saving is done, and the question of saving is for most people precisely as "moral," no more and no less, than other questions in the field of consumption. In discussing the question it will help us to distinguish between saving for some single object, as for a house, the education of the children, or a grand piano, and saving for the support of a family deprived of its breadwinner or for old age. The first kind of saving may, in fact, be dismissed from our discussion here as involving merely an extended application of recommendations already given as to forethought in consumption.

In the case of providing some means of support for the family if its breadwinner should die we have a problem of risk which a family of slender resources can best meet by insuring the life of the father. It would be quite impossible to expect savings to meet this risk in the early years of family life. According to its means the family must decide whether or not the policy can be made large enough so the family can live in whole or in part on the income received from it as invested, or whether the capital sum must be spent in tiding over the period until the survivors can become self-supporting. Low-paid wage-earners quite generally carry burial insurance, in policies running from one hundred to five hundred dollars; this pays for the funeral and carries the family a few weeks until the mother can find work or, in some states, secure her pension.

The emergency of the death of the wage-earner is very definitely a possible need to be provided for, and provisions for this possibility should take their place with other necessities of family living. In the United States, this is quite generally done. Insurance is not essential if other provisions are made but in most cases some life insurance is the most satisfactory provision because it can be so definitely adjusted in advance to the conditions of an emergency. Insurance of any kind, when placed with a reliable company, has the additional advantage of usually being a safe means of investment. Theoretically a person could choose just as safe investments with slightly higher rates of interest in the general investment field, but in actual life an untrained man or woman is at a disadvantage here. Too many already have placed their hard-earned savings in the hands of some smooth-tongued salesman or over-enthusiastic friend, and bought their experience at a price they could ill afford. Insurance companies make a great point of the fact that saving to meet insurance payments compels habits of regularity in saving, which for some families is a service.

It is not so easy to give recommendations for saving for old age. One flat rate, such as 10% of income, can certainly not be advised for all or even for any large proportion of actual cases. In making recommendations the past savings of the family, its future prospects as to income and expenses, including dependence of children, and its hopes for the future, are all points just as important as the present income of the family. What is more, the general price level may change, and this is not predictable.

It will help the family in making its plans to know at what annual rates old-age annuities of different amounts can be purchased. The family certainly should be informed of the rate at which savings increase at compound interest. A hundred dollars saved annually during forty years of working life does not seem very much in itself—four thousand dollars—but the twelve thousand dollars or so which it has become at compound interest is another matter. The knowledge of these facts of increasing return is encouraging to people who find it hard to save, and people who are in danger of saving too much are given pause by them. Many banks furnish tables showing the rates at which money increases, and some of them have advisors who will help people on the basis of conditions prevailing in individual cases. One reason why specific printed advice about proportions to save is not acted upon more generally than it is, is that people suspect it is not altogether sound advice for their circumstances, and their suspicions are usually correct. The question should be treated as a matter of economic common sense.

In some foreign countries the aged are provided with old-age pensions which come, of course, from the taxes paid by other citizens. Where the distribution of wealth and income rests on old vested interests or where the economic system is essentially corrupt, such pensions are one partial solution of problems of poverty and of social justice. Many people have claimed in the United States that the ordinary man would never learn to save, but the ordinary man with the help of the insurance companies has already begun to disprove that contention. There are still many cases of real poverty in the United States, where saving is impossible or not to be recommended. Such poverty in the United States, however, is more usually a result of defect, ignorance, or misfortune than of persistent economic evils, and with the removal of the causes it is growing less and less common. The principle of old-age pensions paid by the state implies that poverty in old age is to be considered more or less normal.

Families who wish to get the greatest value for their money, and these are all families, must have some advance plan for their spending, though they may carry it in mind rather than on paper. As a means for checking expenditures with the budget some families get much aid from keeping household accounts, at least occasionally. There is, of course, such a thing as wasting good time in fussy account keeping. The author has had considerable experience in helping families with accounts, and has found that the simplest forms of bookkeeping present the greatest advantages. Elaborate forms are very rarely kept, whatever the family's initial enthusiasm. One column for food, one column for clothing, and one for "all other" is about as complicated a plan as most families will hold to, and all necessary results may be easily deduced from it. The more unsatisfied wants are felt by a family the more need there is for them to keep a check in some way over their expenditures.

THE EXPENDITURES OF THE INDEPENDENT SINGLE INDIVIDUAL

The independent single individual, whether man or woman, fits into typical schedules even less satisfactorily than the family does. In the case of independent single individuals we have to consider not only those differences which exist between different parts of the country and between city, town, and country, but also the very considerable differences caused by whether or not the individual is living at home or away from home. The age of the individual makes a notable difference so far as expenditures for clothing are concerned. Relatively the largest expenditures for clothing among both men and women come in the years immediately preceding the normal age for marriage, say between twenty and twenty-five.[1] Relatively the largest expenditures for amusement among men come at the same period. The independent single individual does not ordinarily have to economize so closely as a family does, and so his personal preferences can play a larger part in determining what his expenditures shall be.

To add to our difficulties in presenting typical or normal practice, we have almost no statistical data dealing with the expenditures of typical single individuals who are economically independent. The statistical data available are practically confined to the budgets and expenditures of girls and young men living on or near a minimum wage; and to the recommendations of banks and personal service departments of clothing stores, which for our purposes are of very little value.

Under these circumstances it would seem to require considerable temerity on the part of any author to submit "typical" amounts and percentages of expenditure for independent single individuals. The data presented in Table XV must be accepted with a good deal of caution. Conclusions as to income are based on the figures of the National Bureau of Economic Re-

[1] Cf. evidence presented in United States Department of Agriculture, *The Farmer's Standard of Living*, op. cit., p. 20.

search, briefly reviewed in the footnote on page 304. Conclusions as to expenditure were suggested in part by data collected by the present author in 1919, 1920, and 1921, when she made some brief surveys of the cost of living of single individuals in various cities for the National Industrial Conference Board; in part by the author's later conferences with independent single individuals.

TABLE XV

ESTIMATED INCOME AND EXPENDITURES FOR THE MAIN BUDGET ITEMS OF INDEPENDENT SINGLE INDIVIDUALS: A "TYPICAL" AMERICAN MAN AND A "TYPICAL" AMERICAN WOMAN

(Author's Estimates on Data from Various Sources)

	Man		Woman	
	Amount	Per Cent	Amount	Per Cent
Income....................	$1,550	100	$1,350	100
Expenditures				
Food.................	416	27	351	26
Clothing..............	185	12	257	19
Shelter (including heat and light)...........	234	15	202	15
Sundries..............	715	46	540	40

The main typical deviations from the figures presented in this table would be the following:

Men and women living at home would spend less than the amounts and percentages given for food and shelter; men and women boarding and rooming at the same place would spend about the same as the estimates; men and women eating at restaurants and living in lodgings would spend more.

Expenditures for shelter would be greater than the amounts and percentages given for people living in the city, less for people living in the country.

Expenditures for clothing would be greater than the amounts and percentages given for young people in the years immediately preceding the normal age of marriage.

As incomes increase, the percentage of expenditure for food declines and the percentage of expenditure for sundries rises in the case of independent single individuals as in the case of families. There is a presumption that the percentage of expenditure for clothing will rise for a time and then decline.

The general principles for improvement in standards are the same in the case of single individuals as they are in the case of families. Since the independent single individual has more of a margin for expressing his personal likes, it is economically easier for him to save than it is for a family, though the greatest incentives to saving usually come in the responsibilities of family life. It would be well if these normal responsibilities could be foreseen sufficiently early so that the real costs of saving could be more equally distributed over the whole period during which saving is possible.

CHAPTER XXIX

THE EVALUATION OF CONSUMPTION

"We want to measure the height to which we have been able to build our 'civilisation' towards the skies; we want to measure the progress we have made in our great dance of life towards the unknown future goal, and we have no idea what either 'civilisation' or 'progress' means. This difficulty is so crucial, for it involves the very essence of the matter, that it is better to place it aside and simply go ahead, without deciding, for the present, precisely what the ultimate significance of the measurements we can make may prove to be."—HAVELOCK ELLIS, *The Dance of Life.*

All our observations on consumption and all our study of it must naturally urge us along to the one great question of the ultimate significance of consumption and of the ways in which this ultimate significance may be measured. Our last chapter on the materials for budget making led us to the outskirts of this question. That chapter was fairly specific and dealt with fairly concrete matters, for it treated of the problems of an individual who attempts at any given time to achieve the best standards within the standards of a group, the standards of the group being themselves taken to a certain extent for granted. But we have not as yet directly touched the profounder and the more complex problem of the evaluation of the points of view and the accomplishments of groups, nations, and cultures.

It was once told of Napoleon that he directed a marshal to set about performing a certain task. Shortly after, Napoleon discovered that nothing had been done. He demanded an explanation. The marshal replied that the task was impossible. It is in something of the spirit of Napoleon's answer that we approach our final chapter. "If that be all," exclaimed Napoleon, "let us set about it at once!"

The questions we shall attempt to answer are these. Are there any statistical tests by which the value of a people's consumption can be directly measured? What, in evaluating consumption, is the real meaning of two tests commonly held to be significant, the average and actual per capita use of wealth and the average and actual per capita status of education among the people?

DIRECT MEASUREMENTS IN TERMS OF STATISTICS

The most searching effort to measure civilization in terms of statistics has probably been made by an Italian, Professor Alfred Niceforo, of Messina and of Rome. In his book *Les indices numériques de la civilisation et du progrès* [1] he discusses such trends as the consumption of coal, the consumption of luxuries (sugar, coffee, alcohol), the consumption of food (cheese, potatoes), the suicide rate, the increase of wealth, the increase of population, the death rate and birth rate, the convictions for crime, the proportions of illiteracy, and the divorce rate. He well understands, however, many of the difficulties in judging the value of a civilization in terms of the rise or fall of such rates. An increase in suicides, though undesirable in itself, is sometimes an accompaniment of a civilization that seems in other respects to be advancing. Crime sometimes increases, for a time at least, under the pressure of a rapidly changing culture, and certainly the discovery of and conviction for such crimes as actually have been committed is a mark of a superior social order. Wealth and absence of illiteracy have an important relation to the problem, as we shall see, but they mean little in themselves as marks of progress.

In the opinion of the present author, the only statistical tests now available which are direct and conclusive tests of the value of a people's consumption are mortality and morbidity data, death and sickness rates. To a belief in the desirability of life and health we are all committed in practice, if not in philosophical theory, and the prolongation of life accompanied by physical and mental health seems to be one thing that in actual living we accept as indisputably good. Even the individual

[1] Paris, 1921. He has written also *La misura della vita* (The Measurement of Life), Turin, 1919.

cases in which we believe the prolongation of a healthy life is of doubtful value are almost non-existent.

In our chapter on consumption as a science of welfare we discussed the actual prolongation of life and saw that the average expectation of life had probably more than doubled in England and in the United States since the Middle Ages. Morbidity data are less exact than mortality data, but there have also been great advances in the conquering of disease.[1] The United States, the United Kingdom, and Western Europe have the lowest death and sickness rates in the world.

Death and sickness rates are only one indication of the value of a people's mode of life, though they are the surest single indication we can name. We must realize that other things may supersede them in importance and other things must always be considered with them. Furthermore, the significance of death and sickness rates in themselves must be judged in relation to their setting. For instance, the lowest infant death rates of the world are in New Zealand. This is due not simply to the superior health facilities of New Zealand but also to the fact that New Zealand, a new country, has restricted immigration in such a way as to avoid some of the more serious problems we are attempting to solve in the United States. It is quite possible that our present inconveniences in handling problems arising from our southern European population may eventually be outbalanced by advantages from such contacts to us and to the world.

The Significance of Material Progress

In the United States, evidences of material progress are frequently used as an argument to substantiate claims that a high type of civilization has been achieved. Average and actual per capita production and consumption are greater here than anywhere else. Yet statistical measurements of material progress such as average and actual per capita real income and expendi-

---

[1] The student interested in this problem is referred to Brownlee, John, *The Use of Death-Rates as a Measure of Hygienic Conditions*, Medical Research Council (of Great Britain), London, 1922.

ture, and average and actual per capita consumption of various goods and services, are, as we have said, no ultimate index of human services received. Even statistical evidences of extent of collegiate education, number of books borrowed from public libraries, attendance at art galleries and symphony concerts, are not conclusive indications of a high type of civilization, as it has now become a sort of fashion in the popular magazines to point out. To answer every gushing Babbitt proclaiming the unparalleled excellences of "God's country" we have now a grim-faced cynic who sees or pretends to see American life as something inexpressibly absurd and pathetic.

Whatever their immediate effects, however, the ultimate consequences of material progress and domination are to provide man with a greater control over the powers of nature. He is able to do more, he is able to have more, as a result. The range of his possible choices is greatly extended. His opportunities for developing his own powers are immensely increased, as the number of stimuli to his thought grows larger. We have no record of any great thinking that was ever done by a member of a race living under the most primitive industrial conditions. It is hard to see how great thinking could be done under such circumstances, for much of man's impetus to great thought comes as a result of his effort to understand complicated situations. Complicated problems of life depend in very considerable degree on complicated conditions of living. The savage and the barbarian are men ordinarily less awakened than we. They have fewer potential points of contact with the stimuli to thought.

The sages of India, who more than other men have preached against the substantiality of material progress, were men who spoke from a considerable background of material progress themselves. Long before they came into existence someone had labored to spin wool, to grind grain, and to make tools and utensils, elements of their culture which they accepted without thought of the material endeavors implied in them. India had attained an appreciable degree of civilization at the time of writing of its sacred books, and its philosophers had been unconsciously stimulated to thought by the very material progress that they considered non-essential. The same is true of the holy men of other ages and of other countries. Quite generally they have spoken against material success, seeing that its immediate effects on individuals were often unfortunate. The Christian admonition is a typical one: "Lay not up for yourselves treasures on earth, where moth and rust doth corrupt and where thieves break through and steal . . . for where your treasure is, there will your heart be also." The New Testament abounds with injunctions not to be concerned with the material world.

It is frequently pointed out that the Christian world of the West is a great paradox. The theory of the founder of Christianity was to despise the world, but the practice of the whole Christian West is to cultivate it and control it. But if men's struggles for material conquest and domination frequently divert them personally from an appreciation of the things that are more excellent, the group as a whole is given the opportunity of attaining greater wisdom as the ultimate consequence of these struggles. Sages and holy men, being chiefly concerned with individuals at a given time, have devoted their attention to the immediate effects of worldly contacts.

This explains what would otherwise be very difficult to explain, the fact that some of the best and wisest spokesmen of moral forces have counselled a course of life that few Westerners can bring themselves, even with the best intentions, to approve in practice.

The specific bearing of all this on the evaluation of consumption is that material progress brings into existence the conditions under which men's powers can be most fully awakened. It is not true that the effects of material progress are necessarily good in all or even in most respects at any given time or in any given country, as, for instance, in the United States today. But it is true that material progress is nevertheless a necessary basis on which other progress rises. There may be greater human development, temporarily at any rate, on a moderate

degree of material advancement as in the case of classical
Athens, than on a relatively much greater degree of material
advancement as in the United States, but the latter situation
is from a long-run point of view the more encouraging. Although
we Americans cannot claim to be the wisest and the best of
men ourselves, we can at least claim that we are helping provide
the substratum on which a wiser and better civilization for someone can arise. From this point of view, education, Ford cars,
motion pictures, and chewing gum for everybody can be looked
upon as good. They are symbols, though it may be in some
cases ugly and even uncouth symbols, of a great step forward.

THE SIGNIFICANCE OF EDUCATION

The development of popular education, which is in many
ways related to, and an outgrowth of, the increase of wealth,
is often cited along with the increase of wealth as an indication
of a high type of civilization. We have already said that it is
no such indication in itself. Everything depends on what the
education is. It is conceivable that we would be better off
without some of the types of education that exist among us.
In some cases individuals have certainly been injured by their
education. Intellectual balance may be cultivated by the
conditions of struggle with nature as well as in the schoolroom.
The fact that we are able in the United States to keep most of
our children in school until they are fourteen or fifteen years
of age and to keep seven out of every thousand in our population
in universities, colleges, and professional schools is presumably
a fortunate fact. But education, like wealth, is a tool by which
a higher type of consumption may be attained rather than a
proof that it is attained.

Nevertheless, the extent of education is probably a better
index of the welfare of the people than is the per capita consumption of wealth. It is certainly true that progress in good
consumption is necessarily very gradual where there is lack
of popular education. Actual contacts and disciplines, the trials
of experience, by which the better can be recognized and the

worse discarded, are so limited in any one life that unless
experience can be shortened by education man learns slowly.

On the positive side, although we have no conclusive proofs
of the value in life of our systems of education, we may have
reason to be encouraged by certain indications within them.
The good life may be learned in many ways, and the principles
of good education may be manifold.   Yet, whatever else it
does, certainly popular education should emphasize the principles of physical and mental health and efficiency and should
bring to the people the wisdom of the most outstanding individuals of the past and the points of view and the philosophies
of cultures unlike their own.   Unless we have had the opportunity to become familiar with all, we cannot know that we
have chosen the best.

To what extent does American education contribute in these
respects to a better consumption?   It is making great efforts
to teach scientific principles of living, and here it seems to be
achieving considerable results.   In this field we can rightly
believe we have made progress.   But American education pays
less attention to the more intangible matters of bringing the
people into contact with the best thought of other times and
other men.   In this particular respect it may do even less than
education elsewhere, though this contention would be difficult
to prove.   The emphasis of American education is "practical,"
that is to say it is aimed at measurable and more or less immediate results.   It is hard for Americans, as for all peoples, to see
themselves in historical or contemporary perspective.   Like all
other peoples, we emphasize one thing and think little about
the importance of the rest.

Our material civilization is now in the way of being accepted
all over the world, and its advantages are coming more and
more to be the common property of all peoples.   That people
which can accept these material successes and the practical
education connected with them, and add thereto the best
thought of the world about the use of wealth, will be the great
people of the future.

APPENDIX

APPENDIX

SUGGESTIONS FOR READINGS AND SPECIAL REPORTS

Ch. I. CONSUMPTION AND CULTURE
General

CARVER, T. N., *Principles of National Economy*, Boston, 1921, Chs. XLI, XLII.

PATTEN, S. N., *Essays in Economic Theory*, New York, 1924, pp. 1–8.

Ch. II. THE BEGINNINGS OF CULTURE
General

FOLSOM, J. K., *Culture and Social Progress*, New York, 1928, Chs. I, II.

HOYT, E. E., *Primitive Trade*, London, 1926, pp. 5–14; 38–41.

WISSLER, C., *Man and Culture*, New York, 1923, pp. 1–12.

A Picture of Life in Early Society

THORNDIKE, L., *Short History of Civilization*, New York, 1927, pp. 1–12.

Development of Art by Prehistoric Man

MACCURDY, G. G., *Human Origins*, Vol. I, New York, 1924, Ch. VII.

Ch. III. HOW AN INTEREST ESTABLISHES ITSELF
General

HOYT, E. E., *Primitive Trade*, op. cit., pp. 34–38; 45–50; 53–57.

WISSLER, C., *Man and Culture*, op. cit., pp. 50–63; 182–186.

The Physiological Explanation of Habit and Culture Complexes

JAMES, W., *Psychology, Advanced Course*, Vol. I, New York, 1890, pp. 104–128; 553–554.

Ch. IV. HOW GROUP LIFE STIMULATES THE INTERESTS OF ITS MEMBERS
General

PLATT, C., *Psychology of Social Life*, New York, 1922, Chs. II, VI.

ROSS, E. A., *Social Psychology*, New York, 1908, Ch. VI.

Pecuniary Emulation

VEBLEN, T., *Theory of the Leisure Class*, New York, 1911, Chs. IV, V, VI.

The Nature and Impermanence of Fads
    BOGARDUS, E. A., "Social Psychology of Fads," *Journal Applied Sociology*, VIII, pp. 239–243.

Ch. V. HOW GROUP LIFE RESTRAINS THE INTERESTS OF ITS MEMBERS
General
    FOLSOM, J. K., *Culture and Social Progress*, op. cit., pp. 157–167.
    OGBURN, W. F., *Social Change*, New York, 1922, pp. 146–165; 170–186.
    PLATT, C., *Psychology of Social Life*, op. cit., Chs. IV, V.
    ROSS, E. A., *Social Psychology*, op. cit., Chs. VII, XIV, XV.
    SUMNER, W. G., *Folkways*, Boston, 1913, Ch. II.

Curious Survivals of Old Usages in England
    WILLIAMSON, G. C., *Curious Survivals*, London, 1923, Chs. XIII, XVI.

Ch. VI. ECOLOGY: MAN'S INTERESTS AND THE GEOGRAPHIC ENVIRONMENT
General
    BUCKLE, H. T., "History of Civilization in England," in CARVER, T. N., *Readings in Sociology and Social Progress*, Boston, 1905, pp. 174–203; 213–214; 235–237.
    CHAPIN, F. S., *Social Evolution*, New York, 1919, Ch. V.
    HAYES, E. C., *Introduction to the Study of Sociology*, New York, 1925, Ch. III.
    HUNTINGTON, E., and CUSHING, S. W., *Principles of Human Geography*, New York, 1921, Ch. I.
    WISSLER, C., *Man and Culture*, op. cit., pp. 227–232.

The Influence of Climate
    HUNTINGTON, E., *Civilization and Climate*, New Haven, 1915, Chs. I, XII.
    SEMPLE, E., *Influences of Geographic Environment*, New York, 1911, Ch. XVII.

The Significance of Metals and Their Distribution
    BAIN, H. F., *Ores and Industry in the Far East*, New York, 1927, pp. 1–27; 204–216.
    HUNTINGTON, E., and CUSHING, S. W., *Principles of Human Geography*, op. cit., Ch. VIII.

Ch. VII. THE HERITAGE OF BIRTH AND RACE
General
    BOAS, F., *The Mind of Primitive Man*, New York, 1911, Ch. X.
    HOYT, E. E., *Primitive Trade*, op. cit., pp. 19–27.
    TOZZER, A. M., *Social Origins and Social Continuities*, New York, 1925, pp. 62–85.

Universal Races Congress, *Inter-Racial Problems* (SPILLER, G., ed.), London, 1911, pp. 24–39.

WOODWORTH, R. S., "Racial Differences in Mental Traits," in CASE, C. M., *Outlines of Introductory Sociology*, New York, 1924, pp. 94–102.

Cultural Effects of the Merging of Races in Mexico

VASCONCELOS, J., and GAMIO, M., *Aspects of Mexican Civilization*, Chicago, 1926, pp. 3–41; 75–102.

Ch. VIII. THE DIFFUSION OF CULTURE

General

CASE, C. M., ed., *Outlines of Introductory Sociology*, op. cit., Chs. XI, XXII.

CHAPIN, F. S., *Social Economy*, New York, 1917, Ch. XVI.

COOLEY, C. H., *Social Organization*, New York, 1909, Chs. VII, VIII, IX.

GOLDENWEISER, A., *Early Civilization*, New York, 1922, pp. 301–324.

KROEBER, A. L., *Anthropology*, New York, 1923, Ch. VIII.

DE LAGUNA, T., *Factors of Social Evolution*, New York, 1926, Chs. VIII, XIII.

SEMPLE, E., *Influences of Geographic Environment*, op. cit., pp. 74–81; 82–100.

WISSLER, C., *Man and Culture*, op. cit., Chs. VIII, IX.

The Diffusion of Arabian Culture in Europe

BLACKMAR, F. W., *History of Human Society*, New York, 1926, Ch. XIX.

THORNDIKE, L., *History of Mediaeval Europe*, Boston, 1917, Ch. X.

Ch. IX. TRADE AND CULTURE

Influences of Trade in Europe in Middle Ages

KNIGHT, M. M., *Economic History of Europe*, Boston, 1926, pp. 199–219.

WEBER, MAX, *General Economic History*, New York, 1927, Ch. XVI.

Foreign Trade and the Culture of the United States

REDFIELD, W. C., *Dependent America*, New York, 1926, Chs. V, VI, IX.

The American Business Man Influences Consumption Abroad

COOPER, C. S., *Foreign Trade*, New York, 1922, Ch. II; passim.

HOUGH, B. O., *The Export Executive*, Scranton, 1925, Ch. V.

Latest report of the Bureau of Foreign and Domestic Commerce.

Foreign Trade and International Relations

LANGE, C. L., "Internationalism," in BAIRD, A. C., *College Readings*, Boston, 1925, pp. 250–259.

REDFIELD, W. C., *Dependent America*, op. cit., Ch. XII.
YOUNG, A. A., "Economics and War," in *Economic Problems New and Old*, Boston, 1927, pp. 1–21.

Ch. X. AGGRESSIVE METHODS OF SALES-MAKING

General

American Economic Review Supplement, March, 1925, various articles, pp. 5–41.
CHASE, S., *Tragedy of Waste*, New York, 1925, Ch. VII.
COMISH, N. H., *Standard of Living*, New York, 1923, Ch. VII.
MAYNARD, H. H. et al., *Principles of Marketing*, New York, 1927, Ch. XIX.
STARCH, D., *Principles of Advertising*, Chicago, 1923, Chs. III, IV.

Ch. XI. PRODUCTION AND CONSUMPTION

General Historical

BLACKMAR, F. W., *History of Human Society*, op. cit., Ch. XXVII.
CASE, C. M., ed., *Outlines of Introductory Sociology*, op. cit., Chs. VIII, IX.
EDIE, L. D., *Economics, Principles and Problems*, New York, 1926, Ch. II.

General Critical

HOBSON, J. A., *Work and Wealth*, New York, 1916, Ch. IX.

The State of Production and the Culture of Athens in the Classical Period

ZIMMERN, A. E., *The Greek Commonwealth*, Oxford, 1922, pp. 213–227; 286–300; 198–209; passim.

Ch. XII. THE REIGN OF THE PRICE SYSTEM

General on Instalment Buying

SELIGMAN, E. R. A., *The Economics of Instalment Selling*, Vol. I, New York, 1927, pp. 14–33; 92–119.
WICKSTEED, P. H., *Common Sense of Political Economy*, London, 1910, pp. 104–108.

General on Price Fluctuations

ELY, R. T., *Outlines of Economics*, New York, 1923, pp. 320–322; 329–334.
MITCHELL, W. C., *Business Cycles*, New York, 1927, pp. 61–90.

The Measurement of Changes in Prices as They Affect the Consumer

International Labour Office, *Methods of Compiling Cost of Living Index Numbers*, Geneva, 1925, pp. 7–44.

Ch. XIII. THE DISTRIBUTION OF INCOME

General Factual

National Bureau of Economic Research, *Income in the United States*, Vol. I, New York, 1921, Ch. III.

General Critical
HOBSON, J. A., *Work and Wealth*, op. cit., pp. 159–170; 176–189.
SKELTON, O. D., *Socialism*, Boston, 1911, pp. 29–37.

Ch. XIV. TAXATION AND TARIFFS
General on Taxation
PECK, H. W., *Taxation and Welfare*, New York, 1925, Ch. XIV.
SELIGMAN, E. R. A., *Essays in Taxation*, New York, 1921, Ch. IX.

General on Tariffs
SMITH, A., *The Wealth of Nations*, Book IV, Ch. II.

Ch. XV. INTELLIGENCE CHALLENGES THE CONSUMER
General
ELLWOOD, C. A., *The Psychology of Human Society*, New York, 1925, Ch. X.
MITCHELL, W. C., "The Backward Art of Spending Money," *American Economic Review*, II, pp. 269–281.
OVERSTREET, H. A., *Influencing Human Behavior*, New York, 1925, Ch. XIII.
TUGWELL, R. G. et al., *American Economic Life*, New York, 1925, Chs. 25, 26, 27.

The Various Kinds of Thinking
ROBINSON, J. H., *The Mind in the Making*, New York, 1921, pp. 33–62.

The Energies of Men
JAMES, W., *Memories and Studies*, New York, 1912, Essay X.

Ch. XVI. THE SCIENCE OF CONSUMPTION FOR WELFARE
General
CHASE, S., *Tragedy of Waste*, op. cit., Ch. V.

Development of Science of Nutrition
FUNK, C., *The Vitamines*, Baltimore, 1922, pp. 19–33.
MENDEL, L. B., *Nutrition*, New Haven, 1923, Ch. I.

What Have We Learned About Good Housing Standards?
GUERARD, A. R., in PARK, W. H., ed., *Public Health and Hygiene*, Philadelphia, 1920, pp. 443–458.
VEILLER, L., in ibid., pp. 293–307.

Ch. XVII. THE TECHNOLOGY OF CONSUMPTION
General
ANDREWS, B. R., *Economics of the Household*, New York, 1923, pp. 293–298; 304–307; 313–320; 329–334; 362–374; 382–389.
CHASE, S., and SCHLINK, F. J., *Your Money's Worth*, New York, 1927.
HARAP, H., *Education of the Consumer*, New York, 1924.

Household Wastes

SPOONER, H. J., *Wealth from Waste*, London, 1918 Ch. VII; pp. 240-253.

Ch. XVIII. CONSUMPTION AS AN ART

General

HAYES, E. C., *Introduction to Sociology*, op. cit., Ch. XXXV.

KYRK, H., *A Theory of Consumption*, Boston, 1923, Ch. XI.

PATTEN, S. N., *Essays in Economic Theory*, op. cit., pp. 164-177.

Recreation That Recreates

FOLSOM, J. K., *Culture and Social Progress*, op. cit., Ch. XV.

KEY, E., *Younger Generation*, New York, 1914, Ch. VII.

PATTEN, S. N., *New Basis of Civilization*, New York, 1907, Ch. VI.

Our Need for Castles in Spain

GALSWORTHY, J., "Castles in Spain," in BAIRD, A. C., *College Readings*, op. cit., pp. 59-73; same in ROBINSON, K. A., et al., *Essays Toward Truth*, New York, 1924, pp. 113-128.

Ch. XIX. ORGANIZED MOVEMENTS TO BETTER CONSUMPTION

General

American Red Cross, *Handbook of Social Resources*, Washington, 1921, passim.

Social Aspects of the Coöperative Movement in Russia

BLANC, E. T., *Coöperative Movement in Russia*, New York, 1924, Ch. IX.

Women's Institutes in Scotland

ROBERTSON SCOTT, J. W., *The Story of the Women's Institute Movement*, Idbury, 1925, Chs. 19, 20.

Ch. XX. GOVERNMENT AID AND INTERVENTION IN CONSUMPTION

General

American Red Cross, *Handbook of Social Resources*, op. cit., pp. 98-123.

CARVER, T. N., *Principles of National Economy*, op. cit., Ch. XLIV.

COMISH, N. H., *Standard of Living*, op. cit., Ch. X.

Latest *Year Book* of the League of Nations for progress in health organization, control of opium traffic, etc.

Nature and Purposes of Sumptuary Laws in Elizabethan England

BALDWIN, F. E., "Sumptuary Legislation and Personal Regulation in England" (*Johns Hopkins University Studies*, XLIV), Baltimore, 1926, pp. 9-11; 192-247; cf. 248-275.

Limits of the Proper Authority of Society over the Individual

MILL, J. S., *Essay on Liberty*.

Chs. XXI and XXII. WHAT IS A CULTURE TYPE? WHAT IS WORTH WHILE TO CONSUME?

General

MAETERLINCK, M. et al., *What Is Civilization?* New York, 1926.

The Cultural Ideas of India

MUKERJI, D. G., *My Brother's Face*, New York, 1924.

Chs. XXIII and XXIV. WHAT IS A STANDARD OF LIVING? THE STUDY OF SCALES AND STANDARDS OF LIVING

General

ANDREWS, B. R., *Economics of the Household*, op. cit., pp. 40–42; 82–85; 88–109.

KYRK, H., *Theory of Consumption*, op. cit., Chs. VIII, IX, X.

National Industrial Conference Board, *Family Budgets of American Wage-Earners*, New York, 1921, pp. 4–50; 69–86.

STREIGHTOFF, F. H., *Standard of Living*, Boston, 1911, Ch. I.

Studies of Family Budgets Abroad

International Labour Office, *Methods of Conducting Family Budget Inquiries*, Geneva, 1926, pp. 55–78.

A Study of the Standard of Living in Japan

MORIMOTO, K., "Standard of Living in Japan" (*Johns Hopkins University Studies*, XXXVI), Baltimore, 1918, Chs. II, XIV; passim.

Ch. XXV. POPULATION, CULTURES, AND STANDARDS OF LIVING

General

BOUCKE, O. F., *Principles of Economics*, Vol. II, New York, 1925, Ch. XX.

BUSHEE, F. A., *Principles of Sociology*, New York, 1923, Ch. XIX.

DUBLIN, L. I., ed., *Population Problems*, Boston, 1926, Chs. III, XIX.

EDIE, L., *Economics, Principles and Problems*, op. cit., pp. 407–415.

FAIRCHILD, F. R. et al., *Elementary Economics*, Vol. II, New York, 1926, Ch. XLII.

PATTEN, S. N., *Essays in Economic Theory*, op. cit., pp. 195–206.

Limitation of Population in Primitive Societies

CARR-SAUNDERS, A. M., *The Population Problem*, Oxford, 1922, pp. 197–236; cf. Chs. VII, VIII.

Chs. XXVI and XXVII. AMERICAN CONSUMPTION; AMERICAN SCALES AND STANDARDS OF LIVING

General

ANDREWS, B. R., *Economics of the Household*, op. cit., pp. 85–87; 96–109.

COMISH, N. H., *Standard of Living*, op. cit., Ch. VI.

McMAHON, T. S., *Social and Economic Standards of Living*, Boston, 1925, Chs. VIII, IX, X, XI.

Poverty, Rural and Urban, in the United States

HOUGHTELING, L., *Income and Standard of Living of Unskilled Laborers in Chicago*, Chicago, 1927, Chs. VII, VIII, IX.

TUGWELL, R. G. et al., *American Economic Life*, op. cit., Chs. 2, 3.

Comfort and Riches in the United States

TUGWELL, ibid., Chs. 4, 5.

Scales of Living of Industrial Workers

National Industrial Conference Board, *Family Budgets of American Wage-Earners*, op. cit., pp. 1–68.

The Living of Farmers

FUNK, W. C., "What the Farm Contributes Directly to the Farmers' Living," U. S. Department of Agriculture, Farmers' Bulletin, 635, Washington, 1914.

KIRKPATRICK, E. L., *Standard of Life in a Typical Section of Diversified Farming*, Ithaca, 1923.

The Negroes' Opportunity to Respond to Higher Standards

REUTER, E. B., *The American Race Problem*, New York, 1927, pp. 216–222; 240–251; 269–289.

The Cultural Status of Typical American Indian Groups

EASTMAN, C. A., "The North American Indian," in Universal Races Congress, *Inter-Racial Problems*, op. cit., pp. 367–376.

LINDQUIST, G. E. E., ed., *The Red Man in the United States*, New York, 1923, Ch. II; pp. 149–158; 359–365.

Standards of Living Among Immigrant Steel Workers

BYINGTON, M. F., *Homestead*, New York, 1910, Chs. VI, XI.

SOKOLOFF, A., "Mediaeval Russia in the Pittsburgh District," in KELLOGG, P. U., ed., *Wage-Earning Pittsburgh*, New York, 1914, pp. 78–95.

Ch. XXVIII. THE INDIVIDUAL AND THE STANDARD OF HIS GROUP—THE MATERIALS FOR BUDGET BUILDING

General

ANDREWS, B. R., *Economics of the Household*, op. cit., Ch. XVI.

CHASSEE, L. J., *Management of Personal Income*, Chicago, 1927.

DONHAM, S. A., *Spending the Family Income*, Boston, 1923.

LORD, I. E., *Getting Your Money's Worth*, New York, 1922.

Insurance, Savings, and Investments

COMISH, N. H., *Standard of Living*, op. cit., Ch. XVIII.

HUEBNER, S. S., *Economics of Life Insurance*, New York, 1927, Chs. IX, X.

KNIFFEN, W. H., JR., "Types of Savings Institutions," in MOULTON, H. G., *Principles of Money and Banking*, Chicago, 1916, Part II, pp. 403–406.

McKAY, J. M., "The Building and Loan Movement in the United States," in MOULTON, ibid., pp. 354–359.

Ch. XXIX. THE EVALUATION OF CONSUMPTION
General

DEWEY, J., "American Education and Culture," in ROBINSON, K. A. et al., *Essays Toward Truth*, op. cit., pp. 65–71.

ELLIS, H., *The Dance of Life*, Boston, 1923, Ch. VII.

FOLSOM, J. K., *Culture and Social Progress*, op. cit., Ch. X.

GEROULD, K. F., "The Extirpation of Culture," in ROBINSON, K. A. et al., *Essays Toward Truth*, op. cit., pp. 44–64.

INGE, W. I., "The Idea of Progress," in *Outspoken Essays*, Second Series, London, 1922, pp. 158–183; same in ROBINSON, K. A. et al., *Essays Toward Truth*, op. cit., pp. 275–305.

TODD, A. J., *Theories of Social Progress*, New York, 1918, Ch. VII.

Criticisms of American culture may be found in the current magazines.

INDEX

Abortion, 264, 265, 269–270
Account-keeping, 312
Adornment of body, 18, 37
Advertising
  types, 98–99
  as a "science," 99
  cost in U. S., 102, 106
  competitive, 107, 110
  examples, 108–109
  See Aggressive sales methods
Aesthetics, 173–175
Agencies for standardization, 180–185
Aggressive sales methods, 90–91, 97–110, 326
  social gain, 103–105
  social waste, 105–107
  way out, 109–110
American Civic Ass'n, 201
American Country Life Ass'n, 201
American Dietetic Ass'n, 199, 200
American Economic Review Suppl., 326
American Federation of Arts, 201
American Federation of Labor, 294
American Home Economics Ass'n, 199, 200
American Institute of Architects, 199, 200
American Medical Ass'n, 106, 181, 199
American Public Health Ass'n, 199, 200
American Red Cross, 328
Andrews, 301 n., 327, 329, 330
Anthropology, 8, 19, 28, 29, 53–54, 65, 72, 325
Anti-Saloon League, 201
Appreciation, difficulty of, 5

Appreciations, part of standard of living, 243
Aristotle, 165, 190
Art, 39–40, 94, 103, 188, 192
  prehistoric, 14, 18, 231
  of other cultures, 224
Art of consumption, 8, 186–198
  relation to science, 187–190
  as utilization of capacities, 190–193
  guidance in, 197–198
Associationism, 25
Athens, 65, 118, 197
Atlantic and Pacific Tea Co., 181
Attitude toward life, 228
  important in culture, 225, 227
  of six cultures, 230–240, 263–265
Automobiles, 6, 30, 39, 90, 121, 125, 284, 285
Ayres, 125

Bader, 100 n.
Bain, 60 n., 324
Baird, 325, 328
Baldwin, 216 n., 328
Bark, origin of use, 56
Basketry, origin of, 56
Beauty, 195–196, 236
Berridge, 130 n., 275 n.
Birth control, 269, 270–272
  See Population
Black Death, effect on standard of living, 247
Blackmar, 325, 326
Blanc, 328
Boas, 324
  on tenacity of habit, 23–24
Bogardus, 41, 324
Bombay, 254, 258, 259 n., 277
Book of the Dead, 233

333

Folsom, 323, 324, 328, 331
Food
  relation to culture, 9
  extension in variety, 16
  and habit, 23
  and geographic environment, 58
  cost in budget, 257–258, 274–275,
    296–297
  consumption in U. S., 6, 275–280,
    286–287, 291, 292, 297
  typical consumption, 303–305,
    314
  guidance in consumption, 306–
    307
Ford, Henry, 121
Forest Hills Gardens, 203
Form, in Greek culture, 236
Free goods and services, 209–213
Frisch, 141n.
Fuel, consumption in U. S., 283, 308
Funerals, 47, 246
Funk, 327, 330
Furniture
  science of, 170
  consumption in U. S., 7, 283, 308
Future life, in Egyptian culture,
    232, 233

Galen, 165
Galsworthy, 328
Galton, 18, 65
Gandhi, 234
Gay, 60 n.
Geographic environment, 53–61
Geography, 8, 324
Gerould, 331
Girl Scouts, 202
Goldenweiser, 325
Good Housekeeping Institute, 185
Government
  finances, 144–152
  services, 119, 182–184, 207–218
Greek culture, 65, 74, 118, 192, 223–
    224, 235–237
  effect on population, 264
Greenfield, 216 n.
Grierson, 75 n., 76 n.
Group life, 33–52

Group spirit
  defined, 33–34
  economy of, 48
Guerard, 327
Guidance in consumption, 197–198
Guilds, 200
Gunpowder, 221, 238–239

Habit
  and interest, 23–24
  tenacity of, 23–24
  social, 45
Hambridge, 174 n.
Handicraft, 113–114
Harap, 185 n., 327
Harvey, 167
Haskins, 164 n.
Hayes, 324, 328
Health, 160, 167–171, 181, 201, 202,
    203, 217, 318
  advantage in culture, 68
  furthered by League of Nations,
    218
  expenditures in U. S., 284
Hebrew culture, 230 n.
Herodotus, 156, 233
Hesiod, 164, 264
Higgs, 253 n.
Hobhouse, 74 n.
Hobson, J. A., 119, 246, 326, 327
Home
  changed by Industrial Revolu-
    tion, 161–162
  hygiene, 170
Home economics, 163, 182, 184, 329,
    330
  cost of daily nutrition, 279–280
Home ownership, 127, 281
Homo sapiens vs. *homo somnians*, 19
Horace, 306
Hough, 92 n., 325
Houghteling, Leila, 252, 330
Housewife problems, 162–163, 178–
    179
Housing, 327
  assistance, 203, 213
  See Shelter
Hoyt, 29 n., 84 n., 323, 324

GETTING AND SPENDING:
The Consumer's Dilemma

An Arno Press Collection

Babson, Roger W[ard]. **The Folly of Instalment Buying.** 1938

Bauer, John. **Effective Regulation of Public Utilities.** 1925

Beckman, Theodore N. and Herman C. Nolen. **The Chain Store Problem.** 1938

Berridge, William A., Emma A. Winslow and Richard A. Flinn. **Purchasing Power of the Consumer.** 1925

Borden, Neil H. **The Economic Effects of Advertising.** 1942

Borsodi, Ralph. **The Distribution Age.** 1927

Brainerd, J. G[rist], editor. **The Ultimate Consumer.** 1934

Carson, Gerald. **Cornflake Crusade.** [1957]

Cassels, John M[acIntyre]. **A Study of Fluid Milk Prices.** 1937

Caveat Emptor. 1976

Cherington, Paul Terry. **Advertising as a Business Force.** 1913

Clark, Evans. **Financing the Consumer.** 1933

Cook, James. **Remedies and Rackets:** The Truth About Patent Medicines Today. [1958]

Cover, John H[igson]. **Neighborhood Distribution and Consumption of Meat in Pittsburgh.** [1932]

Federal Trade Commission. **Chain Stores.** 1933

Ferber, Robert and Hugh G. Wales, editors. **Motivation and Market Behavior.** 1958

For Richer or Poorer. 1976

Grether, Ewald T. **Price Control Under Fair Trade Legislation.** 1939

Harding, T. Swann. **The Popular Practice of Fraud.** 1935

Haring, Albert. **Retail Price Cutting and Its Control by Manufacturers.** [1935]

Harris, Emerson P[itt]. **Co-operation:** The Hope of the Consumer. 1918

Hoyt, Elizabeth Ellis. **The Consumption of Wealth.** 1928

Kallen, Horace M[eyer]. **The Decline and Rise of the Consumer.** 1936

Kallet, Arthur and F. J. Schlink. **100,000,000 Guinea Pigs:** Dangers in Everyday Foods, Drugs, and Cosmetics. 1933

Kyrk, Hazel. **A Theory of Consumption.** [1923]

Laird, Donald A[nderson]. **What Makes People Buy.** 1935